ORGANIC GARDENING

ORGANIC
GARDENING

ROY LACEY

*Foreword by Lawrence Woodward, Director of Elm Farm
Research Centre and Chairman of the Soil Association.*

APPROVED BY THE SOIL ASSOCIATION

David & Charles
Newton Abbot   London

All photographs by the author, except p29 and
p121 East Anglian Daily Times; p42 BBC
p46 Michael Warren; p65 Europa Manor.

British Library Cataloguing in Publication Data

Lacey, Roy
   Organic gardening.
   1. Great Britain. Gardens. Organic
   cultivation – Manuals
   I. Title
   635′ .0484′0941

ISBN 0-7153-9175-5

Typeset by ABM Typographics Limited, Hull
and printed in Portugal
by Resopal
for David and Charles Publishers plc
Brunel House   Newton Abbot   Devon

CONTENTS

FOREWORD

It is not often that society's consciousness changes in a fundamental way. However, the last few years have seen a major reappraisal of the way we judge our food and how it is produced. Concern about diet, food additives and the agro-chemical armoury has grown and is bringing about real changes.

This can be seen in the remarkable increase in demand for organic food. One survey found that over sixty per cent of shoppers questioned would be prepared to pay a premium for organic food if they could find it. Spurred on by this demand, supermarkets throughout the country are stocking a wide range of organic produce: something unthinkable even a couple of years ago.

Yet why buy from the supermarket when you can grow it yourself? The wholesome taste of fresh, organically grown vegetables from your own garden should be experienced by everyone. In any case, while society castigates the farmer for polluting the environment and food by using agro-chemicals, we should not overlook the 'pall of poison' that hangs over the gardens of our cities, towns and villages. The range of chemicals, all of them toxic, most of them alien to nature, used by Britain's gardeners is truly horrific.

Organic Gardening tells you how to produce your own healthy food in a way which is safe – to yourself, your family and your environment. Roy Lacey is an acknowledged expert on 'gardening without chemicals'. He is also a gifted writer. The fruit of this combination is a book which is stimulating and practical.

Lawrence Woodward

1

WHY ORGANIC?

You might think it perverse, at a time when 'high-tech rules OK' and the only limit to man's ingenuity is time itself, that there are ever-increasing numbers of sane people who want to return to old-fashioned ways of doing things.

Why that should be is due to several factors: in ever-more complicated circumstances there's a natural wish to simplify; when the competitive spirit gets too heady, there are those who wish to opt out; and there are those who believe that in some important respects progress has not always been for the better.

Something is very wrong with expertise that enables us to explore space yet fails to discover the answers to big basic problems on our own planet. We can produce massive yields of pest- and disease-free crops only for them to be stored until they are nutritionally valueless, or dumped or burned. Mountains of food are an insult to our civilisation. They are immoral, an inordinate waste of resources that are mostly non-renewable and an obscene testimony to the greed of the people of the western world. And is it an acceptable consequence of technological progress that mankind must live in daily fear of a nuclear accident, such as Chernobyl? Will it be Sellafield next, or Sizewell?

At a more mundane level there is a fundamental fault in a supermarket society that tolerates battery hens being housed in bizarre, inhumane conditions to lay eggs that are of such uniformly poor quality that colouring has to be added to the birds' feed so that the yolks may appear more wholesome.

The less said about intensive pig production the better. To exploit intelligent creatures in the way that the modern pig farmer does is to debase the principles and practice of animal husbandry.

In a relatively free society, however, there is room for manoeuvre. We aren't forced to eat pigmeat or veal or the pathetic little carcasses of 'spring chicken'. We can say 'No' and many of my children's generation are doing just that. The years of factory farming might well be numbered.

There are other aspects of modern food production that give cause for concern. Every day each of us in Britain eats an average of twenty-three aspirin-sized 'drugs'. That's what my friend Dr Peter Mansfield discovered when he was investigating the use of additives and flavourings in our food. There are several thousand kinds of these chemicals in use by the food industry about whose safety we know too little. Dr Mansfield says:

We know that the drugs we use deliberately often have unwanted or harmful side effects. We also know that drugs interact with each other to alter both their wanted and unwanted effects. We have no reason to suppose that chemicals used in food behave any differently just because we do not call them drugs. How much harm is all this doing to us?

Truly nobody knows. But there is plenty of scope. Con-

LACEY'S LORE

BAD FOR BABIES

Heinz, one of the world's largest manufacturers of canned foods, in 1987 ordered American growers to stop using twelve pesticides on crops grown for its baby foods.

The pesticides include alachlor, aldicarb, captan and cyanazine, and Heinz warned its farmer-suppliers that it would test the crops for residues of the pesticides to enforce the ban.

The move followed reports in the United States that babies, because of their low body weights, are especially susceptible to possible harm from pesticide residues, and all twelve of the pesticides banned by Heinz were under special review by the US Environmental Protection Agency.

A Heinz spokesman said: 'A lot of these chemicals are going to be proved safe, but we don't know which ones, so we are adopting a conservative position.'

A spokesman for the British Agrochemicals Association at Peterborough commented: 'Heinz has over-reacted to the fads and fears of the consumer movement. The salt in baby foods is likely to be more harmful than any of the pesticide residues they may contain.'

sider how often we and our children are vaguely miserable or unwell; how allergies, nervous diseases, bowel disorders, cancer, heart disease and arthritis are all widespread, probably increasing and inadequately explained.

Preservation of food is obviously necessary if we are to continue free of botulism, typhoid and other epidemic scourges of mankind. There is, however, nothing that can be said for straight chemical substitution of valuable ingredients with non-nutritious chemicals. Whatever virtues food manufacturers can claim to their credit, junk food dealings are downright dishonest, shameless profiteering at their customers' expense.

But, of course, chemical inputs into our food start earlier in the production chain, with the farmer and grower. Man has been growing food for thousands of years, but in only a brief fifty years or so has he been using large inputs of chemicals to increase yields of his crops. Yet there is adequate convincing evidence that if you exploit the soil in this way the result is a gradual breakdown of soil structure, so that it loses its vitality and there is a decrease in overall yield. The loss of a viable soil structure is accelerated by constant inputs of a vast range of insecticides, herbicides and fungicides whose residues actually destroy the bacteria that are essential for a living soil.

Toxic substances enter our bodies from the day we are born – some even before then. No doubt that some of the most dangerous are the organo-phosphorus compounds developed from wartime research into nerve gases, and the organo-chlorine compounds, such as DDT. These are synthetic substances. Their molecules differ from naturally occurring ones because nature cannot take them apart for recycling. They break down very slowly into other materials and can build up

A well-designed border in a small town garden in its fifth year from scratch. Fed only with home-made compost, the soil, once cold and heavy, has developed a good crumbly structure. You can add interest to a herbaceous border by giving plants unobtrusive labels with name of variety and planting date

in our body fat. They are a major factor in the swing towards a more natural way of growing food, the organic way.

Organic gardeners try to avoid using pesticides, but when they do they use safe ones of vegetable origin which quickly break down and spare natural predators and other helpful insects, such as bees.

In July 1986 Richard Lloyd, technical adviser to the agro-chemical giant Bayer, said: 'Virtually any weed, disease or insect pest can develop the ability to survive the application of a chemical treatment which was previously fully effective in its control.' That means the agro-chemists must constantly find new formulations to knock down pests, eliminate weeds and control fungal growths. It's a chemical treadmill, and getting off it needs determination and self-control. It is rather like giving up drug-dependency or smoking. But the effort can be extremely rewarding, not only because of the saving in hard-earned cash, but also because of the contribution one makes to a safer, cleaner environment and because organically grown food can be of superior quality with maximum flavour and maximum wholesomeness. If you grow it yourself and take it straight to the kitchen, you have the bonus of maximum freshness.

Those who have to buy their vegetables complain that more and more money now buys less and less flavour. Why? Because commercial varieties have been bred for the supermarket buyer first and the supermarket customer second. The com-mercially grown greenhouse tomato is a classic example of this: bred for maximum yield, maximum eye-appeal on the super-market shelf, the ability to grade, pack and travel well and to ripen in transit, but totally without that tangy taste that tomatoes used to have thirty or more years ago. When a farmer grows a field of cabbage or a market gardener plans the crop-ping of his plots and poly tunnels, maximum yield is a top priority. This invariably means a regime involving large inputs of fertiliser and water, and a major casualty when you are fighting to get the maximum weight of cabbage to the acre or the top yield of tomatoes from a tunnel is flavour.

The organic grower also wants to get the best possible yield from the space available, but it must be consistent with the best possible flavour from his crops. In stimulating growth for maximum yield the inorganic grower uses chemical fertilisers that are as expendable as North Sea oil. Nitrogenous fertiliser can be made by extracting nitrogen from the air, but this takes power. Five tons of coal equivalent are needed to produce one ton of fertiliser, so that's a highly questionable use of resources. When you add to the equation the loss of as much as forty per cent of all water-soluble fertilisers down drains, into ditches and water courses, causing nitrate pollution of our drinking water or simply ending up in the sea, then the cost of chemical fertilisers becomes a big element in the price we pay for food, including the Common Market's mountains. Arable farmers in Britain alone use over a million tons of artificial fertilisers every year and burn, as unwanted waste, about seven million tons of straw after the harvest. At a very conservative estimate that straw is worth £25 a ton, so that's £175,000,000 going up in air-polluting smoke every summer. But the waste doesn't end there.

Britain's livestock farms produce about 190 million tons of manure a year, but only a third of it is returned to the soil, the rest has to be dumped. According to Dr R. D. Hodges, of Wye College, there are more than seven tonnes of manure available for every acre of crop-producing land in Britain, more than an adequate amount to replace the nutrients lost when arable crops are grown, for example. Yet under a third of all crops and grass receives any farmyard dung or pig slurry. So although agriculture, including fruit and vegetable production, should be a producer of energy, turning the sun's energy into energy-giving food, it is actually a net consumer, and a very wasteful one.

THE SURVIVAL CYCLE

Modern agriculture's contribution to the energy crisis, says Professor Howard Newby, of Essex University, is that each of us eats the equivalent of approximately 100 gallons of petrol a year. 'As oil resources become more scarce by the end of the century, can agriculture continue in its present form? And at what cost to the consumer?' he asks.

Organic growing is more efficient than inorganic growing because it utilises the natural cycle of returning animal and vegetable matter to the soil. When you give back to the soil the waste products from your flower, fruit, vegetable and animal crops you are taking part in the cycle by which the world continues to survive. It is a process that has been going on for millenia. Trees shed their leaves, plants die, fruit falls and animals add their dung, and, in time, this organic matter decomposes and becomes compost. That, as we shall see, is at the heart of organic gardening. The fact that there is now such widespread interest in a return to this natural way of feeding the soil is in no small way due to the pioneering efforts of the Soil Association, which was founded in 1946, and the more recent Henry Doubleday Research Association.

For much of the life of the Soil Association its members were seen by the farming tycoons, the agro-chemical industry and the Ministry of Agriculture as a rather weird bunch of extremists, the muck and mystery brigade. Even the greatly talented Dr E. F. Schumacher, one of the most influential figures in the organic movement, became a target for derision by the far Right in politics along with the Confederation of British Industry, the Country Landowners' Association and

LACEY'S LORE

SPECIFIC PROBLEM

Every time a grower decides to apply a pesticide to any of his crops, he puts it at risk from chemical injury, says consultant entomologist in horticulture, Ted Dennis. This is because the product, though painstakingly developed in trials, still represents a complex chemical substance that the plant rarely meets in its natural environment.

Each pesticide carries with it its own specific problems caused by its active ingredient or the other complex chemicals used to formulate it. When other environmental features such as temperature, humidity and nutrient status are added, the physiological responses to the treatment, expressed as chemical injury, would appear limitless.

the National Farmers' Union. This was largely because of the best-selling book *Small is Beautiful* in which Dr Schumacher spelled out the message that man is pulling the earth and himself out of equilibrium by applying only one test to everything he does: money, profits and giant operations. But what about the cost in human terms, in happiness, health, beauty and conserving the planet?

'The case for hope,' said Dr Schumacher, 'rests on the fact that ordinary people are often able to take a wider view, and a more "humanistic" view, than is normally taken by experts. The power of ordinary people, who today tend to feel utterly powerless, does not lie in starting new lines of action, but in placing their sympathy and support with minority groups which have already started.' And that is exactly what has been happening. Membership of the Soil Association, HDRA, Friends of the Earth, the Green Party and other minority groups is growing steadily, so too is the vocal opposition of the establishment in the form of the NFU, CLA, the British Agro-chemicals Association and others opposed to the changes envisaged by Dr Schumacher. In 1984, for example, members of the National Association of Agricultural Contractors were urged to go on the offensive against the 'emotive, biased, vicious and ill-informed campaigns' being mounted against chemical farming.

A report on spray drift prepared by the Soil Association was described by the agricultural contractors as 'simply another addition to the flood of dubious, pseudo-scientific but definitely anti-chemical documents which are reinforcing the farmer-bashing campaign'. 'We are entitled to refute the foul allegations made against us by the Soil Association, the Friends of the Earth and all the other beardy-weirdies from the urban area,' they continued.

The same year, at the Royal Agricultural College conference on 'Organic Food Production', Prince Charles sent a message which included these words:

For some years now modern farming has made tremendous demands on the finite sources of energy which exist on earth. Maximum production has been the slogan to which we have all adhered.

In the last few years there has been an increasing realisation that many modern production methods are not only very wasteful, but probably also unnecessary.

The supporters of organic farming, bio-agriculture and optimum production are beginning to make themselves heard, and not before time.

With such Royal patronage 'the beardy-weirdies' had no need to respond to the crude remarks of the agricultural contractors and even the men at the Ministry were stirred, faint-heartedly, into action. It was discovered, to everyone's total consternation, that the mighty Agricultural Development and Advisory Service, with regional offices throughout the country, an army of advisers and a bill to the taxpayer of many millions of pounds a month, had no one on its staff to give advice on conversion to organic growing.

Two years later there was still little evidence of government support for the organic movement. ADAS sent two of its officers, Martin Phillips and John Whitehouse, on a tour of organic farms and market gardens in West Germany and Holland, and in February 1986 they published their report. They said they found the governments of both countries they visited regarding money spent on organic research as money well spent. This was because organic growing was attracting increasing interest from farmers and market gardeners who were fed up with high-input conventional methods; moreover, organically-grown crops were commanding high premiums. Mr Phillips and Mr Whitehouse told the Ministry: 'The demand for organic produce is increasing, as is the demand for advice from ADAS. To provide this, a sound research and development base is essential.'

And how did the Ministry react? They shelved the report. The time was not ripe, they said.

YOUR CONCERN

Whitehall always lags behind public opinion particularly when the established way of doing things is brought into question. But help for the organic movement will come, of that you can be certain, because as Dr Schumacher noted, 'Ordinary people are often able to take a wider view.'

Farming's dependence on agro-chemicals and what they do to the soil and the environment are not the province solely of the farming community and the chemical industry. This is a matter that is your concern and mine, as consumers, as voters, taxpayers and, perhaps, more appropriately, as gardeners. There are a lot of us in Britain. Some eighty-four per cent of all adults – 36,750,000 – have a garden, and about half of that total grow vegetables. We could and should set an example to the food producers by demanding healthier food of higher quality.

The quality of our food depends on the health of the soil, so that means we must insist that farming changes direction to prevent further damage to the soil, the environment and wild-life; that the waste of finite resources is halted; and that the use of potentially hazardous additives, growth promoters and flavour enhancers is phased out along with ethically unacceptable livestock systems.

We can set an example by growing our home-produced vegetables and fruit the organic way. At the start there are bound to be a niggling doubt or two, or more: What if my garden or allotment becomes a haven for all manner of pests and diseases?

Will all my efforts in raising the crops be in vain because they end up uneatable?

And what about yields? If I don't use artificial fertilisers, will the volume of food fall off to the point where the space I have available is too small?

Will I need more land to produce the same amount?

Will I ever be able to get together enough garden waste to make enough compost?

And so on.

I hope this book will settle those doubts and allay any other fears that the uncommitted gardener might have. In steering you along a path towards organic growing I have no wish to condemn everything about inorganic growing or to suggest that the organic movement has all the answers to the alternative way of crop production. We are having to rediscover a lot of what our forefathers knew instinctively about working with nature rather than fighting it with a costly armoury of chemicals. This means using recycled animal and vegetable waste to feed the soil and to retain and enhance its living structure. It means using natural insecticides and predators; using natural nitrogen fixation; and using crop rotation and resistant varieties of crops to control soil-borne pests and diseases.

2

UNDERSTANDING
YOUR SOIL

Kate Mares and the compost that has helped fashion a highly-productive market garden out of barren heathland

A couple of miles north of the postcard-pretty Suffolk village of Westleton is Brick Kiln Farm. Isolated, yet on the bustling holiday route to Dunwich, this two-acre market garden has been fashioned out of barren heathland by two middle-aged people, Kate Mares and Desmond Morrell.

It has taken them five years to bring the soil, so light and sandy that the wind and rain have scoured and rutted fallow land nearby, to its present highly-productive level. But not a solitary drop of herbicide, fungicide, insecticide or chemical fertiliser has been used in the process of putting heart into the soil.

'It hasn't been a question of taming the land, but of working with it,' Kate told me. 'That means understanding the limitations of husbanding this sandy soil and all the time trying to increase its capacity for improvement.'

We were at Brick Kiln Farm with a BBC Television film unit to shoot a programme in the Allotment Show series. I'd been asked by the producer, Eric Robson, to nominate a viable organic market garden, and I could think of no better place than Kate and Desmond's holding.

With us was Henry Noblett, recently retired head of horti-culture at Cumbria College of Agriculture. A very wise man is Henry and very conventional in his gardening philosophy. Nowadays, he reckoned, you just cannot grow things well enough without the help of the agro-chemist. But what we saw at Westleton altered his view fundamentally – it was 'astonishing, amazing, a fantastic achievement'.

No question but the couple have worked very hard indeed and no question that they have a relationship with the good earth that is both primitive yet built on the soundest of agricultural principles. Even so, Henry could still shake his head in disbelief that such crops, such a bountiful harvest of crops, could be produced without the use of artificial fertilisers and without pest and disease damage.

Kate Mares has the slightness of a ballet dancer, but a grittiness of character and a conviction of her place in the scheme of things horticultural that stifles comment about the good life.

'What we are doing is wholesome and satisfying. We earn as much as we need and no more. We don't exploit the land or ourselves, everything is in balance,' she said.

And that sums up growing the organic way: achieving a balance between what you give to the soil and what you borrow by cropping. It means reviving the old tradition of husbandry that when you hand over your particular piece of land it is in better heart than when you took it on. To do this you need to understand the character of your soil and measure its strengths and weaknesses.

There are many different types of soil, although only a few

Burdock, grown for its highly-flavoured root, gives complete weed-free ground cover at Kate Mares' smallholding

FACT FILE The pH scale

This measures the hydrogen ion potential: the balance between hydrogen ions and hydroxyl ions. It is a logarithmic scale so that pH 5.0 is ten times as acid as pH 6.0, and pH 4.0 is 100 times as acid as pH 6.0.

Below 4.5	pH extremely acid
4.5 – 5.0	very strongly acid
5.1 – 5.5	strongly acid
5.6 – 6.0	medium acid
6.1 – 6.5	slightly acid
6.6 – 7.3	neutral
7.4 – 8.0	mildly alkaline
8.1 – 9.0	strongly alkaline
9.1 and over	extremely alkaline

basic groups, and all have some features in common. All soils are composed of mineral matter derived from the weathering of rocks with the addition of water, air and organic material in varying proportions. The mineral content of the soil is the key to whether it is light, open and sandy or close, wet and sticky, although very few soils are at either extreme. Generally speaking, the larger the mineral particles the more open the soil, while the finer they are the nearer to pure clay the soil becomes.

Clay particles are at least a thousand times as fine as coarse sand, but in between will be a large range of mineral particles. True heavy clay consists of nearly fifty per cent clay particles, while a true sandy soil has less than ten per cent of these particles. Clay loam is eighteen to thirty-five per cent clay, while sandy loam has fifteen to eighteen per cent clay. You can judge the amount of clay in your soil by a simple hand test.

Take a small handful and moisten it, then knead it to break up any lumps. Does it feel gritty? Is it impossible to roll into a ball? If yes, then the sample is a sandy soil. If it can be made to form a ball, you have a loamy sand or a sandy loam. The difference is not important. If the handful of soil does not feel gritty, but forms into a ball that is weak and easily broken, the soil is a silt loam with more clay than sandy particles.

As we move towards the heavier clay soils the moist sample more closely resembles dough or plasticine and ranges from medium loam and clay loam to sandy clay, then clay.

So to two vital components of the soil: air and water, and one is largely dependent on the other. Flooded soil with waterlogging means an almost total loss of soil air and that spells death to both plants and the living organisms in the soil. Without any moisture the soil becomes barren and, eventually, a desert.

Earthworms are a great aid to aeration and proper drainage of the soil, particularly in those soils with fifteen per cent or more of clay. But there are many other living creatures in the soil and their presence or absence determines whether the soil is living and evolving or sterile and dead. I mentioned earlier the main groups of soil. They are clay, sand, clay loam or clay silt, sandy loam or sandy silt and peat.

Clay is cold and wet, difficult to work in the winter and slow to warm up when spring arrives. In summer it often dries out rock hard, making life very difficult for seedlings and shallow-rooted plants. On the credit side, clay soils are usually far richer in plant nutrients than the sandy ones and have better water retention during dry spells. It is a distinct advantage with clay to dig in the autumn and let the winter's frosts break down the lumps to make them more workable. Clays also need regular

FACT FILE The pH preferences

Asparagus	pH 6.2 – 6.6	Potato	6.0 – 6.4
Bean	5.8 – 6.4	Rhubarb	5.5 – 6.4
Beetroot	6.2 – 6.6	Spinach	6.6 – 7.0
Broccoli	6.2 – 6.6	Swede	6.5 – 6.8
Cabbage	6.2 – 6.6		
Carrot	5.8 – 6.4	Apple	6.1 – 6.7
Cauliflower	6.2 – 6.6	Cherry	6.7 – 7.5
Cucumber	5.8 – 6.4	Pear	6.1 – 6.7
Endive	5.5 – 6.4	Plum	6.5 – 7.2
Leek	7.0 – 7.5	Currant	6.1 – 6.5
Lettuce	6.7 – 7.0	Gooseberry	6.1 – 6.7
Onion	6.7 – 7.0	Raspberry	6.0 – 6.7
Parsnip	6.5 – 6.8	Strawberry	6.0 – 6.5

Three tips for digging. 1 Always dig with the spade held at ninety degrees to the soil. 2 Keep the blade clean and sharp. Scrape off soil immediately after use and, if the edge needs sharpening, file the back of the blade. 3 When the spade is put away for a time, wipe over the blade with an oily rag

dressings of lime or calcified seaweed because they tend to be acidic and they need plenty of organic matter worked into them.

At the extreme opposite is sand, which is light and dry, and often called early but hungry. It is gritty to the touch and can be cultivated at any time of the year, so turning it over is best left until the turn of the year. Sandy soils are usually poor in plant foods, especially potash, which is why they are called hungry soils, and they do not retain moisture readily. But because they can be worked at any time and warm up more quicky in spring than clay, they are early soils.

Like clay, sandy soils are often quite acid, so a watch needs to be kept on the acidity or pH level of the soil, especially as large quantities of organic material are needed to improve the soil structure and water retention.

In between the clay and the sand is a group of soils called loam, and anyone with a good loam in their garden or allotment is indeed blessed. Loam is a blend of sand and clay usually moderately well stocked with plant foods, easily dug and readily crumbled to make a good tilth, and well drained; maintaining a reasonable pH level is not difficult by occasional liming or an application of calcified seaweed every third year. It is possible to over-manure this group of soils which is why a yearly check on the pH level is a good precaution against the soil becoming too acidic.

Two other groups of soil are worth mentioning although their distribution is not widespread in the UK. In the premier hop- and cherry-growing areas of Kent you'll find a loam over a deep layer of chalk, while in the Fens, parts of Lancashire, Cheshire and the North East there are extensive areas of peat.

Hops and cherries flourish on the loam over chalk soils, but too often the soils are very shallow and rather starved of plant nutrients. A fairly commonly encountered lime-induced condition of plants grown on limey soils is called chlorosis, where there is stunted growth and yellowing of the leaves. But limey soils respond very well to yearly additions of organic material and can become highly productive.

Because we have become accustomed to using peat as a growing medium in various composts and in growing bags, it might seem to be the ideal soil to have in one's garden. But peaty soils have their snags. They are often waterlogged and very acid, but are plentifully supplied with humus, are warm because they absorb the sun's heat and are easily cultivated. The addition of farmyard manure to peaty soils is not recommended; it is better to add well-made compost as a mulch although, of course, the compost can contain a proportion of composted dung.

CURRENT ACCOUNT

So far we've seen that soil consists of mineral particles, air and water. But it is home also for a vast population of living organisms so microscopically small that it is reckoned there are about two thousand million of them in each teaspoonful of soil. These are the bacteria and fungi that quickly attack plant residues, such as the roots of harvested crops, and animal dung and convert them into organic matter and carbon dioxide. This is the soil's current account wealth.

The residue of less readily decomposable material is what we call humus. Along with the soil's banked deposits of the major plant foods, minor nutrients or trace elements the humus is the soil's investment account capable of giving a very good and profitable return to the organic gardener.

Where aeration of the soil is restricted due to bad drainage, panning of the surface or lack of earthworms, breakdown of plant residues and other material is inhibited and activity by the beneficial bacteria and fungi is far slower.

You can check on the humus content of your soil by this simple test. Take a two-pound jam jar or Kilner jar and three-quarters fill it with water. Now take a soil sample from your garden by using a trowel and collecting a sample just below the surface. For the test you'll want about half a cupful of soil. Put the soil in the jar of water and stir a few times. Now put it on a shelf and forget about it for at least thirty-six hours when you'll find the soil has settled into clear layers. At the top is the humus material and at the bottom is the sand and small stones. In between is a layer of muddy water containing the clay. If the layer of humus is 6mm (¼in) deep or more, your soil is rich in humus; if it is a barely visible layer, then you need to take steps to improve matters because humus is a vital factor in soil fertility.

Humus encourages plant roots to grow by pushing their way into the pores and cracks in the soil and then expanding so there is a continuous system of pores connecting the roots to the air above. Humus also enables water-soluble nutrients to be held in suspension, like water in a sponge. This is important because it slows down the loss of these plant foods by leaching through rain. Humus is truly a wonder material. It makes both sands and clays more crumbly and loamy and gives heart to unstable soils where there is high rainfall or wind erosion. At Brick Kiln Farm, Westleton, for example, plentiful humus in the top few inches of soil helps to prevent wind erosion when the land is free of crops and gives seedlings and transplants a good start in life because of nutrient and water retention. Lower down where accumulated dressings of compost have been taken by cultivation and the action of earthworms, there's a rich reservoir of plant foods and moisture for the deeper rooting crops such as carrots, parsnips and burdock. Because of this sponginess, humus helps to prevent panning of the soil by the pressure of men, machines and animals.

So, to summarise, a good humus content in the organic gardener's soil:

- Helps plants to develop a strong, searching root system which gives the plants anchorage against wind rock.
- Holds nutrients and moisture like a sponge at a level where the roots can reach them and helps to resist panning of the surface.
- Makes clay soils less doughy and sticky and assists drainage.
- Gives sandy soils more body.
- Gives stability to unstable soils.

There are several ways of providing humus: even digging in weeds and the green residues of crops such as peas, beans and potatoes. But this type of green manuring, including the growing of special green manure crops, has to be undertaken with care because often the decomposition of the plant material will cause a rapid rise in the bacterial population and this will rob the soil of some of its nitrogen. Other humus making materials are forest bark, which is very useful for mulching (see pp 57–9) but contains virtually no available plant nutrients; leafmould, particularly when it is made from beech and oak

LACEY'S LORE

PLANTS AS INDICATORS OF SOIL CONDITION

Acid soil The main weeds will include dock, thistle, daisy, plantain, creeping buttercup; and the main plants might include heather, rhododendron, azalea and camellia.

Alkaline soil The main weeds will include clover, campion, while the main plants will include beech. Leaves of acid-loving plants may show yellow patches.

Badly-drained land Rushes and sedges may be present with moss or green slime on the surface.

Fertile soil Weeds include nettles, fat hen, sow thistle, chickweed and groundsel.

leaves; spent mushroom compost which is nowadays made mostly from composted straw and lime; peat, either sedge or sphagnum, which can be dug in or used as a mulch; seaweed, which adds both humus and trace elements to the soil; straw, of which there is such a vast surplus in East Anglia; and farmyard manure.

However, all these materials and several others listed in the next chapter are best composted before being added to the soil either dug in or as a mulch.

Properly made compost, as well as providing humus and food for the soil, also encourages the activity of mycorrhizas which assist in the transfer of some nutrients, particularly nitrogen, and moisture from the soil to the plant roots. Mycorrhizas – myco means fungal and rhiza means root – have a symbiotic relationship with some eighty per cent of all flowering and food plants; they help the plants to feed and in return take carbohydrates from the plant roots.

Compost helps the mycorrhizas to flourish, but many of the chemical fertilisers in use today inhibit or prevent the work of the mycorrhizas. Chemical fertilisers also discourage the earthworms whose role in draining, aerating and enriching the soil makes them the gardener's best friends.

Charles Darwin, more than 150 years ago and streets ahead of his time, was the first great champion of the earthworm and his book *The Formation of Vegetable Mould* is an absorbing account of his studies. Of the earthworm he said: 'It may be doubted whether there are any other animals which had played so important a part in the history of the world, as have these lowly organised creatures.'

More recently Dr W. E. Shewell Cooper wrote:

The earthworm is naked and blind, and has no teeth or claws, in fact, no weapons of defence or offence. It has no mind to be afraid, and no feet to run away. It is the earthworm which continually renews and maintains the valuable film of top soil. All the waste products of life, the dead vegetation, the manure and dead animal residues are the chief source of earthworm food. It has been said that animal life, in all its forms, from man down to microbe, is the great transformer of vegetable matter into the food for the earthworm.

Even the animal itself, in the end, becomes earthworm food, for whatever has lived and died can be said to be food for the earthworm.

Darwin ended his book with these words:

The whole of the superficial mould over any expanse has passed and will pass again every few years through the bodies of worms.

The plough is one of the most ancient and valuable of man's inventions, but long before it existed the land was regularly ploughed, and still continues to be ploughed by earthworms.

Unhappily, that is not the case today. The use of chemical fertilisers, fungicides and herbicides on the scale we have today reduces the earthworm population. In fact, in some parts of the arable region where I live when the plough turns the stubble there's not an earthworm to be seen.

INTERNAL PLOUGHING

Given the right conditions, and that means the right organic conditions, there can be as many as eight million earthworms to the acre. Their contribution to soil fertility is enormous. Each worm can ingest about 4.5kg (10lb) of soil a year, producing worm casts that contain:

- Five times more nitrogen.
- Seven times more available phosphates.
- Eleven times more potash.
- Forty times more humus than is found in the top six inches of the soil in which the worms are living.

The work they do to help the gardener goes on for much of the year. I used to think that the worms hibernated in winter until I realised that organic matter left on the surface of the soil was being taken by fractions into the topsoil. Worms only go deep and pause from their internal ploughing of the soil during drought or hard frost.

Modern mechanical cultivation methods in the long term could be doing untold, permanent damage to the soil by reducing the microbial activity, decimating the earthworm population and so altering the soil structure that there could be both severe subsoil panning, particularly of clays, and loss of topsoil through wind erosion, particularly on light soils.

In a paper for farmers presented by Dr Victor Stewart, senior lecturer of the Soil Science Unit at University College of Wales, the warning was given that the structure of much of the arable land in Britain is being damaged by ignoring the 'sound biological husbandry principles which place emphasis on drainage and a vigorous soil population sustained by an adequate lime status and a high level of organic matter return to the soil'.

Anyone who fears that phasing out the use of chemicals in horticulture and agriculture will involve an alarming decline in the yield of crops should bear in mind that the days of our present methods making enormous demands on non-renewable resources are certainly numbered. It helps no-one at all simply to sit back and knock the efforts of those who are offering alternatives both to farming and growing methods and the Western life style.

Organic production is not less efficient because it relies on re-cycling: there need be little loss in re-cycling if we didn't waste so much. A good example of what I mean is the allotment. Many of Britain's half million or so allotments are entirely fed by compost, animal dung and other organic materials, and they are the most fertile and productive pieces of land in the country. Some allotments have been in continuous use for hundreds of years and generations of gardeners have farmed them, mucked them and passed them on that much better than when they took them over.

The acidity of the soil is another factor in fertility and we measure it on a pH scale which is the abbreviation for the hydrogen ion concentration. On this scale 7.0 is neutral; values above this mean increasing alkalinity with 8.1 to 9.0 strongly alkaline, and 9.1 and above extremely alkaline. A soil is slightly acid in the pH range 6.1 to 6.5; 5.6 to 6.0 is medium acid; 5.1 to 5.5 is strongly acid, while below 4.5 the soil is extremely acid.

In our temperate climate calcium is constantly being leached from the soil by rain, so most soils in Britain tend to be acidic rather than alkaline and, fortunately, most plants prefer a slightly acid level in the soil on the pH scale 6.0 to 7.0. If the soil becomes too acid, at pH 5.0 and below, key nutrients, especially the phosphates, become locked up in the soil, while minor ones, such as magnesium and calcium, can be washed out of the soil. Similarly, when the pH level rises too high above 7.5 the soil becomes so alkaline that essential plant foods are locked up and crops show signs of chlorosis or other symptoms of mineral deficiency.

A further complication today is acid rainwater which tends

FACT FILE Changing the pH level

Acid soils

It is far easier to modify an acidic soil than it is to change an alkaline one, especially over a wide area. Most vegetables thrive in soil that is medium to slightly acid – pH 5.6 to 6.5 – and regular dressings of compost usually provide just the right pH with, possibly, an application of dolomitic limestone, hydrated lime or calcified seaweed every three years.

On my highly fertile allotment land I apply calcified seaweed as a routine measure every three years at the rate of 113g (4oz) to the sq m/yd, although up to 226g (8oz) to the sq m/yd would be recommended if the pH dropped below 5.6.

I prefer calcified seaweed (lithothamnium calcareum) to other calcium providing treatments because there are other benefits. It improves soil structure and aids flocculation (improved

Kilogrammes/pounds square metre/yard of hydrated lime needed to raise the pH level to 6.5

Starting pH	Sandy soil	Medium loam	Peat or clay
4.0	1.70 (3¾)	2.04 (4½)	2.26 (5)
4.5	1.36 (3)	1.58 (3½)	1.81 (4)
5.0	1.02 (2¼)	1.24 (2¾)	1.47 (3¼)
5.5	.68 (1½)	.90 (2)	1.02 (2¼)
6.0	.34 (¾)	.45 (1)	.68 (1½)

crumb structure) in heavy soils. It contains 46 per cent calcium oxide, 4.8 per cent magnesium oxide, sulphur, copper, zinc, iodine and cobalt, plus about 20 trace elements. Calcified seaweed contains more minerals and trace elements than the old and popular basic slag.

Ground limestone or ordinary chalk (calcium carbonate) can be applied before planting or sowing a crop, as can calcified seaweed, but hydrated lime or quicklime is best applied in late autumn or winter and lightly raked into the surface. It should not be applied at the same time as animal dung.

More lime will be needed to raise the pH level to 6.5 on clay soils than on sandy ones, as you can see from the table.

Alkaline soils

Large dressings or organic matter help to lower the alkalinity of the soil. If there is evidence of waterlogging an efficient drainage system will also help to take away some of the chalk in the soil.

If the soil is pH 8.0 and above, apply flowers of sulphur at the rate of 113g (4oz) to the sq m/yd on sandy soils, and at 226g (8oz) to the sq m/yd on clay. Repeat annually, if necessary.

---

to exacerbate a natural tendency towards acidity in the soil and as the pH level slides down the scale, so the earthworms move out to more hospitable conditions, the helpful micro-organisms become less and less active, and dangerous diseases, such as clubroot in brassicas can flourish.

So it is important for the organic gardener to know the pH level of his soil from year to year so that action can be taken to bring it into the acceptable margins. To keep tabs on the pH is simple with either the Rapitest or the Sudbury pH testers (see addresses of suppliers). Both testers have a metal probe which is inserted a few inches into the soil and the pH reading is immediately registered on the dial of the meter. Also available from Rapitest are chemical testing kits for measuring pH, and

for checking the levels of nitrogen, phosphorus and potash in the soil or compost.

When you take over a neglected garden or allotment the weeds growing there will give some idea of the condition of the soil. On acid soil the main weeds will include dock, thistle, daisy, plaintain and creeping buttercup. Weeds on alkaline soil will include clover and campion, and any acid-loving plants will show yellow patches on the leaves.

Badly-drained sites are readily recognised by the presence of surface water with moss or green slime and, perhaps, rushes and sedges, while if you are in luck and you are taking over a nicely-fertile plot or patch of garden, the weeds will include nettles, fat hen, sow thistle, chickweed and groundsel.

3

MAKING AND USING
COMPOST

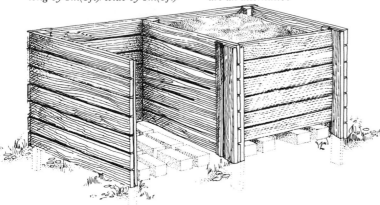

This is a good design of compost bin with two compartments and a removable slatted front. It should be no smaller than about 2m(6ft) long by 1m(3ft) wide by 1m(3ft) *tall and should have a cover to keep out the rain. The bricks at the base are optional. Brassica stalks and other woody material are an alternative*

The compost heap or bin is the kitchen garden's kitchen. It is the place where you make the food to feed the soil to feed the crops to feed the family. It's the powerhouse of the organic garden and while the making of compost deserves to be treated seriously, there's absolutely no need to invest it with muck and mystery, myths or degrees of magic. It is an entirely natural process.

To make good compost you first need the material, then the know-how. Good books have been written about making and using compost (see Further Reading) and they are worth your attention. But when you have finished reading this section of this book you should have acquired enough information to make your own plant food and will exercise your skill and judgement to make best use of that food. In the kitchen a cook can so make a hash of things that the food is uneatable, if it gets as far as the table. But with compost even if things go wrong it will still be good food for the garden or allotment.

I mentioned earlier that by giving back to the soil the waste products from your crops you are taking part in the cycle which ensures the world's survival. As organic gardeners, we both control that process and speed it up and, for those who have yet to try it, making sweet, friable compost from waste organic material is one of the most satisfying of all gardening activities, and one of the most useful. Unfortunately, some people hesitate to start making their own compost fearing they will end up with a stinking, gooey mess. Dick Kitto in his book *Composting* has some calming words to say about this:

The cycle of birth, growth, death and decay is one of the most inevitable laws of nature and, whatever you do, nature will be on your side and will come to your rescue.

So do not be put off by the experts who say, 'Oh, you should have done this or that', do not worry if your compost heap will not heat up or smells funny or seems to be waterlogged.

None of these things is a total disaster and even if you do nothing about them, you will get compost of a sort eventually.

The first and only major decision is whether you want quickly-made compost or are content to wait up to a year for the finished product. And that might depend on the size of your garden and the time it takes to collect enough material to start the process. The quick way with compost is called the aerobic method, while the slower way is called anaerobic and what quite often happens is that one starts with the decision to use the aerobic method and ends up with an anaerobic heap.

The key difference between the two systems is the aerobe, a micro-organism that can only live and flourish in the presence of oxygen. To produce good compost in as little as eight weeks, the aerobic heap must have an adequate supply of oxygen. In the aerobic heap you are achieving a sort of biological bonfire. The energy of the countless billions of bacteria at work in breaking down the compost materials creates heat. As the temperature rises different species of bacteria take over the work of consuming, transforming, excreting and recycling the

Well-made compost ready to return to the soil all the goodness plants need

You can make compost in a plastic sack pierced with holes. Almost as simple is this structure. The walls are of wire-netting and straw held in position by stakes. It has a cover over it, not shown, to keep out the rain

material. At the peak of the decomposition process the temperature in the centre of the heap will be about 65°C (150°F), which is high enough to destroy weed seeds, pests and diseases.

The aim with the aerobic heap is to maintain an adequate supply of air throughout the decomposing period, and the only way of doing this is to turn the heap inside out so that the micro-organisms have a chance to work on the outer undecomposed material. Several turnings may be necessary and at each turning the heat of the heap falls and takes longer to build up again. By the time the heap has cooled for good all the aerobic action will be over and the partly-made compost will gradually be colonised by anaerobic armies, including *Eisenia foetida* worms – the angler's brandlings which have a section to themselves on page 24 – earthworms, mites and insects, who all help to complete the decomposition. *(cont on page 26)*

This well-designed compost container has slatted sides to admit air, a cover to keep out rain, and a removable front for easy access for turning or removing the compost

YOUR OWN WORM FARM

The ability of the young to take an old idea and make it their own newly-discovered wonder is both charming and infuriating. We've all done it.

On a train journey to London a couple of years ago to attend a council meeting of the Soil Association another passenger, young, married and uprooted by British Telecom to work and live in Suffolk, told me he had invented a way of getting earthworms to turn kitchen scraps into compost. I hadn't the heart to tell him I'd been doing it for at least five years and that Jack Temple and Mary Appelhof had given it official recognition in the organic world by writing booklets about it.

Putting cooked kitchen waste on to the compost is inviting rats and mice to take up residence over the winter, while in summertime it is a magnetic attraction to flies. The answer is to start a worm farm using manure worms – *Eisenia foetida* – commonly known as brandlings which occur naturally in any heap of decaying vegetation and which can be bought from any angling shop because they are used as bait.

Unlike the aerobic compost heap which relies on a combination of bacteria and heat to decompose the material placed on it, the compost produced by brandlings is the product of the worms' digestive system. The worms digest and break down the waste material and convert it to a clean, organic compost that is rich in plant foods.

All you need to start your own worm farm is a plastic dustbin, some peat, a quantity of calcified seaweed or ground limestone, plus a regular supply of food scraps and waste vegetable matter and, of course, the brandlings – you'll need about 100 to get things going. To make your bin suitable quarters for the worm colony, it will need to have the right ventilation and humidity together with a close-fitting lid, to keep flies out.

Ventilation is achieved by boring holes in the lid using a drill or heated metal skewer. There will be some seepage so to allow this to escape and be collected in a drip tray for use as liquid manure, make small drainage holes in the bottom 15cm (6in) of the bin. Fill this bottom 15cm (6in) with a mix of pebbles and sand, then add water until it

Black, crumbly and with the sweet smell of wet earth, this is worm compost from kitchen waste

A plastic dustbin with close-fitting lid makes an excellent worm farm. When full, it will weigh about 75kg (1½cwt) so if you want to move it about, give it wheels, like this old sack barrow

seeps out of the drainage holes. This provides just the right level of humidity. Place wooden slats on top of the sand and stones so that when you fork out the compost you don't disturb the bottom layer of sand. Now add about two bucketfuls of peat or a mixture of peat and well-rotted manure or spent mushroom compost and you are ready to introduce the worms.

Add the worms to the peat, then the first load of well chopped household waste with a few sheets of moist shredded newspaper as a starter. The layer should preferably be about 10–15cm (4–6in) deep and should be sprinkled with the calcified seaweed or limestone, about a yoghurt carton-full, and a light covering of moistened peat. Manure worms are very sensitive to acidic conditions, so the calcified seaweed or limestone is necessary to maintain a neutral pH. They cannot survive if the compost dries out, so try to ensure that all the material is moist, but not wringing wet.

'At first you will need to be patient,' says Jack Temple in his booklet *Worm Compost*, 'for the colony will grow only slowly. But as the numbers increase the rate of multiplication will also increase and before long you will have a population explosion – myriads of worms converting your kitchen waste into compost swiftly and efficiently.

'Bearing this in mind, don't go and fill the bin too full to begin with: the infant colony will cope better with small quantities.'

All organic kitchen waste and leftovers are suitable except those that have been saturated in vinegar or fat. The more varied the diet, the more your worms will flourish. Each adult worm produces two to five cocoons a week, each containing ten to fifteen hatchings. These mature in seven to eight weeks. If you make your own beer, then add the spent yeast, along with crumbled stale bread, biscuits and cakes, stale milk and cheese. The more protein, the better. In fact, Jack reckons that if your kitchen waste is short in protein, the first two layers should include generous dollops of chicken mash or similar meal. We feed our dogs on one of the proprietary complete foods and have found that the dusty scraps at the bottom of the sack when moistened make a good starter meal for the worms,

but a stale loaf of bread would be equally as good.

This first dose of protein-rich waste should be added about two or three weeks after starting the farm when you should see signs of tiny worms hatched from the cocoons of the starter colony. Once you see these signs of population increase you can add further loadings of material, but don't fill the bin right up to the top. Sprinkle every 15cm (6in) layer with the calcified seaweed and peat. Some worm farmers recommend that you fork the new material into the existing contents, churning it thoroughly, but I've found this is unnecessary because the worms work their way up into the new material.

The compost is ready when it has turned dark and spongy like friable soil. This takes up to six months from starting, but is a mite quicker in the summer. The contents of the bin can be forked into an open-ended sack for storage, freeing the bin for another worm colony. Use a little of the starter compost for the next colony and so on indefinitely.

When dry, the worm compost can be sieved and handled like a concentrated manure. It is rich in the main plant nutrients and all the vital trace elements. It is ideal for use in potting composts and can be used as a plant food for the flower and vegetable plots sprinkled over the surface

of the soil and lightly hoed in.

Because heat plays no part in the making of worm compost don't add any garden waste containing weed seeds.

In the winter the activity of the worms decreases as the temperature falls until below about 8°C (45°F) the worms simply rest up, so if your bin is outside in the garden for much of the winter your worms will not be operating but the kitchen scraps will be gathering volume. You can encourage the worms to continue working by moving your bin into a shed or garage and providing some form of insulation for it. This could mean wrapping it around with a length of old carpet or similar material.

If the idea of having your own worm farm doesn't appeal, you can buy worm compost in a variety of forms. As a result of research at Rothamsted Experimental Station at Harpenden, Herts, a company called British Earthworm Technology was set up in 1983 to look into methods of exploiting that research commercially. Now the company markets what it calls vermicompost in a wide range of formulations under the label Betagro together with equipment and the know-how for the production of the worm compost by farmers at home and abroad.

Cross section through a dustbin worm farm with its first load of kitchen waste, from a drawing in the Soil Association booklet Worm Compost *by Jack Temple*

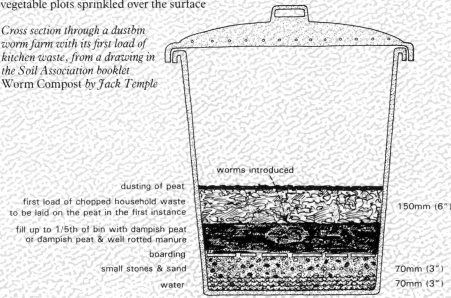

worms introduced

dusting of peat
first load of chopped household waste to be laid on the peat in the first instance
fill up to 1/5th of bin with dampish peat or dampish peat & well rotted manure
boarding
small stones & sand
water

150mm (6")

70mm (3")
70mm (3")

Finished compost is clean, sweet-smelling and full of food for the soil

At the end of it all each of your nine barrow-loads of garden waste will have become one barrow-load of valuable organic material that feeds the soil, improves its structure whether clay or sandy, and provides your crops, whatever they may be, with all the major nutrients and trace elements necessary for healthy growth.

In my experience it is always better to aim for an aerobic heap, even if it is only partly successful. This means putting your raw material in a bin or container of some sort, putting a cover over it and using an activator to get the decomposition off to a good start.

The choice of what you use to make your container is very wide. At Otley College we have a very successful compost container made from ordinary chicken wire netting walls, stuffed with straw and with four strong stakes as the corner posts, and we start off each making of compost with 15cm (6in) layer of straw. Over the top we throw a square of old carpet.

Go to almost any allotment site in Britain and you will see a good old mix of compost-making structures, although most will be stronger and longer lasting than our straw and netting affair. You can use bricks, corrugated iron sheeting, second-hand timber or straw bales, but the finished container should be no smaller than about 1.22m (4ft) deep by 1.22m (4ft) wide and 1.06m (3ft 6in) or 1.22m (4ft) tall and should have gaps in the side to enable air to enter the heap. It should also have a cover to prevent it becoming rain-sodden and a removable panel so that the material can be turned and the compost removed without having to dismantle the structure.

BIG ADVANTAGES

For those who want to make just a small amount of compost there are several proprietary compost bins, some of which we have tested at Otley. They all make rather optimistic claims about how quickly the compost is made; one even claims that it can turn garden waste into rich, brown compost in just three weeks. We found that in late spring and summer compost was made in this rotating barrel in six to eight weeks, while in the autumn and winter it took very nearly twice as long.

Two of the big advantages of the plastic bin or barrel compost makers is that turning the material inside out is not needed and a start can be made with quite a small amount of waste material. Although the experts say that anything that has lived is suitable for putting on the compost heap, I always exclude cooked meat and fish scraps and other kitchen waste that might attract rats. This material goes into my worm farm (see page 24).

With the anaerobic method you can make a start with just a modest amount of weeds, hedge clippings, lawn mowings, potato peelings, leaves, tea leaves, straw and so on. If you can also add some animal dung or bird droppings this will make an excellent activator and should give your anaerobic heap a right good aerobic start. However, the heat generated will be insufficient to destroy weed seeds and perennial weeds, so I'm afraid they will have to go on a bonfire along with any pest-ridden or diseased material. If you start an anaerobic heap during the winter, it will become well-rotted ready to use compost next autumn. Start in April or May and your compost will be made in about seven months providing you can keep the heap reasonably dry. Waterlogging is to be avoided like the plague because it slows down or even stops the activity of the micro-organisms. Most of the slimy gooey messes in compost heaps are due to too little air and far too much water getting into the heap.

Manufacturers of chemical fertilisers can play around with the balance of the main plant foods, giving a bit more nitrogen here, a little more potash there. When you make your own plant food in the form of compost, you might think that the

A plastic-walled proprietary compost maker

balancing of nutrients is a hit-or-miss business. It isn't. The process of decomposition results in a finished material that has a balanced amount of the nutrients required for strong, healthy growth of your charges, whether they are roses, raspberries or radishes.

However, if you decided to try to make your compost out of just lawn mowings or straw or potato haulms, for example, the aerobic process would be difficult to sustain. You would have either too much nitrogen content in the vegetable waste or too much carbon content.

To ensure both a proper balance and correct composting, one should aim to secure a correct ratio of carbon to nitrogen because adequate nitrogen is needed to start the process of decay and then to keep it going. The table of carbon-nitrogen content of materials is helpful to achieve that balance (see page 31). In some garden waste there are between thirty and seventy parts of carbon to each part of nitrogen, but the ideal C:N ratio for the heap is twenty-five parts of carbon to each part of nitrogen. If the C:N ratio is too high at, say, 100:1, the decomposition will be slow to start and nitrogen and phosphates will be lost. That's why it is not good gardening to dig raw vegetable waste straight into the ground – the resulting slow decomposition will rob the soil of some of its banked reserves of nitrogen and phosphates. Similarly, if you dig fresh manure into the ground the high nitrogen content will be largely wasted by evaporation as ammonia gas.

When you are building your heap try to achieve a balance in the carbon-nitrogen ratio of your materials, but if you know the total carbon content is getting on the high side, don't be too concerned as the activator will help to even things out. You could also add a bit of organic fertiliser in the mix to improve the nitrogen ratio.

The table shows the approximate carbon-nitrogen values of some of the commonest compost materials, with shredded newsprint – not the colour supplements – offering just carbon, and urine and dried blood giving high levels, proportionately, of nitrogen.

Two very good activators are fresh animal dung and fresh stinging nettles. In a 1.22m (4ft) by 1.22m (4ft) heap you will need a 7.5cm (3in) layer of either dung or nettles to every 15–22.5cm (6–9in) of compost materials.

Other good activators are powdered seaweed or liquid

FACT FILE Steps in making compost

1 Prepare the site by forking over the ground and, if dry, water well twenty-four hours beforehand to encourage earthworms towards the surface.

2 Build your container or place your ready-made structure in position. If it has solid walls of, say, breeze blocks, railway sleepers, corrugated iron or rigid plastic sheeting, you will need to lay down an aeration layer of staggered bricks, drainpipes or large lumps of rubble. If you are using ventilated sides, you can put down a layer of woody stems, such as prunings or brassica stumps.

3 Now add a 15cm (6in) layer of vegetable waste. It should be moist but not sopping wet. Follow with the activator of seaweed meal, dried blood, fresh nettles, fish meal, poultry manure, urine or a proprietary compost accelerator such as QR herbal compost maker, Fertosan or Bio Recycler. If you use urine – household liquid activator – dilute one part of it with three parts of water.

4 Add a second 15cm (6in) layer of waste and incorporate a sprinkling of calcified seaweed, 113g (4oz) to the sq m/yd, then the activator.

5 Continue building the heap in this way, but in between adding the layers of waste material always cover the heap with old carpet or sacking to keep the heat in, then put a wooden lid or plastic sheet on top to keep the rain out.

6 When the heap is finished it should heat up to about 65°C (150°F) within a fortnight. Test it by putting a metal rod probe into the centre, leave for a few minutes, then withdraw. The end of the probe should be hot to the touch.

7 Top up the heap, if you have enough material, when it has shrunk by about a third.

8 After four or five weeks turn the inside of the heap to the outside and cover again.

9 Test the heap with the probe occasionally and once it has cooled the second stage of decomposition is under way.

10 The heap should be mature in from twelve to sixteen weeks after starting. It will then be dark, friable and smelling of warm earth after rain.

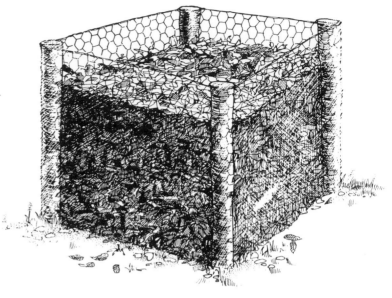

If you can collect a good quantity of fallen leaves, make a simple structure like this to turn them into humus-rich leafmould. See also page 41

seaweed extract, non-toxic sewage sludge, fishmeal or a proprietary brand of activator in powder or liquid form such as QR herbal compost maker, Bio Recycler or Fertosan compost accelerator. These are inexpensive and simple to use.

One of the best activators of all costs nothing. It's what the Victorians called night soil and following the precedent of Lawrence Hills what we'll call HLA. Household liquid activator is a mixture of one part urine to three parts of water, sprinkled over every 15cm (6in) layer of compost material. You can also use the contents of Elsan lavatories, providing each layer is immediately covered with soil or further mix of compost material.

As I've mentioned, you can make your compost heap from anything that has lived. However, some materials, such as sawdust and wood shavings, should be avoided because they slow down the aerobic process. Evergreen prunings are also unsuitable, along with manmade fibres. For this reason don't use the contents of the vacuum cleaner bag as many carpets no longer have any kinship with sheep.

SURPLUS SOIL

Try to avoid having too much of any one material. If you have, for example, a splendid lot of pea and bean vines, with a three-star rating for nitrogen and only one for carbon, you can balance the ratio with, say, autumn leaves or shredded newspaper. Crushed egg shells, feathers, bracken, tea leaves, bonfire ash and the hair from pet grooming can all be added to the heap in small doses. Bracken should be cut while it is still green.

Weeds should be added with the roots intact, although surplus soil should be shaken off, unless, of course, you are planning to add perennial weeds such as thistle and dock. With these weeds only the above ground growth should be added to the heap; the roots must go on to the bonfire. However, the ashes of the bonfire, when cool, can be sprinkled on the heap. Too much soil in a compost heap is a bad thing, so if you have a number of unwanted turves or a biggish pile of grassy weeds with the soil clinging to them, stack them separately and when they have decayed thoroughly use the loamy material as a potting compost. Similarly, if you are fortunate enough to have a large quantity of fallen leaves, make up a separate container and use the leaves when decayed as leafmould. A simple cylinder of wire-netting makes an excellent leafmould maker.

Unfortunately in our twentieth century industrialised society even garden compost made in our own garden cannot be entirely free of pollutants. Principal ones are cadmium and lead, mainly tetraethyl lead discharged by vehicle exhausts. This is a major contaminant of sewage sludge. Cadmium is found in industrial effluents and may also occur in sewage sludge. It is possible to extract this metal by an electrical process, but industry must be forced to do so.

Copper sulphate, used by pig farmers as a fattening agent, will contaminate pig manure and in extreme instances will gradually build up in the soil to a toxic level for some plants. Question your pig manure supplier about this and try to avoid dung from intensively-reared animals.

In the anaerobic heap the carbonic acid level can become too high, so you will have to watch the pH reading and correct the material mix with extra lime or calcified seaweed.

I am indebted to Soil Association members Joan and Peter Roberts for an interesting recipe for making what they call yeast compost. I haven't tried it yet, but I intend to.

You need a good supply of waste vegetable material, sufficient to make a heap 1.83m long by 1.22m wide by 90cm high (6ft by 4ft by 3ft); a good quantity of soil; a water supply, preferably by hosepipe; 448g (1lb) of fresh baker's yeast; 9 litres (2gal) of hand-hot water. Mark out a suitable site and cover it with the vegetable material about 7.5 to 10cm (3 to 4in) deep, then cover this with a 5cm (2in) layer of soil. Add a further 7.5cm (3in) layer of vegetable waste, then more soil and repeat until the heap is 22.5cm (9in) high.

Now prepare the yeast solution by stirring the yeast into .75 litre (1½ pint) of cold water. Next take .25 litre (½ pint) of the yeast mixture and stir it into 9 litres (2gal) of hand-hot water. Add one tablespoon of sugar and allow the yeast to start working. At an air temperature of 18–21°C (65–70°F) this will happen within a few hours. Below 18°C (65°F) it may take three to five hours.

Water the yeast mixture all over the surface of the heap which should be on to a layer of vegetable material, not soil. Continue building the heap in alternate layers and at about

FACT FILE Municipal composting

Early in 1987 in the Soil Association quarterly publication *Review*, Ulrike Oehlschlagel and Joe Lopez-Real, of Wye College, University of London, described some of the municipal composting operations in Western European countries.

Bottom of the league with just one sewage sludge plant producing 1,200 tonnes a year is the United Kingdom. Britons should hang their heads in shame. At the top is France with over 100 composting plants, producing 800,000 tonnes of compost, while the Federal Republic of Germany has 82 plants producing 715,000 tonnes of compost.

Much of this compost is derived from household refuse, although farmers are encouraged to contribute organic waste and local authorities compost sewage.

In the article, the authors note that:
In the State of Hesse in the Federal Republic of Germany, with the Green Party in the state's government, it was decided to re-define organic wastes **as valuable materials which become valuable materials again through the process of composting** *and back it up legally.*

In the case of both Witzenhausen, in Hesse, and Wurzburg, in Bavaria, compensation is also paid for not tipping organic refuse, and this extends the life-span of landfill sites.

Member States of the EEC produce the truly vast total of 2,300 million tonnes of waste every year, of which 1,600 million tonnes is organic waste. Because of the diminishing availability of landfill sites and the increasing cost of transport, alternative ways of dealing with this waste have been tackled vigorously by almost every country except Britain.

'Composting,' says the *Review*, 'is an attractive option due to a number of inherent advantages including bulk reduction of the waste, stabilisation, removal and control of offensive odours, elimination of pathogenic organisms and the production of an aesthetically acceptable and potentially marketable compost end product.'

If our politicians were more environmentally minded, we might one

Bill Skinner with Chicory, one of his goats. A founder member of the Soil Association, he has been committed to the organic movement for more than forty years. He lives at Great Waldingfield, Suffolk, with his wife Briar in a 400-year-old cottage. For his acre of crops Bill feeds the soil with compost produced by the Indore process using straw bales as the retaining walls, goat manure and plenty of nettles

day see the establishment of municipal composting plants, like those in most other European countries. One of the most vociferous advocates for this extremely sensible idea is Bill Skinner, of Great Waldingfield, who has been involved with the Soil Association since it was founded in 1946 and has been an organic market gardener in Suffolk and Lincolnshire for many years. He has bombarded the Ministry of Agriculture, Anglian Water

and the farming press with calls to set up a pilot plant to compost some of the vast quantities of organic materials that are now either dumped in the sea, into landfill sites or, like the seven million tons of surplus straw, are burned.

Anglian Water alone spent £119 million a year in 1986 on sewage disposal. Included in this is the cost of taking 11,000 tonnes from treatment works in Suffolk and Essex by tanker out to the shallow North Sea where it is pumped overboard. Many of us reckon that this could be damaging, in the long term, to marine life. It is certainly a costly waste of a potentially useful material. In the summer of 1986 a Greenpeace research vessel cruised along the East Coast of England sampling water at several places where there are both holiday beaches and outfall pipes pumping thousands of tons of sewage straight into the North Sea. Greenpeace found chilling evidence that at some of the most popular resorts sewage was drifting back from the outfall pipes causing tideline contamination so bad that no right-minded person would risk paddling let alone bathing in the water. Someone said, 'You don't swim, you go through the motions.'

On the positive side, Anglian Water is hoping an experiment at five sewage works in its region will cut costs. The plants are using a German invention in which reed beds are planted to do the work of sewage disposal.

When one considers the truly vast amounts of wasted sewage, the 100 million tons of wasted animal manure, the many millions of tons of wasted straw and other crop residues, there exists the raw materials to produce enough rich compost to fertilise and improve every acre of food-producing land in the UK, including our back gardens and allotments.

'It could create a revolution in farming practice and get us back to a healthier system for producing food,' says Bill Skinner.

Meanwhile, we have to rely on our own resources and, as one of my more cynical correspondents wrote, 'Compost is rather like money. It's hard to make, easy to spend and there's never enough to go around.'

45cm (1ft 6in) add a second yeast solution made as before. Continue to build the heap up to about 70cm (2ft 3in), then walk over the surface once or twice to compact the material. Water the top surface with the third 9 litres (2gal) of yeast solution and sprinkle the sides of the heap as well. Continue building up the heap in layers until it is 90cm (3ft) high then finish with a layer of soil.

LACEY'S LORE

COMPOST FOR SOIL HEALTH

Beneficial organisms which are formed during composting animal or vegetable waste may attack disease micro-organisms in the soil, so protecting crops against soil-borne infection.

Work at the Faculty of Agriculture, Hebrew University, Jerusalem, has confirmed that when properly-made compost is added to potting media,

harmful soil-borne organisms are reduced or suppressed.

If the materials are not properly composted or are sterilised after composting, the benefits are lost. The germination rate of seedlings and their subsequent growth rate is also increased when compost is added to the growing media.

Throughout the building of the heap ensure that the material is moist but not sodden; if too dry water with the hosepipe. After about five or six days the heat will have built up and the heap should be turned inside out. Turn a second time about ten days later and after about fourteen days the heap should be ready for use. While making, always protect the heap from heavy rain by covering with a sheet of thick plastic.

RECYCLER METHOD

Another interesting and, this time, well-tried composting technique is the Recycler method devised by Pan Britannica Industries. It both 'challenges and rejects many of the old rules of compost making' says the firm and was trialled in 1980 by some 200 horticultural societies and gardening clubs with considerable success.

The Recycler method uses mixed garden waste or just lawn mowings. Lime is not added, but a vital ingredient is soil in 2.5cm (1in) thick layers, and no turning of the heap is necessary. Bio Recycler is an organic-based material which provides the energy source for rapid bacterial development in the heap. The compost can be made in an open heap, an enclosed heap, a plastic bin or a hole in the ground. There are just five steps:

- Make a layer of greenstuff or lawn mowings about 22.5cm (9in) deep.
- Sprinkle Bio Recycler evenly over the surface. Two small handfuls should cover about one sq m/yd.
- Cover with 2.5cm (1in) layer of soil.
- Continue with another layer of vegetable waste or mowings, then the Bio Recycler, then the soil until all the material for composting has been used.
- Cover the top to keep out the rain.

The firm says that the purpose of adding soil between the layers of vegetable waste or grass is to help heat conservation, provide an abundance of bacteria and to absorb the water and gases which might stop or delay decomposition.

Hortichem Ltd supplies a complement to compost activators called Microgest, formulated from earthworm digested animal manure which has been air dried. Why a complementary substance should be considered necessary is not clear.

A frequently-asked question is whether pet litter from rabbit, guinea pig and hamster cages and dog's excreta should be added to the compost heap. We have three dogs and are very much opposed to owners who take out their dogs not so much to exercise them as to allow them to excrete in public places.

Our dogs mostly perform in their own garden and their excreta are collected and added to the compost heap. If they are taken short while out, their droppings are collected and brought home, and that should be a rule for all dog owners.

Providing the dogs are wormed regularly there is absolutely no health hazard to humans from dog excreta that have been properly decomposed. But if you are unwilling to use this material in your compost, you can buy a Dog Loo container for your garden which acts on the same principle as an Elsan closet and converts the droppings into an innocuous material for incorporating into the soil. Rabbit, pigeon, hamster and other caged pets produce a very useful material for composting providing they are kept on hay or straw. If the bedding is sawdust or wood shavings, don't add it to the heap, but use it as a mulch in the soft fruit department of the garden where it is helpful in controlling weeds and conserving moisture and, eventually, breaks down to humus substance.

Disposing of the woody stems of Brussels sprouts, cabbages and cauliflowers can be a problem. Normally, mine are placed as the aeration layer at the bottom of the compost heap. After two or three makings they are sufficiently decomposed to be added to the body of the heap.

TRENCH COMPOSTING

If your heap is already made, however, you can use the trench composting technique and, when complete, it becomes an excellent site for growing the runner beans.

In early winter take out a trench a spade wide and as long as you wish. Take out the soil to a depth of 30cm (1ft) and fill the bottom of the trench with a layer of about 15cm (6in) of the brassica stumps. Add any other vegetable waste and kitchen

FACT FILE
Carbon-nitrogen ratio of common compost materials

Material	Carbon	Nitrogen
Urine		★★★★
Dried blood		★★★★
Bone meal	★	★★★★
Fresh nettles	★	★★★★
Poultry manure		★★★
Pig manure	★	★★★
Stable manure	★	★★★
Pea and bean vines	★	★★★
Spent hops		★★
Lawn mowings	★★	★★
Potato haulms	★★	★★
Tomato haulms	★★	★★
Uncooked kitchen scraps	★★	★★
Annual weeds, plant debris	★★	★★
Cabbage, lettuce leaves	★★	★★
Fresh seaweed	★★	★★
Peat	★	★
Fallen leaves	★★★	★
Wheat straw	★★★	★
Shrub prunings	★★★	★
Newspaper, shredded	★★	

FACT FILE When things go wrong

If your compost heap fails to heat up properly, you can either resign yourself to it becoming an anaerobic heap which means waiting longer for your compost, or you can remake the heap and hope for success the second time around.

Here's a check list of points to remember:

1 Failure to heat up could be due to too dry a condition of the material or too wet. Make sure the heap is protected from rain and snow but is as damp as a well-squeezed sponge.

2 Don't forget to pre-mix the material and chop up any extra large pieces.

3 Too much soil on the roots of weeds and other plants will slow down decomposition. Shake off surplus soil before consigning the plants to the heap.

4 If the carbon-nitrogen ratio is heavily out of balance in favour of carbon, increase the amount of compost activator used between the layers, and don't make the layers of waste material too thick.

5 Do provide a square of old carpet or blankets to cap the heap and retain the heat.

6 Don't add material a little at a time, save it up in a covered container or plastic bag so that you can get maximum loadings of material.

7 Do ensure that air can enter the heap either from the bottom or at the sides.

8 Don't rush things. In winter the decomposition process slows down considerably. Try to organise matters so that your heap is finished in the autumn. The compost can then be used for mulching over the winter or turning in during the early months of the year.

scraps, but not cooked fish or meat pieces, then cover with soil to within 2.5cm (1in) of the surface, making sure that it is well compacted over the stumps. Add the remaining soil in April when there will have been further compaction after the winter's rain and snow. Runner bean seeds can then be sown directly into the trench in May or June or plants set directly into the trench.

The ability of the bean roots to fix nitrogen will assist rapid decomposition of the brassica stumps, and any overwintering eggs of mealy aphis and cabbage whitefly will be destroyed. Do not use any stumps which are infected by clubroot. They should be burned or put in waste disposal bags for burying by your local authority.

One of the most simple of all composting systems is the Brian Furner heap, named after its inventor. You pile all your waste vegetable matter and kitchen scraps into a stack-like heap or pyramid then cover it with heavy gauge black polythene sheeting. You don't add an activator or turn the material, all you have to worry about is whether or not this pleasantly warm pile has become the very desirable home for all the rats in the neighbourhood. That's what happened to my Brian Furner heap and when I got around to using the compost in early spring, after it had been working away for six months, I found a very sleepy hedgehog had also taken up residence and missed being speared by my fork by a whisker. You will also need to anchor the sheet against the wind. The Brian Furner heap does not heat up enough to destroy weed seeds and the roots of perennial weeds, so do not add them to the heap.

A retired United States Navy officer, Captain Macdonald, is responsible for another method, called the Californian composter, which is portable and especially suitable for the smaller garden where limited supplies of vegetable waste prohibit the use of something more substantial

You will need a roll of wire mesh 4.25m (14ft) long by 1.22m (4ft) high which is formed into an upright cylinder with the ends securely fastened. This is now lined with several thicknesses of newspaper, brown paper or cardboard cartons opened out and sown into position on the inside of the wire mesh. It needs an air course of old bricks on which you can place a layer of cabbage stalks or other woody material, then continue adding material to the cylinder with an activator as you would for any aerobic heap. When the filling in the cylinder has sunk by about a third you can lift it off and start another heap, using the undecayed top and bottom of the original filling. It doesn't make much compost at a time, but it does make good compost.

FACT FILE Increased Output

Here are some ideas that might help you gather more material together to increase your output of compost:

- Give your non-organic friends a plastic bag and ask them to collect their kitchen waste, weeds and lawn mowings for you. Give them a few of your organically-grown vegetables in return.
- Ask your local park-keeper if you can help yourself to the grass cuttings and the autumn piles of fallen leaves.
- Behind every supermarket you will find masses of unsold lettuce, fruit, cabbages, and other assorted fodder for your compost heap that the firm pays to have carted away and dumped. Ask the manager if you can take away some of that wasted produce and explain why.
- If you live within easy reach of the coast, find where and when the seaweed comes ashore. Usually this is in late autumn and winter when the gales loosen the seaweed's grip. A few plastic bags-full will cost nothing except the labour of collecting it and the petrol you use, but you will have a very valuable addition to your store of compost material.
- Grow a green manure crop especially to compost (see page 46).
- Old straw stacks offer a useful supply of material. Check with the farmer that they are unwanted and offer to relieve him of a bale or two.

Having made your compost, the important principle is to use it wisely, that's to say, it should be used where the plants want it at the time it will do most good. If you have enough to use as a mulch, that's fine. But unless your soil is a truly heavy clay, don't put it on the surface to overwinter. Spread it out in early spring.

For all plants and seeds that are sown or set out in shallow trenches or drills, place a 2.5–5.0cm (1–2in) layer of compost in the bottom of the drill or trench and sow into the compost.

When planting leeks with a dibber put a small handful of compost in each hole, drop in the leek, then trickle water into the hole so that the roots quickly get to grips with the nutrient-rich compost.

When planting seed potatoes with a trowel or spade or in prepared trenches, use a generous handful of compost with each tuber. Transplanted brassicas should also have a generous dollop of compost placed in the planting hole.

For planting herbaceous perennials, rose bushes, ornamental shrubs and fruit trees, it is important to incorporate compost beneath the roots at planting time. This helps to encourage a good rooting system and guards against drying out in late spring when we normally have a longish dry, hot spell.

The site should be prepared at least a month before planting to allow the soil and compost to settle. Use at least a bucketful of compost per tree or shrub, mixed half and half with the topsoil and add a bucketful of water before planting.

For the vegetable patch here is a programme for applying compost:

March/April Give the seedbed a generous quantity, and early potatoes, early peas and onions.

May Greenhouse borders and pots, asparagus bed as a mulch, strawberries, raspberries, gooseberries and currant bushes.

June Runner beans, maincrop peas.

July Planting out brassicas, celery, celeriac, leeks.

August Planting out brassicas.

September Spinach, planting out seakale, but not the spring cabbage.

October/November Broad beans.

The rotation of vegetable crops according to their feeding needs is described in Chapter 6.

FACT FILE
Make your garden safer still

The organic garden is a safer place for people of all ages, for pets and wildlife than the garden where poisonous sprays and powders are used. But you can make it safer still by following these rules.

- Keep children and pets well away when using power tools.
- Do not leave tools lying around. Store them tidily.
- Use a cylinder lawnmower: statistics show they are the least dangerous.
- If you prefer a rotary or hover mower, choose one with a plastic blade that can cut all types of grass for year-round safety.
- Don't use any electrical appliance in the rain or on very wet grass or hedges.
- Always wear proper outdoor shoes or boots when you are digging, forking or mowing.
- If you cut or entangle the electric cable of whatever machine you are using, immediately unplug at the mains socket before touching the cable or machine.
- Fit a residual current device for additional protection from electric shocks.
- Always unplug an electric machine or tool at the mains socket or switch off a petrol-powered machine before leaving it unattended.
- Check that electric equipment is properly wired. If using an extension cable, ensure that the pronged connector is fitted to the lead from the machine and regularly inspect the cable for wear and damage.
- Don't try to free metal blades with your fingers, even if the power is switched off.
- Some berries – honeysuckle and yew, for example – are attractive to birds and toddlers. They don't harm the birds, but can cause severe vomiting in children. Teach young children never to touch berries of any kind. As they grow older, tell them about the edible berries in the garden and show them the right way to harvest them.

4

FERTILITY,
THE KEY TO SUCCESS

The golden rule of gardening is to make the soil fertile and to keep it that way. That very wise plantsman, R. P. Faulkner, former head gardener of University College, Nottingham, said: 'If we ignore such factors as aeration, moisture retention, temperature and soil condition which makes for free root expansion, in a word, the physical condition of the soil, and apply substances whose sole value is their plant food content, then we run a grave risk of ruining the physical condition of the soil, and when we have done this we shall find that our crops will be poor, although we load the soil with concentrated plant foods.'

There's no doubt that high inputs of chemical fertilisers have enabled Western agriculture to achieve highly-profitable levels of production, even over-production of some major crops, but in doing so it has created massive problems for future generations. When the soil has been exploited on the scale of the 1970s and 1980s, when its performance has peaked at incredibly high levels, what on earth can it do for an encore? We are just beginning to count the cost of this blind disregard for good husbandry, this lack of love for the soil, and the organic movement believes it is an unacceptably high cost to pay for what is a relatively short-term advantage.

The purpose of this section is to describe the organic alternatives to the chemical fertilisers that are used so freely today by conventional farmers and growers.

Conventional is the wrong way to describe chemical farming, a technique that is comparatively speaking so young. Mankind has been growing crops for thousands of years using entirely organic methods. It is only in the last hundred years or so that artificial fertilisers and chemical herbicides, pesticides and fungicides have been used. So the traditional way is the age-old one in which animal dung was stacked and rotted or composted with vegetable waste to provide the main source of plant nutrients, while crag, marl, chalk or clay were used to improve soils.

In my part of Suffolk crag or shell-marl was once an important soil improver. Crag is the shelly deposit laid down in the shallow seas of the Pliocene and Pleistocene periods and although it was used widely in the West Country in the seventeenth century, it was not 'discovered' in Suffolk until about 1718 by farmer Edmund Edwards at Levington, a village near Ipswich which more than two hundred years later was to become the site for the chemical giant Fisons Levington Research Station.

Arthur Young in his *Farmer's Tour through the East of England* in 1771 tells how he tested crag.

I brought away half a bushel and have since tried it in strong vinegar, but it has not the least effervescence nor any ebullition; and yet it undoubtedly enriches the soil far more than any marl, for the farmers here lay on ten or twelve cart loads

an acre, and the effect is amazingly great; with this uncommon circumstance the soil is ever after greatly the better for it; nor do they in twelve or fifteen years, as is common with such small quantities of marl, find the benefit declining fast. But there is a strong notion among them that the land can only be cragged once; if it is afterwards repeated, no advantage is found from it.

This part of my intelligence I doubt very much, and especially as they find it very advantageous to form composts of crag and dung, which they practise much, carting the dung to the crag pits and there making the compost tips, turning it over twice and sometimes thrice.

The redder the crag is the better they reckon it. The effect of it is so great that, on breaking up the poor heaths of this county, they have had a succession of exceedingly fine crops of all sorts from such parts as they have manured with it, while at the same time other parts unmanured have scarcely yielded the seed again.

The farmers here are very attentive to all sorts of manures; they raise large quantities of farmyard manure, and cart it all on to crops and mix it either with crag or virgin mould, and this universally.

Norman Smedley, the historian, says crag, which contains phosphates and nitrates, was also much used to bring marshland into arable production, and the marsh soil itself was carried to the sandy areas.

LACEY'S LORE

DON'T PUDDLE

Puddling, the old idea of dipping the roots of plants and shrubs in a doughy mix of clay and water, was reckoned by the Victorian gardeners to be the best technique for giving transplants a good start.

Now we know that this can actually delay the settling-in period by creating a barrier between the fine feeding roots of the plant and their new environment.

Roots need air every bit as much as water, so it is better to water the planting hole before and after planting, not cake the roots with clay.

Chalk was taken quite long distances to the light soils in the east of Suffolk, but a widespread practice was claying. The boulder clay which covers a large part of East Anglia contains quite a lot of chalk and this, when mixed with farmyard manure, gave a well-balanced, humus-rich fertiliser. Clay was applied to the light land at the rate of thirty to forty cubic yards to the acre and after spreading in the autumn, the frost helped to break down the clods. Clay was also spread on and turned into the peaty soils of the Fens to help to consolidate them.

The value of coprolite was discovered by John Stevens Henslow (1796–1861) who was at one time Professor of Botany at Cambridge and Rector of Hitcham, Suffolk. Coprolites are the fossilised dung of prehistoric animals and are rich in phosphates. There were extensive beds of coprolite in Suffolk, and Henslow suggested that Edward Packard, of Snape, should exploit their possibilities as fertiliser. This he did with great success, first in a converted flour mill, then moving to Ipswich in 1849 and establishing a factory at Bramford in 1857. This was the foundation of the Fison fertiliser firm.

In Staffordshire we lived in Marlpit Lane, Moss Pit, and I suppose marl pits are remembered in this way at many other places. Marling was the equivalent of today's liming: a way of improving the fertility of light land and of adjusting the pH level of all soils. It is wrong and rather foolish to assume that previous generations of gardeners cultivated the soil without any science. Farmers and their workers husbanded the soil with the accumulated wisdom of generations and this was applied to the tending of cottage gardens every bit as much as the broader acres of the farm.

Crop rotation to enable plants to utilise nutrients to the best of their ability and to avoid the carry over of soil diseases, such as clubroot in brassicas, wasn't the invention of Townshend and Coke in the eighteenth century. It is mentioned in Virgil's poem on agriculture, *The Georgics*. Marl, a mixture of chalk and clay, was spread on the land in much the same way as modern farmers spread lime. Pliny says that the Britons marled their land in pre-Roman times and dug pits more than a hundred feet deep for the material. Townshend marled the light land of Norfolk with truly spectacular results.

Sheep on the light, sandy soils of east Suffolk were considered an essential part of farming. George Ewart Evans in *Ask the Fellows who cut the Hay* says:

Some of the older people say that it was a bad day when they left sheep out of farming in this district. For, they say, sheep fertilised the land, giving back to it the goodness taken away in the form of crops; and giving it back more efficiently than can ever be done by artificial manures.

It is fairly certain that in the past no farming at all would have been possible in the light, sandy soil or heathland of this district had it not been trodden and manured by countless generations of sheep.

There are few districts in England where the old proverb – the foot of the sheep turns sand into gold – could be repeated with more truth.

JUNK FOOD

What is it about these old techniques that could make them of any relevance to modern gardeners? What's wrong in giving plants their food in exactly the right doses of chemicals for maximum growth? In some respects it's much the same as offering a child the choice of junk food or wholefood.

To a child the eye-catching highly-flavoured meal of processed food, doctored with chemical additives, flavours and colours, is a far more appetising proposition than the wholefood alternative that relies on a natural content of vitamins, trace elements and roughage. You can't blame the child for choosing the junk stuff. Some unfortunate children are fed almost exclusively on processed, de-natured food and they look well enough on it, although there may be early signs of podginess and a tendency to catch every ailment around. But what happens later on when the child becomes adolescent, then adult? Why are bowel disorders, gastric problems, allergies, heart disease and obesity becoming so commonplace? Why is our nation's health steadily worsening? Could it be connected with the deteriorating health of the soil and an increasing dependence on junk food? Many experts believe that the connection has been proved convincingly and that there must be a radical change of attitude in both the way we grow our food and in what we eat.

You can grow plants by feeding them just the three main plant foods in chemical form – nitrogen, the leaf maker; phosphate, the root maker; and potassium, the flower, fruit and seed maker. And you don't even need soil. Using hydroponics or the newer nutrient film technique, the plants are given their food as soluble chemicals diluted in water. But plants grown this way lack the vigour and stamina to resist pests and diseases, would find it impossible to live outside the strictly controlled environment of the glasshouse and, as food crops, cannot compare in flavour with organically grown produce. The same goes for plants grown in soil that is fertilised only by artificial fertilisers. In time, the problems of pests, diseases, soil instability and declining yields become more and more marked.

Organic fertilisers feed the soil. They improve its structure, its crumbiness and so improve its drainage and aeration. They encourage the earthworms and the bacteria that help to release the nutrients from the soil to the plants. It's slow and steady, unlike the effect of chemical fertilisers which too often give a short sharp boost from too-rapid nitrogen uptake. Vegetables fed in soil enriched with organic fertilisers have a superior flavour and longer storage life in the case of root crops because their dry matter content is higher. Cabbages and cauliflowers have tighter hearts, Brussels sprouts have tighter buttons with that marvellous nutty flavour, onions keep longer, potatoes cook better and taste far, far better, carrots are more nutritious, peas are sweeter, and so on.

Sceptics call the organic gardeners the muck and mystery brigade. But the only mystery to me is why more people aren't growing the organic way. One reason, of course, is the power of the chemical companies who spend vast sums of money on promoting their products. In contrast only a tiny amount is spent by charities such as the Soil Association and Henry Doubleday Research Association in trying to promote the organic way of growing food and in trying to revive some of the time-honoured skills of husbandry.

Most soils in mixed farming – where animals, grass and crops are raised – contain adequate amounts of the main plant nutrients, but our gardens and allotments are another story.

INTENSIVE REGIME

Where we are growing food crops we expect to get maximum output from quite small areas. In fact, it is reckoned that most allotment plots are far more productive than the farmland they once were. But this highly intensive regime of growing calls for regular replacement of the nutrients taken by cropping and lost by leaching, particularly of nitrogen and phosphates.

Regular and adequate feeding of the soil with farmyard manure or compost is usually enough to maintain and build up the fertility of all except the poorest, lightest soils. When the organic gardener needs to supplement his soil-feeding programme because of a shortfall of manure or compost or because of the special demands of his crops, there are organic fertilisers and ground minerals available, such as bone meal, seaweed in dried, powdered and liquid forms, hoof and horn meal, dried blood, fish meal, rock potash, rock phosphate and dolomitic limestone. The purist might argue that there is little difference between providing potassium to a garden soil as a straight chemical or as the ground mineral rock potash. Lawrence Hills in his booklet *Feeding the soil the organic way* has summarised the argument like this:

The basic problem is the solubility of chemical fertilisers. This makes them available all at once, in massive concentrations, and they are leached away almost as suddenly.

This criterion allows the organic grower to draw the line between chemical fertilisers like superphosphate, and ground minerals like rock phosphate or between sulphate of potash and rock potash.

Organic fertilisers, which include ground minerals, have to be made available by the action of bacteria, fungi and plant root secretions. The following list of organic fertilisers gives some idea of their value as whole foods for the soil and as supplementaries when there are deficiencies. Not all are widely available and most are, initially, more expensive than the chemical versions, but it must be remembered that they may last up to three years or more in the soil, slowly releasing not only the main plant foods but also the vitally important trace elements which can be locked up out of reach of plant roots by the use of chemical fertilisers.

The use of potash and phosphate artificial fertilisers by farmers and growers has remained relatively static since 1949 compared with the nitrogenous fertilisers. These have rocketed from 185,000 tonnes in 1949 to 1,588,000 tonnes in 1984. Nitrogen is the plant food required in the greatest quantity by most crops, and it's certain that all the time cereal production remains highly profitable – despite the EEC grain mountains – so the use of nitrogenous fertilisers will continue to increase.

Because the cost of nitrogen fertiliser is closely linked to oil prices, as crude oil prices shot up in the 1970s, so fertiliser prices followed suit. Yet anything up to sixty per cent of the nitrogen in chemical fertilisers is wasted either because when it is distributed as granules it fails to hit the target of accurate placement near the plant roots or because the rain rapidly leaches it through the soil, or both. Nitrogen leached through the soil enters our drinking water as nitrates. In some parts of the country, notably where I live in East Anglia, the nitrate level is well above the EEC limit of fifty milligrams per litre.

In 1979 the Royal Commission on Environmental Pollution reported that: 'It appears . . . that if action had to be taken to reduce nitrate levels in water it would be more cost effective for the (water) authorities to install plants for nitrate removal than to impose restrictions on fertiliser use.'

Since then the grain mountains have grown and, as 1987 moved to a close, a tax on the use of nitrogenous fertilisers seemed to be the soft option most favoured by the Euro MPs. From the table on page 47 you can judge the value of each of the organic fertilisers in terms of the main plant nutrients, although many will also give quantities of the minor nutrients and trace elements, such as calcium, iron, magnesium, boron and zinc. You will see that seaweed, for example, is a balanced fertiliser. But it is particularly valuable for the wide range of trace elements it contains, while the alginate content breaks down into humus to improve as well as nourish the soil.

If you would like to prepare your own well-balanced organic fertiliser, mix by weight one part of seaweed meal, one of dried blood, one of hoof and horn and two parts of bone meal. Use this at about 113g (4oz) to the sq m/yd in early spring for all your root crops, brassicas, peas and beans and work into the top 15cm (6in) of soil.

ANIMAL HAIR

Not, perhaps, available in bulk, but those of us with pets might like to know that the hair we get from grooming is a good, slow-release source of nitrogen.

In the compost heap spread it and mix it as thoroughly as possible because it is slow to break down. If not composted, turn the hair in to the top 15cm (6in) of the soil in winter.

Calcified seaweed, one of the most versatile organic fertilisers

BONE MEAL

Sometimes available also as bone flour and crushed bones. This fertiliser is a good source of phosphates and is excellent for all crops. The bone flour releases its nutrients over a full growing season, the meal does so over about two years, while the crushed bones will go on releasing nutrients slowly and steadily for as long as ten years.

Bone meal and crushed bones are especially valuable on light soils where leaching of phosphates can be a problem.

For bone meal the rate of application is 85g (3oz) to the sq m/yd in early spring. When planting shrubs, roses, fruit bushes and raspberry canes, give 113g (4oz) to the sq m/yd or to the individual planting hole, well mixed with the soil.

BRACKEN

Only valuable when cut green and composted or burnt. Cut the bracken while still green in late summer and burn it in a slow bonfire to provide a good source of potash. Store in a damp-proof container, such as a tightly tied plastic bag, and apply in April at the rate of about 450g (1lb) to the sq m/yd. This is particularly appreciated by gooseberries and strawberries.

CALCIFIED SEAWEED

One of the most versatile of organic fertilisers because, as well as its richness in calcium, magnesium and trace elements, it can be used as a tonic for established soft and top fruit plantations, as a compost activator, as an ingredient of the home worm farm (see page 24) and in place of lime as a soil sweetener and conditioner.

Calcified seaweed is a calcareous magnesium algae resembling coral and known to marine botanists as *Lithothamnium calcareum*. It is dredged from the seabed off the Cornish coast, crushed and cleaned, graded and packed by the Cornish Calcified Seaweed Company. As a marine product it is, of course, insoluble in water, and it is very attractive to soil bacteria which quickly colonise the granules and start to break them down, releasing their nutrients. This increase in bacterial activity helps to build a better soil structure, especially of the

Many plants benefit from foliar feeding in spring and summer. A seaweed spray, such as SM3, helps plants to fight attacks by pests and diseases and to stay in production longer. This is a rechargeable battery-operated electric sprayer that is ideal for those with weak or disabled hands

heavy soils, and so enables the plants to develop a strong, thrusting root system.

I much prefer calcified seaweed to lime in keeping my soil sweet at a pH range for my vegetables of 6.0 to 6.5. Lime is readily lost through leaching and, although calcified seaweed has a lower neutralising value, it has a longer neutralising effect than lime and there is far less risk of over-neutralising with a consequent locking up of trace elements. As a combined fertiliser and neutralising agent use calcified seaweed at the rate of about 113g (4oz) to the sq m/yd every three years.

CHILEAN NITRATE

This is an unrefined but water soluble salt whose use is no longer permitted by the Soil Association for its Symbol licencees, but is still allowed in moderation by Organic Farmers and Growers Ltd. It is found in large deposits in Chile and contains about sixteen per cent nitrogen and twenty-six per cent sodium. Being a soluble salt, it is very quick acting and starts working within three days of application.

I have never used this material, but I believe it would be a very useful top dressing for the lawn and a good fertiliser for swedes and turnips. The snag is, I know of no firm that offers Chilean nitrate in smaller lots than a 50kg (110lb) bag, so if you want a supply the best plan would be to order a bag through your gardening club or allotment association and dole it out in smaller units. Rate of application is about 56g (2oz) to the sq m/yd.

DOLOMITE

Dolomitic limestone contains about sixty per cent calcium carbonate and forty per cent magnesium carbonate. It is a ground rock and can be used instead of lime or calcified seaweed as a neutralising agent both on the soil and in the compost heap. It is also very useful in preventing or correcting magnesium deficiency sometimes encountered with crops that demand a lot of potash, such as tomatoes, potatoes and gooseberries. For general use about 113g (4oz) to the sq m/yd is the dosage.

DOLOMITE AND GYPSUM

This is a clay soil conditioner rather than a fertiliser. Used as a mixture of about eighty per cent gypsum and twenty per cent dolomite, it is a valuable flocculator; that's to say, it causes the fine particles of clay to coagulate and form larger fragments or crumbs.

The improvement in soil structure after applying this mixture can be considerable and nutrients that were once locked up by the clay are made available to the plants.

One application is not enough to effect a radical change, however. So the drill on a heavy clay is to apply the 80–20 mix at the rate of 340g (12oz) to the sq m/yd in the early spring and hoe it into the top few inches. Apply a second similar dressing in October or November and hoe it in again. Repeat the treatment the following year and in subsequent years just give a dressing of 85g (3oz) to the sq m/yd.

The gypsum, which is mainly calcium sulphate, is neutral pH, although it also contains silica, aluminium oxide and other minerals.

DRIED BLOOD

Just after the end of the 1939–45 War, Chesthunt Research Station produced a scale to compare the amount of available nitrogen in fertilisers which would be released to the plants within twenty days. At the top was urea with a score of 170, but well up among the nitrogen leaders were dried blood, and hoof and horn, both with ratings of 100. Of the two, dried blood used as a liquid fertiliser is the faster acting, giving a rapid boost to leafy crops when applied in early spring. It never causes flagging through sappiness as chemical fertilisers do, but is best followed by a supportive organic fertiliser, such as hoof and horn. Use of dried blood is restricted for Soil Association Symbol holders. It is best used in liquid form at the rate of 56g (2oz) in 1.12 litres (1 quart) of water per sq m/yd. Place the powdered dried blood in a glass or plastic container and allow to soak for at least three days, stirring now and then. Use round the plants having first moistened the soil if it is dry. If that is not possible, sprinkle the powder round the plants then water with a fine rose on the watering can and tease into the surface.

FEATHERS

The fillings from old feather pillows or feathers from home-raised hens provide a good source of nitrogen and should be dug in on medium and light soils, not clay, at the rate of about 140g (5oz) to the sq m/yd during the autumn and winter.

FISH MEAL

Once the most popular of the organic fertilisers, fish meal is now both scarce and costly, so one is usually offered an organic version of the compound Growmore chemical fertiliser as fish, blood and bone fertiliser. This contains, on average, 5.1 per cent nitrogen, 5 per cent phosphorus and 6.5 per cent potash, although you could maybe find your own supplies of the ingredients and vary the balance a bit.

Work this compound fertiliser into the top few inches of the soil in early spring at the rate of 56g (2oz) to the sq m/yd and repeat when the crops are about half grown.

The potash in this mixture is usually finely ground rock potash and if this fertiliser is used year after year there is a tendency for the potash to build up a reserve in the soil. This can cause the magnesium in the soil to be denied to the plants and a typical symptom is the yellowing of tomato leaves.

As with all fertilisers, always wash your hands after using fish, blood and bone; store the container in a cool, dry place away from children, pets and foodstuffs, and always stick to the recommended rate of application.

FOLIAR FEEDS

Feeding plants through their leaves is well-established horticultural practice. There are numerous feeds on the market, many of them with an organic base but with added chemicals.

For the organic grower liquid foliar feeds with a seaweed base are popular and versatile. Some of the new ones, involving enzymes and amino acids, are still being investigated by the Soil Association. Seaweed extracts have been used for many years and their value is well proven. They contain proportions of the main plant foods, many trace elements, cytokin growth hormones and alginates which act as a wetting agent and seem to discourage sucking insects such as aphids. Because of this sticking effect of seaweed liquid preparations, many gardeners and commercial growers use such a product when applying organic insecticides, such as derris and pyrethrum, or the fungicide sulphur.

Foliar feeding with seaweed liquid is an important remedy for trace element deficiency. The liquid should be sprayed or watered on the plants every fortnight until the symptoms disappear.

SM3 (Sea Magic) is a concentrated form of selected seaweeds and land plant tissues which can be used as a soil conditioner, house plant fertiliser and foliar feed.

Farmura is the commercial equivalent of the old technique of hanging a sack of farmyard manure in a barrel of rainwater. It contains the main plant nutrients and many trace elements and is widely used by soft fruit and top fruit growers and is especially valuable for potato and tomato crops.

GOAT MANURE

An excellent fertiliser containing all three major plant foods. It is best composted, but otherwise should be allowed to rot with a generous amount of straw or other vegetable material. It also makes a good liquid manure. Simply hang a sack of it in a drum of water, allowing about a pailful of manure to three pailfuls of

water. Put a decent sized stone in the bag to stop it floating on the surface and leave it for a week. Before use, the liquid must be diluted until it is the colour of weak tea. You can add water to make up the previous volume until the liquor loses much of its colour. The old manure can then go on the compost heap and fresh manure be placed in the sack.

Although an organic liquid fertiliser such as this made from goat manure will not scorch foliage, as will some chemical preparations, it is always better to use the liquid on the weak side rather than too strong. Two applications of a weak liquid manure are far more beneficial than one dose of over-strong stuff.

GREEN MANURES

This is one of the best ways to improve soil structure, provide humus and nutrients and prevent soil erosion and nutrient leaching, so it is a major subject in itself and is fully dealt with in Chapter 5 starting on page 46.

HOOF AND HORN

This is becoming scarcer every year and therefore more expensive. It is a medium to slow release nitrogen source and for best effect should be applied as a base dressing when preparing the soil in winter or early spring. The rate is 112g (4oz) to the sq m/yd. Add about 56g (2oz) to each bucketful of potting soil when repotting plants.

For the fruit garden use hoof and horn meal at the rate of 112g (4oz) to the sq m/yd when planting new stock of all the soft fruits. Apply at the same rate to Brussels sprouts when the plants are transplanted. Do not use on spring cabbage, spinach, Swiss chard or sprouting broccoli which has to stand the winter.

HOPS

If you can get hold of a supply of spent hops from a friendly local brewer, use the material as a soil improver rather than as a fertiliser, although you could add a general organic fertiliser to the hops to remedy the deficiency of nutrients. Dig in the spent hops at the rate of about 1–1.5kg (2–3lb) per sq m/yd.

HORSE MANURE

Becoming somewhat easier to get as more and more riding stables are set up, but not all the establishments use straw as a litter — some use wood shavings. If you can find a stable that uses straw, buy the manure as fresh as possible in as big a load as possible and rot it down using the Brian Furner heap technique (see page 31). If the heap is loosely stacked and gets too dry, it will be infected by firefang fungus and lose some of its value.

Use the well-rotted manure at the rate of a barrowload to each 4.5m (15ft) row, turning it in from October to March.

LEAFMOULD

There's only a miniscule amount of plant food left in dried, fallen leaves, but they are a good source of humus and so leafmould is a useful soil conditioner. Beech and oak are best, but avoid evergreens.

Dig in at the rate of 2.25kg (5lb) per sq m/yd in autumn and winter or apply to the shrubs in the garden as a mulch at any time when the soil is moist. Always rake aside any mulch still in situ during the winter to allow the birds to find and eat any pupating pests. Restore the mulch in early spring, having first given a light surface dressing of a balanced organic fertiliser if you feel the need for it.

LIME

As I have explained elsewhere, I no longer use lime on my vegetable patch as I prefer the longer-term benefits of calcified seaweed. Nowadays, regular liming is necessary for many areas where the effect of acid rain can be measured in a marked swing down the pH scale.

Lime is a definite source of plant food which is continually being leached from the soil. A 300sq m (10-rod) allotment, for example, can lose as much as 12.6kg (28lb) of lime a year. Lime sets free otherwise unavailable reserves of nitrogen and phosphates and gives great encouragement to the earthworms. It has a sweetening effect on all soils, but is particularly recommended for breaking down heavy soils.

It is available as hydrated lime, quicklime, dolomitic limestone and carbonate of lime. Quicklime is the most concentrated form of lime and is sold in lumps that are caustic. Before use in the garden it must be slaked, unless ready-slaked lime can be supplied.

Quicklime should be spread at any rate to a maximum of 750g (1½lb) to the sq m/yd.

Hydrated lime is sold as a fine, non-caking powder, harmless to growing crops, although it should not be spread within fourteen days of seed sowing. Use at the rate of 250g (½lb) to the sq m/yd on heavy soil, and about 112g (4oz) to the sq m/yd on light and average soils.

Dolomitic limestone gives a long-lasting source of lime with the bonus of a generous supply of magnesium. Use it at the rate of up to 500g (1lb) per sq m/yd.

Carbonate of lime is generally recommended on light soils instead of hydrated lime because it is less soluble and not so readily leached out of the soil. The rate is about 168–250g (6–8oz) to the sq m/yd.

MANURE AND PEAT

Several proprietary brands are sold and they are usually a combination of cow manure and peat or horse manure and peat, composted together. Some firms add seaweed meal, so as well as supplying humus and the major plant foods, their product also gives a broad spectrum of trace elements.

In general, these products are very useful for those with a poor soil, but they can work out pretty expensive. They should be used according to the instructions on the bag.

MUNICIPAL COMPOST

If my friend Bill Skinner had his way, every large town and city would have its own composting plant to turn household and shop waste into recycled compost to make a useful addition to the soil with a consequent reduction in the rates.

Some of the more enlightened local authorities already do this, taking dustbin refuse and composting it with sewage sludge. It is then sold as a dark-coloured powder with a low nitrogen content, but a good source of humus. However, sewage sludge will contain some heavy metals which could build up in the soil, so try to get hold of an analysis before use and don't be tempted to use municipal compost exclusively. It is not an acceptable alternative to your own home-made compost.

Municipal compost may contain fragments of glass and plastic, so do not use as a top dressing. Dig it in at the rate of about 1.5kg (3lb) to the sq m/yd in winter or early spring and always use a shovel or trowel to handle it, never your bare hands.

MUSHROOM COMPOST

This is very variable in quality and composition, so before you buy ask a few questions about how the compost was made. Avoid compost made entirely from straw composted with chemical activators and without any horse manure. Almost all mushroom compost will contain insecticide residue, so the safest way of dealing with it is to add it to your compost heap.

Compost showing signs of firefang fungus will have lost value as a source of plant food but can still provide humus.

Good mushroom compost contains a fair balance of nutrients and makes an acceptable alternative to home-made compost and should be used at the rate of a barrowload to each 4.5m (15ft) row whether dug in during the winter or early spring or spread as a mulch.

Dr David Bellamy holds bladderwrack seaweed during one of his BBC TV series. Seaweed is the nearest thing to a complete organic fertiliser, and is an excellent activator for the compost heap

PIG MANURE

This is often shunned by organic purists because most of it comes from factory farms where the animals are kept under intensive conditions. It should certainly not be used year after year. Pig feeds include copper that can accumulate to a dangerous level in the soil. Never use pig manure until it has been stacked and rotted for at least eight months and, if possible, compost it with plenty of vegetable matter.

Use at the rate of a barrowload to each 4.5m (15ft) row, dug in at any time from October to March.

There have been fears that pig manure could be the means of spreading the virulent Aujeszky's disease, also known as pseudo rabies, from infected pigs to dogs and cats. However, thanks to the government's policy of eradication of infected herds, the danger of cross-over infection has been minimised.

PIGEON MANURE

A richer source of plant foods than poultry manure. It should be used moist as a compost activator or when dried used in the same way as poultry droppings at the rate of about 250g (8oz) to the sq m/yd.

POULTRY MANURE

This contains about four times as much plant food as farmyard manure. It tends to make clay soils even stickier, so is best composted, when it makes an excellent activator. Deep-litter and battery-poultry units often have a major problem in disposing of their manure and opponents of factory farming wouldn't touch the manure from broiler units and battery cages with a bargepole.

The muck from poultry houses is usually flash dried and sold as a powdered material which can be used as a top dressing when crops are growing well and is especially valuable for leafy crops and onions. Use at the rate of about 250g (8oz) to the sq m/yd.

PLANT ASH

Most of the nutritional value of plant material goes up in smoke when it is put on the bonfire, while the smoke itself is highly carcinogenic, so plant debris is best composted unless it is too woody.

If you do have a garden bonfire to burn diseased material, shrub prunings and any rotten bits of wood, don't waste the ash. Collect it as soon as it is cool enough to handle and store it in a damp-proof container.

Use the ash at the rate of 500g (1lb) per sq m/yd, scattered over the surface in spring and lightly hoed in to provide potash.

RABBIT DROPPINGS

If large quantities are available or simply the efforts of the pet rabbit, the litter should be composted, with plenty of straw added if necessary.

The manurial value of rabbit droppings is only fair, but is improved after composting. Use at the rate of about 4.5kg (10lb) to the sq m/yd when composted with straw or about 450g (1lb) to the sq m/yd if dried and powdered.

ROCK PHOSPHATE

Few soils in Britain are naturally well supplied with phosphate, although most contain adequate amounts for normal crop requirements. Gardens, allotments and smallholdings that have been regularly mucked with farmyard manure or compost usually have good reserves of phosphates.

However, phosphorus is often deficient in areas of high rainfall, such as the West Country and parts of the North of England, parts of Scotland and Ireland; where land has been over-manured and the pH reading slides to below about 5.7; and where the topsoil is thin and overlies chalk.

Regular use of bone meal, poultry manure or seaweed meal is recommended to boost the phosphate level, but where semi-permanent crops are planned, such as strawberries, raspberries and gooseberries, rock phosphate should be applied at the rate of 450g (1lb) per sq m/yd. This is a slow-release source of phosphorus: one dressing will last at least three years.

ROCK POTASH

This holds ten to twelve per cent of potassium in tiny particles of rock, exactly in the form in which the roots of plants take it out of the soil. It is sold as Highland rock potash or Adularian shale; it will last about three years in the soil during which time it will not be leached or locked up and made unavailable to the crops.

Gooseberries, tomatoes and ptatoes are all potash-hungry crops particularly when grown on light soils. Use at 224g (8oz) to the sq m/yd.

SEAWEED

Living within shouting distance of the North Sea has its problems when gardening, but has a bonus in the form of plentiful supplies of one of nature's most marvellous fertilisers – seaweed.

After the first of the autumn gales had dredged up this free harvest we would take plastic bags to the beach and gorge them with bladderwrack. But over the past few years the seaweed harvest has declined in quantity and quality. Too often what seaweed there is to be taken is contaminated with sewage debris from the outfall a little way up the coast or, worse still, with thick evil-smelling oil. Fresh seaweed as a mulch for the beetroot gave a superb flavour to this crop, and with carrots it helped to ward off the carrot fly. The Brussels sprouts and purple sprouting broccoli had the first helpings, however, and by April most of the seaweed on this part of the vegetable patch had disappeared, having been pulled underground by the worms.

Though fresh seaweed may not be available to all who would like to use it, the dried and powdered version is plentiful. It is the nearest thing to a complete natural fertiliser with 2.8 per cent nitrogen, 0.2 per cent phosphate and 2.3 per cent potassium. It is expensive, but worth every penny, and should be used quite sparingly: 56g (2oz) to the sq m/yd is about right. Spread it close to the growing crops and lightly tease it into the surface.

On lawns use it in early spring as a tonic at the rate of 112g (4oz) per sq m/yd.

Seaweed either fresh or dried is an excellent compost activator because the alginates promote rapid development of the bacteria of decomposition. Seaweed is also available as a liquid manure. It contains all the trace elements needed by plants in a form that the leaves can take in readily when used as a foliar feed: boron, bromine, calcium, copper, iodine, magnesium, manganese and sodium.

One of the most widely used seaweed liquid preparations is Chase SM3 made by a low temperature process from a blend of seaweeds harvested in northern waters. These are said to be richer in their main components than seaweeds farther south. Chase Organics told me that as well as the major and minor plant foods and trace elements SM3 contains gibberellins, vitamins, cytokinins and betaines. A lot still needs to be learned about how seaweed foliar feeds affect plant growth, but it is known that while the nutrients and trace elements play their part, the major effect comes from the cytokinins and the betaines.

Cytokinins are naturally occurring plant hormones which are involved in plant growth through cell division and enlargement, protein synthesis and the production of chlorophyll.

Betaines are modified amino acids closely concerned with the plant's osmotic processes in which moisture or a solution of salts or sugars reaches throughout the plant's living tissue. When plants are sprayed with the seaweed extract nutrients are drawn into the leaves with the cytokinins and betaines acting as metabolic reservoirs.

Tests have shown that plants sprayed with SM3 exude extra root secretions which are utilised by the mycorrhizal fungi and these, in turn, unlock additional nutrients for the plant's use.

Seaweed foliar sprays also help plants to resist attacks by pests and diseases and to slow down the ageing process so that they stay in production longer.

SEWAGE SLUDGE

Only digested sludge that has been treated at a sewage plant should be used, then the risk of passing on pathogens is minimised. Farmers are permitted to use untreated sewage although conditions of use are carefully controlled.

Sewage sludge even after treatment contains heavy metals, such as zinc, cadmium and lead, whose effects can be toxic if allowed to accumulate in the soil. On the credit side, sewage sludge contains useful proportions of plant nutrients and is perfectly acceptable as an organic fertiliser if bought as a dried product, sold in plastic bags. It contains more nitrogen, phosphorus and potassium than the best quality farmyard manure, but is rather less valuable for its humus content.

Mix three parts of dried sewage sludge with one part of seaweed meal for an excellent activator for compost used at the rate of 112g (4oz) to the sq m/yd.

As a general plant food in both the vegetable and flower garden use the dried sludge at the rate of about 168g (6oz) to the sq m/yd in early spring and again when the plants are about half-grown.

It can also be used on the lawn before the first mowing of the spring at about 224g (8oz) per sq m/yd.

SHODDY

This is the waste material from wool and cotton manufacturing and, as the UK has steadily declined in this department, it is seldom available for the gardener. It is bulky and very difficult to spread, but is an excellent source of slow-release nitrogen for crops such as the currant family.

Because of its bulkiness it is also an excellent source of humus, especially on light soils. If you are offered any old mattresses, pillows or cushions for use as shoddy, ensure that they are not filled with manmade fibre. If they have a filling of good old-fashioned wool, dig in from September to December at about 450g (1lb) to the sq m/yd.

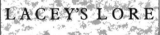

LACEY'S LORE

GARDEN LAW

No-one has a right to enter your garden; anyone who does so without consent is trespassing.

Similarly, if you want to trim a boundary hedge or prune a tree that overhangs your neighbour's garden, don't go on to his land without first getting his agreement.

LACEY'S LORE

USEFUL FEED

Horsetail and tansy, soaked for a week in rainwater, make a useful liquid fertiliser for strawberries, tomatoes and onions. A bucketful of the weeds in four of water is about right.

SOOT

Another material no longer widely available. Its value as a plant food is suspect although it was highly regarded by our grandfathers. Its principal value lies in darkening the soil early in the year and so hastening the warming up period. Some gardeners also use it round slug-attractive plants such as young lettuce and delphiniums to ward off the pests.

Never use soot fresh from the chimney sweep. It will contain toxic substances, so always place it outdoors in an open container to allow it to weather and rid itself of toxicity.

WOOD ASH

Ash from wood fires as distinct from coal fires and garden bonfires is rich in potash. The best ash comes from thinnings of trees and the prunings of fruit trees. This contains about ten to fourteen per cent potassium carbonate, while ash from felled timber may contain only a third of this amount.

Ash must be stored very dry and it is a good idea to mix some charcoal with it in an airtight container. Apply in the spring at up to 450g (1lb) a sq m/yd and hoe lightly into a moistened soil.

WORM COMPOST

One of the most interesting developments in the organic world has been the follow-up to research into vermiculture started at Rothamsted Experimental Station in 1980. It follows quite naturally on the classic study of earthworms by Charles Darwin and recent work by Dr C. L. Curtis, of Connecticut, USA, which established that earthworm casts contain five times more nitrogen, seven times more available phosphates, eleven times more potash and forty times more humus than is found in the top 15cm (6in) of the soil in which the worms may be living.

A company, British Earthworm Technology Ltd, was founded in 1983 at St Ives, Cambridgeshire, to produce worm compost or vermicompost, as they call it, on a large commercial scale using equipment and technology designed and developed by the National Institute of Agricultural Engineering.

Basically, the technique exploits the earthworm's capacity for converting organic waste into compost that gives high levels of slow-release nutrients with a low level of ammonia, good water-holding capacity, high cation exchange capacity and with a high microbial population. British Earthworm Technology told me that in their trials a single batch of pig waste (faeces, urine and straw) was processed by worms in less than a third of the time it took to compost the same material using a professional composting system.

Worms can process a 6.25cm (2½in) layer of straw-based waste in less than a week and the compost so produced can be used immediately, although it can be stored without loss of value.

Now worm compost is available in a wide range of types, marketed under the Betagro label. They are entirely organic and offer a first class alternative to composts that contain chemical additives.

You can produce your own worm compost, as I do, using very basic equipment. The technique is described in detail, starting on page 24.

5

GREEN MANURING

FACT FILE How to use organic fertilisers

The stars give an indication of relative values in terms of Nitrogen (N), Phosphates (P), Potash (K)

Material	N	P	K	Application rate	Material	N	P	K	Application rate
Animal hair	**			250g (8oz) to sq m/yd	Lime	Neutralising agent			Depends on pH of soil
Bone meal	*	***	*	85g (3oz) to sq m/yd. 112g (4oz) when planting shrubs, fruit bushes	Limestone	Neutralising agent			500g (1lb) to sq m/yd
					Manure and peat	*	*	*	Follow instructions of supplier
Bracken			**	500g (1lb) to sq m/yd, burn when green	Municipal compost		*	*	1.35kg (3lb) to sq m/yd
Calcified seaweed		*	*	112g (4oz) to sq m/yd every 3 years	Mushroom compost	*	*	*	1.35kg (3lb) to sq m/yd
Chilean nitrate	***			56g (2oz) to sq m/yd	Pig manure	*	*	*	38kg (¾cwt) to 4.5m (15ft) row
Compost	**	**	**	Barrowload to 4.5m (15ft) row	Pigeon manure	**	**	**	250g (8oz) to sq m/yd
Dolomite and gypsum				250g (8oz) to sq m/yd, lightens clay	Poultry manure	**	***	***	250g (8oz) to sq m/yd
Dried blood	***	*		56g (2oz) in litre (quart) of water to sq m/yd	Plant ash			**	500g (1lb) to sq m/yd
					Rabbit droppings	*	**	*	500g (1lb) to sq m/yd when dried
Feathers	**			140g (5oz) to sq m/yd	Rock phosphate		***		500g (1lb) to sq m/yd
Fish meal	**	**	**	85g (3oz) to sq m/yd	Rock potash			***	250g (8oz) to sq m/yd
Goat manure	**	**	*	50kg (1cwt) to sq m/yd with straw	Seaweed meal	**	**	**	56g (2oz) to sq m/yd
Green manures	**	**	**	See separate table on page 50	Shoddy		*	*	500g (1lb) to sq m/yd
Hoof and horn	**	*		112kg (4oz) to sq m/yd	Wood ash			***	500g (1lb) to sq m/yd
Horse manure	*	*	*	Barrowload to 4.5m (15ft) row	Worm compost	**	**	**	Use in potting compost
Leafmould		*		2.25kg (5lb) to sq m/yd					

The organic movement's dependence on an input of animal manure into the soil fertility cycle attracts criticism from, among others, vegetarians. Some are opposed in principle to the use of farm animals in this way, while there's a group of people who believe animal manures are a pollutant. Kenneth Dalziel O'Brien, for example, in his book *Veganic Gardening*, published in 1986, says animal organics, like chemical fertilisers, create a soil imbalance. He writes:

For . . . the domestic animals' ancestors lived in an environment where, overall, a naturally balanced soil was maintained despite their presence . . . any isolated local imbalances would have been adjusted when the animals instinctively moved on so as not to destroy their source of food, giving the worms, insects and microscopic soil workers time to do their work of rendering the animal wastes as harmless as possible. In this way herbage and soil were kept in a reasonable healthy state.

It seemed fair to introduce this view that Mr O'Brien calls the veganic philosophy although there isn't the space to develop his argument or to counter it. However, for those gardeners who are opposed to the use of animal manure, or who cannot get regular supplies of it or who simply want to augment their compost-making efforts inexpensively, green manuring is the answer.

Green manuring was practised by the Chinese 3,000 years ago and has been in continuous use in Mediterranean countries since early Greek times. It took much longer to make a mark in northern Europe generally, while in Britain it seems to have been popular in the eighteenth century, then for some reason fell out of favour. In *Green Manures*, a booklet published by Elm Farm Research Centre, the editors Lawrence Woodward and Pat Burge say that a strict definition of a green manure is a green crop produced solely for the purpose of being incorporated in the soil. 'We are in favour of a wider definition which identifies green manuring as the practice of enriching the soil by the addition of undecomposed plant material, either in place or brought from a distance, whether or not it was grown solely for the purpose', they say. And we won't quarrel with that.

Green manuring was never an important part of British farming, but elsewhere in Europe it has played 'a central role in organic farming'. Because of this, the know-how of green manuring has had to be collected from foreign-language sources and translated, both literally and pragmatically, by experts such as Lawrence Woodward and his Elm Farm colleagues to help the ever-increasing numbers of UK farmers, smallholders and gardeners who are converting to organic growing. I have drawn on this information, but have tried to put it in the context of the back garden and allotment. It would be unjust to overlook the work done over several years by the Henry Doubleday Research Association, first at Bocking in Essex, now at Ryton Gardens, near Coventry, to attract more gardeners to the benefits of green manuring. Unfortunately, perhaps, HDRA has tended to concentrate on two crops, comfrey and Hungarian grazing rye. Compared with Continental practice that's rather like limiting our food choice to bread and cheese.

The green manure menu for the soil is a substantial one. The table on page 50 lists a range of crops each offering value for green manuring, although the choice in the UK could be somewhat circumscribed by local difficulty in securing the seed. The principle behind green manuring is easy enough to grasp and applies equally to the use of compost, animal dung and other organic fertilisers.

Gardening involves making intensive use of a parcel of land whether for growing edible crops, flowers, shrubs, trees or grass and this means taking nutrients out of the soil. But, as organic gardeners, we aim to put back as much as we take out and, hopefully, a bit more as well. If every suitable scrap of material is given back to the soil via the compost heap, the net loss in nutrients is accounted for partly by the vegetables and fruit we eat, because in Britain and other 'civilised' countries human excreta is not returned to the soil – unlike China where, as with green manuring, this has been normal practice for thousands of years.

The other item in the debit account is the loss of nutrients through the leaching action of rain and weathering of the topsoil. On light soils, particularly those lacking the sponge-like action of humus, this natural leaching can be severe enough to require supplemental feeding to maintain the correct degree of fertility. Nitrogen is the most readily leached of the three main plant foods, and the loss is most noticeable with a hungry crop such as cauliflowers.

As a bonus, green manuring helps to maintain a good soil structure and keeps both annual and pernicious weeds in check. Even if you are fortunate enough to be able to maintain your soil's food reserves without the need for green manuring – and I'm in that happy position – it makes good sense for vacant bits of the vegetable plot to have an overwintering leguminous crop for turning in during the early spring. Some of my allotment neighbours pooh-pooh this and instead let their vacant areas become weed-ridden. They argue that the weeds serve exactly the same purpose as a green manure crop of, say, broad beans and at a good deal less cost and bother. This is true, but there's a snag. By the time you come to turn in the weed cover many of the plants will have seeded and even though you may be meticulous in burying them a good 25cm (10in) deep, that won't be the last you'll see of them.

You can use a green manure crop in several ways. For instance, you could choose a good bulking crop, such as sunflower or comfrey, to provide extra material for the compost heap; you could grow a nitrogen-fixing legume, such as vetch, clover, lupins, peas or beans, and use the above-ground growth as compost material while leaving the nitrogen-rich root systems in the ground for a nitrogen-loving following crop; you could undersow a green manure crop with another one of a different type or with one of your mainline vegetable crops; you can use mustard to rid the plot of wireworm (see opposite) or, come to the autumn, and there are bits of vacant land, you can sow an overwintering crop, such as broad beans, winter tares or Hungarian grazing rye, and turn it in during the spring digging.

Those with particularly heavy soil might prefer to see as much of their land as possible dug over in the autumn – rather than given over to green manuring – so that the soil benefits from the action of frost and snow. But those working light soils certainly can derive maximum value from an overwintered green manure crop that will hold nutrients in situ instead of having them leached by the rain and, in especially exposed areas, will prevent soil erosion through strong winds. I am extremely fortunate in having a humus-rich medium loam to work with. Its only drawback is that it is rather shallow and, in hot, dry East Anglia, can rapidly dry out. So my green manuring is confined to an overwintered crop of broad beans on vacant land that would otherwise carry weeds.

Before considering the main green manure crops, it is important to note that very little comparative experimental work has been carried out on these crops in Britain, although a considerable volume of research has been undertaken abroad, notably at the National Research Institute of Biological Husbandry at Oberwil, Switzerland.

The information in these pages has been compiled from Roger Wyartt's contribution to the Elm Farm publication

FACT FILE Compost, manure and organic fertilisers analysis

	Water %	Nitrogen %	Phosphorus %	Potash %
Strawy cow dung	66.17	0.54	0.31	0.67
Rotted cow dung	75.4	0.59	0.45	0.49
Farmyard manure	76.0	0.65	0.23	0.32
Mushroom compost	53.14	0.80	0.63	0.67
Deep-litter compost	50.20	0.80	0.55	0.48
Indore compost	76.0	0.50	0.27	0.81
Comfrey compost	68.0	0.77	0.29	0.92
Brian Furner compost	47.8	0.67	0.31	0.50
Urine activated compost	46.29	0.80	0.29	0.41
Huker bin compost	50.6	0.71	0.11	0.30
Rotol bin compost	56.2	0.88	0.22	0.36
Dried blood		9–13.0	0.8	
Hoof and horn meal		6.5–13.2	0.20	
Bone meal	0.2–14.0	0.30–4.60	14.1–33.2	1.0
Bone and meat meal	6.0	3.90–12.30	0.90–19.0	1.0
Fish meal		6.30–8.90	6.0–8.90	1.0
Seaweed meal		2.80	0.22	2.29

THE FLOWER GARDEN

In this book the emphasis is on the organic cultivation of vegetables and fruit because plants that are raised for food have the most direct effect on our health. When we grow our own food crops without the use of chemicals we are making a significant statement about personal values and the quality of our lives.

However, there are many people, whose gardening is confined to the care of a lawn and flower beds with, perhaps, a few shrubs, containers and house plants, who feel equally strongly that the environment would be safer and healthier if everyone used far fewer garden insecticides, fungicides and herbicides.

Certainly, in gardens used by children and pet animals – and that includes public parks and play areas – pesticides should be outlawed. As adults, we are able to exercise caution about where we walk and what we touch, but children, dogs and cats are very vulnerable to residues of poisonous sprays that may still linger on foliage, grass and soil.

At home it is a firm commitment to the safety of the family to rid your shelves of any insecticides, fungicides and weedkillers. Some local authorities make special provision for the safe disposal of such bottles and packets. If your council cannot help in this way, speak to the environmental health officer for advice on safe disposal. This doesn't mean tipping the contents of the bottles down the lavatory pan or an outside drain. Once the first step has been taken and the poisons have gone, working with nature becomes easier and the temptation to resort to the bottle is removed. The garden becomes a safer haven for you, your family, your pets and the wildlife visitors.

Similarly, as taxpayers and ratepayers we should bring every possible pressure to bear on local authorities that use weedkillers in public places to stop because all weedkillers kill wildlife. They can also be fatal to pets and harmful to children. At the very least, local councils should publish warnings about their intention to spray and name the particular poison they intend to use.

Many of the problems of modern gardens come about because of over-dependence on chemicals to provide nutrients for the plants and on poisons to control insect pests, fungi and weeds. Giving plants their three basic nutrients of nitrogen, phosphates and potassium in the too-easily assimilated form of artificial fertilisers does nothing to give long-term nourishment to the soil. Instead it leads to lush growth that readily succumbs to attack by insect pests or harmful bacteria. Aphids, in particular, find the soft, sappy growth of such plants irresistible and they are the pests most commonly encountered in the garden.

If you follow the advice on improving soil structure, the use of mulches and the hoe for weed suppression and of organic fertilisers when necessary, together with the help given on composting and controlling pests and diseases without destroying the predators and fouling the environment, your flower garden can readily and painlessly be converted to the organic way.

For more detailed advice on the cultivation of flowers, shrubs and trees the 'Expert' books by Dave Hessayon are inexpensive and comprehensive and you can ignore the chemically-biased bits. There are also many first-rate titles in David & Charles' book list.

Green Manures and from the Soil Association technical booklet No 5 *Green Manuring*.

MUSTARD

The best known and probably most widely used green manure, capable of producing a good bulk of material in about eight to ten weeks, but it has the drawback that it is a Cruciferae and should therefore be part of the brassica rotation.

Mustard is also a shallow-rooting plant so to grow it well requires a soil in good organic condition and not lacking in nitrogen. It is a spring and summer crop with very low resistance to drought.

Sown broadcast in June, the crop can be turned in in September to give a highly satisfactory increase in organic matter and a slow release of nitrogen the following spring when soil temperatures rise.

As already noted, mustard is an excellent cleansing crop on wireworm-infested land, and when used for this purpose a rather denser sowing rate is recommended. For normal purposes the rate is about 28g (1oz) to 7sq m/yd, while for pest control it is 28g (1oz) to 5sq m/yd.

CHINESE RADISH

This is similar to white mustard, but can be sown in May at the same rate as mustard. It gives rather less bulky material than mustard, but a bit more nitrogen and potash. It is not winter hardy and must be rotated with the brassicas.

RAPE

The third of the Cruciferae group of green manures has rather more nitrogen than mustard or fodder radish, and about the same phosphorus and potash content. It is sown broadcast in July or August at the rate of 28g (1oz) to 10sq m/yd and cut for turning in during early September, or cut and carried to the compost heap in October.

GRAZING RYE

For overwintering, this is one of the best choices, although the timing of the crop is rather critical to avoid the stems becoming woody. Sow in September at the rate of 28g (1oz) to 3sq m/yd and dig it in during March or early April when it has grown to

FACT FILE Green manuring crop summary

Crop	Sowing rate	Sowing time	To maturity	Comments
Alfalfa	28g (1oz)/sq m/yd	May/Aug	14 weeks	Legume
Beans	15cm (6in) each way	Oct-Nov	20 weeks	Legume
Buckwheat	28g (1oz)/4 sq m/yd	May	12-14 weeks	Attracts hoverflies
Chicory	28g (1oz)/sq m/yd	April-Aug	16 weeks	Deep rooting
Chinese radish	28g (1oz)/7 sq m/yd	May	10-12 weeks	Rotate with brassicas
Clover, crimson	28g (1oz)/8 sq m/yd	May	26 + weeks	Legume
Clover, white	28g (1oz)/8 sq m/yd	April-June	26 + weeks	Legume
Clover, sweet	28g (1oz)/10 sq m/yd	June-Aug	26 + weeks	Mice deterrent
Fenugreek	28g (1oz)/4 sq m/yd	May	10 weeks	Legume
Grazing rye	28g (1oz)/3 sq m/yd	Sept	24 weeks	For digging in
Lupins	5cm (2in) apart	April-May	12-14 weeks	Good for light land
Mustard	28g (1oz)/7 sq m/yd	June	8-10 weeks	Clears wireworm
Phacelia	28g (1oz)/10 sq m/yd	May	16 weeks	Bulks well
Rape	28g (1oz)/10 sq m/yd	July-Aug	10 weeks	Rotate with brassicas
Winter tare	28g (1oz)/2 sq m/yd	Aug-Sept	20 weeks	Legume

about 60cm (2ft) tall. When it is young and tender it decomposes rapidly and makes available a high level of nitrogen in the soil at the expense of organic matter. As it gets older and the leaves and stems become tougher, decomposition poaches some nitrates, but the slower rate of decomposition makes for more slow-release nitrogen and a greater volume of organic material.

WINTER TARE OR VETCH

This is a legume and its principal value is in covering otherwise bare soil over the winter to give a nitrogen-rich start to a following crop in the spring.

Seed is sown at the rate of about 28g (1oz) to 2sq m/yd in late August or September and the crop is turned in before it flowers. As well as a good bulk of organic matter, it adds about 450g (1lb) of available nitrogen to 36sq m/yd and this is much appreciated by a following crop of autumn-hearting cabbages.

BROAD AND FIELD BEANS

A richer source of nitrogen than the vetches and, if you save your own broad bean seed, an economical crop for overwintering. Sow at 15cm (6in) each way in late October or early November, but be prepared for losses if the winter produces severe frosts. Dig the crop under in March or early April or cut the top growth off at soil level and use on the compost heap while leaving the root system in the soil to release its nitrogen to the following crop.

TREFOIL

The most important green manure for the British organic farmer because it is easily cultivated and can be undersown in a cereal crop even in a wet season, is inexpensive and can be grazed by sheep. It is a legume, but to achieve its full potential needs twelve weeks of growth after a spring sowing, and this makes it a doubtful proposition for the garden or allotment.

CRIMSON CLOVER

A very attractive plant with upright stem and brilliant crimson flower heads. Roger Wyartt says: 'A crop in full flower is a quite magnificent sight, unrivalled by virtually any other agricultural crop grown today.'

It is a legume and is rather slow to establish and grow in the autumn and is therefore not highly recommended. My own experience is that as a forage crop or one to attract the bees, crimson clover is unbeatable.

RED CLOVER

This used to be called claver and is widely grown to give large crops of high protein hay or silage, while the nitrogen from the root system is available for the following crop.

WHITE CLOVER

An agricultural green manure, usually undersown with rye grass and grazed to increase the nitrogen-fixing root system.

WHITE SWEET CLOVER

This one cannot be undersown because it is so fast growing that it would overtake the accompanying crop. The exception is when it is used in the greenhouse. As with the other clovers, it is a biennial and is winter hardy, so needs a full year's growth to achieve its full potential.

For the gardener without stock to graze the clovers or bees to take advantage of the flowers, their value as green manure crops is limited. However, the seed is relatively cheap, the crop is easy to establish and, sown in August at about 28g (1oz) to 10sq m/yd, it will be ready to be turned in during the spring. White sweet clover is also said to rid the garden of mice.

FENUGREEK

A quick-growing legume which, if left, is self-seeding. Sown in May, it is ready to cut ten weeks later before the flowers become seed pods. I took the cut material to the compost heap and dibbled leek plants into the fenugreek roots with excellent results.

CHICORY

This is agricultural chicory, not the edible horticultural type. It can be sown at any time from April to August at the rate of 28g (1oz) to the sq m/yd broadcast and its main use is on light soil. It is very deep rooting and its tap roots will bring minerals to the surface and leave the soil in better condition than beforehand.

LUPINS

Another excellent green manure crop for light land. It is a deep-rooting legume which will grow well in infertile, acid soil. Seed is sown in drills 5cm (2in) apart with the rows 15cm (6in) apart in April or May; 28g (1oz) of seed will sow about three 4.5m (15ft) rows.

It can be a large bulk producer for the compost heap and would be cut about twelve to fourteen weeks after sowing. If sown after old turf has been dug in, this crop will stop the denitrification as the grass rots.

My Soil Association colleague Peter Segger says of this crop: 'It is not known exactly how much nitrogen is made available to succeeding crops by growing lupins and we could hope that some enterprising university department will give us answers one day.'

It is claimed that lupins possess bacteria in their root systems which have the ability to convert normally unavailable phosphates into available plant nutrients. The crop must not be allowed to flower if it is intended to dig in the top growth because the stems become very woody.

ALFALFA

A member of the clover family, this is a deep-rooting perennial which will go on growing and penetrating deeper into the soil year after year. Seed of alfalfa – or lucerne – is available, along with many other green manures, from Chase Organics, who say that alfalfa stores more nutrients than it needs to grow and is rich in calcium, magnesium, phosphorus, potassium, nitrogen, manganese and zinc, making it almost a complete natural fertiliser.

Although it is a perennial it can be sown in spring at the rate of about 28g (1oz) to the sq m/yd and turned in during late autumn, or will overwinter from a summer sowing. Alfalfa should not be used where there are grazing animals.

BUCKWHEAT

A fast growing crop that is an excellent choice for improving soil structure because it not only produces a good volume of organic material for digging in, but it also has deeply penetrating roots that help to open out heavy soil. It has the big bonus of attracting bees and hoverflies.

Sow in late May at the rate of 28g (1oz) to 4 sq m/yd broadcast, and dig it in during the late autumn or when the frost has cut it down.

SUNFLOWER

Widely grown on the Continent but not popular in Britain as a green manure crop. It needs a long time to mature and is difficult material to compost.

PHACELIA

Another popular crop on the Continent that is little grown in the UK, although I know of several people who are trialling it.

It is a very delicate-looking plant with an attractive pale blue flower yet is capable of producing a heavy volume of organic material for sheet composting or adding to the compost heap; 28g (1oz) of seed sows about 10sq m/yd when broadcast. Sown in May, the crop is ready to cut or turn in during the autumn.

A point worth making about a green manure crop that is cut and then turned in is that it should be allowed to wilt thoroughly for a couple of days. If there is a considerable amount of green material, decomposition in the soil will cause some subsidence as well as difficulty in securing a good surface for seed growing, so it is generally preferable to allow as long as possible for compaction and to follow the green manure crop with a transplanted crop.

I have tried to give some idea of the characteristics of the individual crops, but it should be remembered that there is big scope for the organic gardener to experiment, using combinations of the crops for particular purposes. For example, white clover and white sweet clover are good crops to undersow with greenhouse tomatoes. White clover is resistant to trampling, while white sweet clover keeps mice out of the greenhouse and is an aid to ripening of the fruit.

6

HUSBANDRY TECHNIQUES: FLOWERS, VEGETABLES AND LAWNS

1 Mark out the required area, 1m(1yd) to 1.2m(4ft) wide and any length. 2 Double dig a trench, removing all traces of

perennial weeds. 3 Fork the bottom of the trench and add at least 15cm(6in) of rotted manure or compost. 4 Return the soil to

the trench with more manure, compost and peat worked into the soil. The bed should have a neatly humped profile

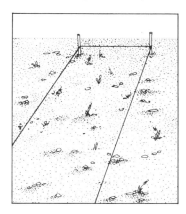
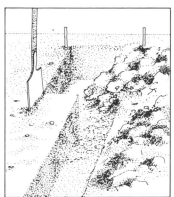

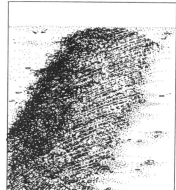

DEEP-BED GARDENING

The idea of a no-dig garden has held a fascination for people for a very long time – and not just among the non-gardening fraternity. Indeed, my friend the late Dr W. E. Shewell-Cooper, author of countless gardening books and founder of the Good Gardeners' Association, was a strong, occasionally fierce advocate for it, with a technique based on a deep mulching of the soil with peat or compost.

The clever Chinese have practised no-dig for scores of centuries using deep beds or what we call the Chinese bed method for raising horticultural crops. While the peat or compost mulching method is entirely satisfactory for shrubs, the flower garden and the soft fruit department, the deep-bed system is eminently suitable for the vegetable plot and the allotment. As the years roll by, the prospect of a no-dig vegetable plot becomes more and more appealing. My spirit is willing enough to carry on wielding the spade. It's the back that's weak. Or, at least, less strong.

The basic idea of the deep bed is that you divide your plot into sections about 4.5m (15ft) long by about 1.20m (4ft) wide, separated by pathways about 60cm (2ft) wide. Each of the sections is dug out to twice a spade's depth, in fact, the double-digging beloved of so many of the old hands. When the soil is replaced, large quantities of compost and, if possible, farmyard manure are incorporated, and all the perennial weeds are removed. After that, the beds aren't walked on or disturbed. If it weren't for the double-digging, I am sure that many more gardeners would embrace the technique with open arms because it has other attractive features.

● It saves space by enabling most of the main vegetable crops to be grown closer on a block system rather than in rows. Access to the beds is by way of the paths, so sowing, transplanting and hand-weeding are all carried out from the paths.

● The soil is never walked on or disturbed after that initial double digging, so it isn't compacted and its structure remains open and free draining while the high humus content holds plant nutrients and moisture at a level most convenient for the plants.

● Time is saved because the beds are far easier to manage than conventional rows of crops, and if the paths are given a mulch of straw or forest bark, access to the beds is a cleaner, easier task even after heavy rain. After one or two seasons' use, the straw or bark can be added to the surface of the beds to increase the humus content, and a new layer put down on the paths.

● Seed is saved because crops grown on the block system require far less thinning than those grown in rows.

● Rotation of crops is a far simpler exercise because of the clearly-defined boundaries of the beds.

● But by far the biggest advantage is that from the same amount of space output of crops can be double or triple that from the traditional rows.

When I started in the no-dig direction some years ago two deep beds were made just to see how things worked out. One was a complete success, the other a total failure, but for that I was to blame, not the technique. Both beds were made 4.5m by 1.20m (15ft by 4ft), although the first to be dug – the successful one – is at the southern end of my plot, while the other is at the northern end where the topsoil is only about 30cm (12in) deep. I dug the northern bed first, intending to give it the full back-breaking two-spit dig, but found my spade going into a typical crag subsoil. So I decided not to disturb it.

At the other end of the plot the soil is a good 12.5cm (5in) deeper, so it got the full double-digging treatment. Knowing that the deep-rooting bindweed and horsetail were a potential problem in beds that were to become no-dig areas, I tried to be as thorough as possible in eradicating them from the soil that refilled the trenches. Unfortunately, I wasn't painstaking enough. The northern bed must have had a hidden mass of couch grass rhizomes and the wire-like fragments of horsetail in the subsoil, just waiting to break cover in the spring. So with that bed I had to start all over again the next autumn.

The other one proved to be a great boon and its success inspired me to carry on with the deep-bed technique although

Deep-bed bottle bank . . . one way of using empty plastic bottles is to cut the base and use them as mini cloches to protect seedlings during early spring

I have made the width of subsequent beds slightly narrower at a metre as against 1.20m to use my cloches, carrot fly guards and Hortopaper mulch to maximum effect.

However, all my plot hasn't been given over to deep beds because there are some crops, such as peas, potatoes and runner beans that are best grown in rows so that the space-saving advantage of the deep bed is then lost.

When the deep bed is prepared the incorporation of large amounts of organic material means that the completed bed has a surface several inches proud of the pathway on either side and, in view of the hot, dry summers we have in East Anglia, I was a mite concerned that the deep bed would dry out very rapidly. That first year's cropping of that first bed coincided with a drought in June and July, but the deep bed came through remarkably well and, in subsequent years, the annual addition of compost as a surface mulch has now raised the beds some six inches above the path level but given the soil a sponge-like texture with a great capacity for moisture retention.

My deep raised beds are 4.5m (15ft) long because that is the width of my allotment plot. But they can be any length one cares to make them, although if they are over-long walking back and forth is time-consuming. The important dimension is the width: it should be no wider than it is comfortable to reach across, for weeding, planting, harvesting and the like, from either pathway. Most people find a metre and a bit is just about right. When planning the layout of the deep beds try to align them so that the length of the beds is on a north-south axis to give the crops maximum benefit from the sunshine, and when planning the cropping of the beds remember to site the tall crops on the northern side so that they do not overshadow the lower growing crops.

The initial manuring of the beds will provide adequate nutrients for the first year's cropping. Thereafter an annual dressing in the spring of blood, fish and bone or one of the more specialised organic fertilisers together with further applications of compost as a mulch will maintain a high level of fertility.

Check the pH of the beds every other year and apply a sprinkling of calcified seaweed or lime at the rates given on page 20 to rectify a natural tendency for the beds to become rather acid. Avoid any major disturbance of the soil if possible, so simply tease the fertiliser, calcified seaweed or lime into the surface – don't fork it in. Because of the superb, open structure of the soil in a well-established deep bed it is possible to harvest deep-rooting crops such as carrots, parsnips, salsify and scorzonera without the aid of a fork: they can be eased out of moist soil by hand pulling.

Close planting in a deep bed. Here kale has been interplanted with cabbage lettuce which will be harvested well before the kale matures
By close spacing you can restrict the size of cabbages so that there's little wasted even when cooking for just two. These Primo, growing in a deep bed, will go to the kitchen at about 1kg (2.2lb) in weight

Researchers at the National Vegetable Research Station at Wellesbourne demonstrated that it is easy to regulate the size of some vegetables by the spacing they are given, and the block system of deep-bed cropping is perfect for this. Take summer-hearting cabbage, for example. Spacing the plants at 35cm (14in) each way gave the highest yield of good 'family size' heads, while increasing the distance to 45cm (18in) each way between the plants gave the same weight of crop, but the cabbages were bigger and a little earlier. With parsnips the maximum yield of large-rooted varieties was achieved with a plant population of three to 30cm² (1 sq ft). With a small-rooted variety such as the canker-resistant Avon resister, maximum yield is obtained when there are six or seven plants to 30cm² (1 sq ft).

For beetroot total yield declines significantly the denser the population. My family are very fond of baby beet, both in salads and for pickling, and I've found that about fifteen plants to 30cm² (1 sq ft) gives a very satisfactory yield of beet a little larger than golf ball size. At a density of twelve plants to 30cm² (1 sq ft) the roots can grow on to maturity without becoming oversize and woody.

I said that I made my deep beds slightly narrower than the usual 1.20m (4ft) because this suits my use of cloches and other gardening aids, and this is worth bearing in mind when planning your beds. You can, for example, get a far earlier start with some crops by covering a bed with black polythene sheeting. Put it in place, anchored at the sides, a fortnight before sowing and it will warm up the soil at the same time as it restrains any annual weed seed growth. Although seed is sown in blocks rather than in rows, there's no reason why you shouldn't run two rows of cloches on a bed for an especially early crop of baby carrots or turnips or beetroot, and the handyman can quite easily and inexpensively construct a plastic-clad frame that can be used over the full width of a bed for marrows, courgettes, cucumbers, melons and bush tomatoes.

As an aid to earlier cropping and as an effective barrier

LACEY'S LORE

A HEALTH FARM

If it were just a question of saving money, this rewarding hobby of growing one's own fruit and vegetables might not be so widespread.

More important to many of us are the facts that growing our own means we can choose top-flavour varieties, grow them without the use of chemical force-feeding or poisonous sprays, pick or lift the crop at the peak of freshness and rush it to the kitchen to take full, immediate advantage of its dew-fresh nutrition.

Not for us the limp lettuce, tired peas, stringy runners, tasteless tomatoes and scrubbed carrots. Even our marrows can be eaten at just that stage – beyond courgette size but well below show-bench proportions – when the whole delicate flavour is perfectly captured and requires only the enhancement of a sauce made with freshly-gathered parsley. As the seasons unfold there's a succession of succulent delights.

In agriculture we measure a farmer's success in terms of yield per acre. The real measure should not be of mere quantity, but the human health value of the crop, because the function of farmed land is to maintain human health.

Using that standard, my allotment plot, fuelled only by compost, manure and my two-handed energy, is in more senses than one, a veritable health farm.

Deep-bed beetroot at a density of about 15 plants to 30cm² (1 sq ft) gives a good yield when the roots are pulled about golfball size

against pests I use Agryl P17, a polypropylene fibre cloth which is just the right width to spread over the crop immediately after sowing or planting out. It becomes, in effect, a floating cloche, capable of protecting the crop from several degrees of frost, but giving good ventilation, light transmission and allowing the rain to permeate evenly.

Once your beds have been made and you revel in their labour-saving high-yielding properties, you can add refinements to the system with, maybe, pathways of secondhand bricks or paving slabs – even old lengths of carpet laid face down among the deep beds. Avoid, if you can, having grass paths; in no time at all the grass will penetrate into the lush feeding ground of the beds and prove very tiresome to eradicate.

LACEY'S LORE

FIGHTING DROUGHT

In June the sun is at its strongest and afternoon temperatures often reach 27°C (80°F). This is when a garden needs close to 2.5cm (1in) of rain per week to replace the water lost by transpiration through plant leaves and evaporation through the soil surface.

Here are some ways to beat the drought:
● Choose the right varieties. Much effort has gone into breeding drought-tolerant varieties, so make use of them.
● Try to provide some shade for non-tolerant plants and give shelter from winds that hasten evaporation.
● Collect rain in a water butt and put waste water from the kitchen sink on to the garden.
● Improve the soil structure by incorporating humus-forming materials so that more available water is held in the soil.
● Mulch in May after a shower and before the summer drought begins.

Hortopaper, made from wood fibre and peat and sold in metre-wide rolls, stretched over a deep bed 4.5m (15ft) wide. After a few days to allow for shrinkage,

plants can be dibbled straight into the bed using the planting grid printed on the paper. Always position the paper when the soil is moist and weed-free

Agryl P17 woven plastic sheeting over a deep-bed trial of spring-sown crops at Otley College

A deep-bed mulching trial with spring cabbage at Otley College organic demonstration unit

WEED CONTROL

Weeding is one of the most time-consuming chores in the garden. Weeds have to be kept in check because they are in straight competition with the cultivated plants, although the mere presence of weeds is not necessarily a problem. In fact, here and there I'm quite happy to see them, particularly those that attract butterflies, hoverflies, bees and other beneficial insects. But when the weeds compete for living room with the flowers, shrubs, grass and edible crops then something has to be done about them, and it has to be done before they seed.

The inorganic gardener uses herbicides of one sort or another and they include some of the most potent poisons freely available to the general public. Paraquat, for instance, has no known antidote, yet is the active ingredient in two of the most widely sold weedkillers.

The organic gardener shuns these products and instead uses one or more of these techniques:
• Covering the soil with a cover crop, mulch or physical barrier to prevent the emergence of weed seeds.
• Hand-weeding, particularly in the flower garden and on the lawn.
• Hoeing, particularly among growing vegetable crops.
• Flame gunning in early spring on land waiting to be sown, on drives and pathways.

If you deny a plant light and air, then even though the seed germinates it cannot survive, and that's the theory behind mulching. Even the most stubborn perennial weeds, such as bindweed and horsetail, eventually give up the ghost with this treatment, whereas with cover cropping or green manuring, pernicious weeds usually survive.

Mulching with peat or forest bark in the ornamental garden

Mulching the pathways between deep beds or sections of the vegetable garden helps to keep weeds controlled and prevents soil from being walked elsewhere on one's boots. Both straw and forest bark are organic mulches that can, eventually, be raked on to the beds and replaced with fresh material

Old carpet pieces laid pattern-side down in early spring between rows of raspberry canes is an effective method of weed control. Alternatively, use a thick layer of newspaper followed by a 5cm (2in) thickness of straw

not only successfully suppresses weeds, it also produces an attractive, decorative finish for the beds and borders. Both these materials are organic ones that add humus to the soil. Used as a layer about two inches deep on flower beds, around shrubs and trees, weed growth is checked, moisture is retained and the soil underneath the mulch becomes a very suitable environment for the earthworm population. In time the earthworms will take the mulch into the soil, so don't regard that initial 5cm (2in) layer as permanent – an annual topping up is necessary and this is best done in early spring when the spring-flowering bulbs are well through.

In terms of cost, there's little difference between peat and the specially prepared pine bark, such as Cambark. Peat, initially, costs less but is more rapidly absorbed into the soil, so more is required to top up. Peat tends to increase the acidity of the soil after a year or so, but is better at water retention.

Cambark is produced from the bark removed from coniferous logs and it seems that the Forestry Commission has an inexhaustible supply. The bark is processed and matured under natural conditions without the use of chemicals. This controls the pH of the product and removes the phytotoxic substances in the bark. It is sold as a straight material for mulching or as a peat and bark mix to which organic fertilisers can be added to make a compost for potting or for use in growing bags. For mulching the coarse grade is the one to use but it – or any other mulching material – must go on to the ground after it has been cleared of weed growth, especially perennial

weeds. Another advantage of the bark mulch is that you can walk on it even after heavy rain, so you can cut roses or deadhead the annuals without compacting the soil or getting your shoes muddy.

Forest bark is now widely used in children's play areas because it gives a springy surface, which cushions any falls, is non-toxic, free of dust and blends in with the surroundings.

In the vegetable garden there's a wider range of mulching materials some of which would be less visually acceptable in the flower garden. Straw, paper, used peat from growing bags, lawn mowings, leafmould, black plastic sheeting, old carpets and rugs can all be used on the vegetable plot, while for deep beds the routine is to mulch the surface with compost and/or well-rotted farmyard manure.

For effective weed suppression, whatever is used for mulching, the layer must be thick enough and dense enough to deny light to the weed seedlings.

Between the rows of raspberries I use a combination of thick layers of newspaper overlaid with straw and this checks not only the weeds but also the suckers that spring up as much as five feet away from the parent canes.

NEW TECHNIQUES

At Dickleburgh in Norfolk Bob Flowerdew, a professional gardener, converted what was a meadow into a low-labour high-output organic fruit, flower and vegetable garden brimful of ideas. It's his own garden and so he has been able to put into practice many new techniques as well as updated old ones.

Contented chickens range free through the orchard and the difference in flavour between their eggs and those from battery hens is the difference between chalk and cheese. Hens respond to humane treatment by giving Bob a plentiful supply of top-quality eggs that are his main source of protein.

As a professional gardener, there's not a lot of time left over to look after his own land, he's too busy looking after other people's. To rid his one and a quarter acres of weeds he used a typically unorthodox technique. For minimum maintenance of his vegetable crops he decided to use deep beds. He mapped out forty beds, each 4.80m (16ft) by 1.20m (4ft), and to prepare them for production he used carpet mulching.

'Most people throw away their old carpets. I use them in the

Suffolk farmer James Juby with his garden rook. It does the work of several tools – draw hoe, Dutch hoe, rake, edger and crome, and is made from hook-shaped narrow *tempered steel with a sharpened outer edge. It is especially useful for working the soil in borders and other confined spaces*

garden and if they are the good old-fashioned wool or cotton ones, they gradually rot down and become humus. Carpet as a mulch excludes the light and offers ideal conditions for the earthworms who can work right to the surface, safe from the birds,' he told me.

Once the perennial weeds had been eliminated by carpet mulching, the next stage was to plant crops through slits in the carpet. In two years each of the forty beds had become free of perennial weeds and in a further two years, after dressings of compost, they were giving an output of entirely organically-grown produce more than double that of a conventional inorganic system. Bob keeps a card index record of the beds to help him keep his rotation orderly and check on crop behaviour and yields.

Hoeing as a weed control technique should be kept as shallow as possible, preferably about half an inch below the surface, and it needs to be done regularly throughout the spring and summer. Between rows of vegetables and in the flower borders and beds a Dutch hoe or the specially-designed Wilkinson 'swoe' are most suitable, while for large weeds a draw hoe that cuts through the soil will chop through the weeds at the right level.

Hand-weeding of the deep beds is no problem. It can be done at the optimum time, just after rain, with a minimum disturbance of the soil, and the weeds are added to the compost heap. With conventional rows of vegetables and wide borders of flowers and shrubs try to keep off the soil as much as possible when hand-weeding. Every time you disturb the soil weeds will be brought to the surface to germinate and every footstep causes compaction.

LACEY'S LORE

CHILDREN BEWARE

The seeds of laburnum and yew are the two main causes of poisoning from plants commonly found in gardens and parks.

Make it a rule to warn children not to eat the seeds, berries or leaves of any plant.

The secret of successful hoeing for weed control is to slide the sharp blade of the hoe into the soil. Keep it shallow so that the weeds are severed just above the roots

On our three-acre smallholding a wheeled and hooded flame gun was an invaluable aid at weed control, especially for large areas in early spring. Now, with a much smaller allotment, a hand-held Sheen X300 flame gun has proved a good investment, although not one I would recommend for a tiny back garden.

The secret of flame gunning is not to try to burn the weeds in one sweep of the gun. It should be used in two stages. The first involves using the gun like a scythe, walking slowly forward and covering a strip about 2m (6ft) wide, holding the gun so there's about 10cm (4 in) of flame visible.

The intense heat causes the plant cells to collapse and after an hour or so the weeds will have withered. Leave them for another 24 hours and, providing there's been no rain, a second pass with the gun will burn the weeds. Otherwise allow dew or rain to dry off the weeds before the second sweep. If the flame should become extinguished, relighting can be a bit tricky so whenever you are flame gunning have a small bonfire burning to make relighting the gun a simple matter of placing the jet of vaporised fuel near to the glowing embers of the bonfire.

CROP ROTATION

The idea behind the rotation of crops is that some vegetables are more hungry for a particular plant food than others and that moving the crops around the plot in a planned sequence doesn't

A flame gun, operating on paraffin, is a useful tool for clearing weeds on paved pathways, patios and gravel drives, but follow the safety rules on page 64

deplete the soil of one nutrient and so lead to an imbalance. Rotation also reduces the risk of a build up of pests and diseases that are prone to attack a particular species.

Normally, the rotation is based on a three-year cycle, although four-year rotations are still practised. Nowadays, with our smaller gardens, even rotating the vegetable patch on a three-year basis is scarcely feasible. It means dividing the space into three and then moving the groups of vegetables from site to site so, for example, the cabbage family doesn't occupy the same position in the garden more than once in three years. Conventional gardening books often go on at great length about the vital need to rotate crops in this way. The argument goes something like this:

Roots, such as carrots, parsnips, beetroot, turnips, swedes and salsify require phosphate with potash, but little or no nitrogen.

Leaf and stem crops, such as cabbage, celery, sprouting broccoli, Brussels sprouts, spinach, lettuce, asparagus and rhubarb require nitrogen with phosphate, but little potash.

Fruiting and seed crops, such as peas, beans, marrows, cucumbers, tomatoes, melons require phosphate and potash, but little nitrogen.

Tubers and bulbs, such as potatoes, onions, leeks, shallots and Jerusalem artichokes require potash and phosphate, but only a little nitrogen. So the conventional plan is to feed the crops with a chemical diet tailored to suit them.

LACEY'S LORE

GROUND COVER PLANTS

Weed control by ground cover in the flower garden is reserved for no-go areas or where maintenance needs to be kept to a minimum.

You can do it in several ways:
● By providing a permanent surface, such as paving slabs or crazy paving, bricks or tiles.
● By use of a semi-permanent cover such as thick plastic sheeting overlaid with a decorative material. You could use gravel, pebbles or forest bark.

● By planting ground cover plants of which there is a wide choice, including specially-raised roses, such as the Japanese-bred Nozomi and those from the German breeder Kordes and from Poulsen of Denmark. Other popular subjects are potentilla, the low-growing varieties of hebe, hypericum, vinca, the creeping polygonum and *Spiraea japonica*.

The organic gardener has a different philosophy. By the use of compost, farmyard manure and green manures the organic gardener feeds the soil not this plant or that, and there is little evidence to support the theory that significant depletion of nutrients results from this, providing the soil is fed on an adequate scale.

However, there is the important consideration to organic

LACEY'S LORE

HYACINTHS FOR CHRISTMAS

Indoor forcing of hyacinth bulbs is good fun and quite easy. To have them in bloom for Christmas you should buy bulbs that have been specially prepared for early flowering and they must be planted by 15 September.

Plant only one variety in a bowl so that they come into bloom together. Earthenware or plastic pots are equally suitable, but if the bowl doesn't have drainage holes, then use bulb fibre as the growing medium.

Leave the nose of the bulbs above the rim of the bowl and scatter some sharp sand over the growing medium to anchor the bulbs, which should be planted close together, but not touching. Water well, but don't waterlog the bulb fibre.

The bowls must now be kept cool, preferably at not more than 10°C (50°F) for about twelve weeks. They can then be placed in a frost-free shed, garage or a plunge in the garden: a hole deep enough to cover the bulbs with about 10cm (4in) of soil, peat or sand (see also page 69). Alternatively you can place the bowls in a box filled with soil. During the twelve-week period the bulbs should be kept moist. They can then be moved into the home to a position where they will get light but not too much warmth. Keep well watered and when in bloom move to a warmer location during the day, but a cool place at night so as to prolong the flowering period.

and inorganic gardener alike of soil-borne disease and pest control. Lettuce root aphid, for example, can survive in the soil from one season to the next, so a change of site for this crop is always a wise move. With pests such as the carrot fly, cabbage root fly, flea beetle and cabbage white butterflies, changing the site of the crop is not a preventive. Three major diseases of important crops make rotation a necessity, although if they occur in a small garden it would be more appropriate to refrain from growing those plants. They are clubroot of the cabbage family, onion white rot and potato eelworm or golden nematode.

Where rotation can be carried out, this three-year plan could be followed:

Year 1	Year 2	Year 3
A	C	B
B	A	C
C	B	A

Plot A This carries all the cabbage family, except spring greens, along with lettuce, radishes, spring onions. Compost and farmyard manure – if available – are applied when the plot is dug in late autumn or winter and lime or calcified seaweed is applied in early spring, if necessary.

Plot B This section is for the potatoes, followed by spring greens, leeks and maincrop turnips. It will have had a compost feed in early spring with a balanced organic fertiliser when the seed potatoes are planted, but no liming.

Plot C This is for the root vegetables – carrots, parsnips, turnips and beetroot – plus onions, peas and beans and only the latter three crops will have need of compost or well-rotted farmyard manure dug deeply into the soil:

Celery and spinach or Swiss chard should be fitted into Plot A, while shallots and garlic would belong with the crops in Plot C.

CHART YOUR PROGRESS

Rotating your vegetable crops, whether in the conventional three-year row system or the deep-bed method means that you must keep a record, however basic. Your gardening becomes even more interesting if you also keep a record of your successes and failures, sowing dates and planting out and harvesting times, pests and diseases encountered and controls used, along with basic data on the weather, and prices of seed and other bought-in materials. There's only one way to find out if Variety X is better than Variety Y on your land and that's by trying it, and if you put the results in a diary or notebook, you won't have to rely on your memory.

LACEY'S LORE

MULCHING GUIDELINES

1 Whatever material is used for mulching, clear the land of perennial weeds before applying the mulch. This means digging out all traces of root or rhizome, although with carpet mulching cutting off the surface growth is sufficient.

2 The mulch should be thick enough to deny light and air to the weed seedlings.

3 Wait for the soil to warm up before applying the mulch and ensure that it is moist.

4 Organic mulches are gradually incorporated into the soil by earthworms, so remember that an annual topping up is necessary.

5 In the winter draw the mulch away from the soft fruit canes and bushes to allow the birds to deal with pupating pests.

6 Every other year check the pH level of the soil under the mulch. If it has become over-acidic (see the pH guide on page 16), remove the mulch temporarily and lightly hoe in a dressing of calcified seaweed or hydrated lime, then restore the mulch.

7 Remember that weeds in pathways, particularly couchgrass, will penetrate into the soil under a mulched cropping area. So unless your grass paths are couchgrass-free, use paving stones, gravel, straw or forest bark instead.

I've been keeping gardening records for more years than I care to recall. Back in 1970 when all four children were at home, the seed list for vegetables was a very comprehensive affair. It had to be; I worked three allotments totalling thirty rods and we were self-sufficient in everything except top fruit and maincrop potatoes. I can remember with the help of my notebooks that planning the cropping of the plots was a Sunday afternoon in winter exercise, involving all six of us.

In those days, maximum effort on the allotment, with all four cylinders firing smoothly, was the prerogative of a healthy

LACEY'S LORE

THINNING TOOL

A pair of tweezers – stamp collector's or eyebrow plucking types – makes an excellent tool for thinning out seedlings grown in trays or pots. Thin as soon after germination as possible. This gives the survivors elbow room so that they can grow on, often without the need for pricking out.

LACEY'S LORE

SWEET LAVENDER

Lavender, when dried, retains its fragrance longer than any other herb. Gather it before the flowers have fully opened and hang the bunches upside down in an airy, dry place.

When thoroughly dry, you can use a hair comb to take the flowers off the stems.

husband with a growing family making maximum demand on the output from the plots. Now I'm in a far more restrained cruising period, but allotment gardening has become a way of life with deep satisfaction that holds as good in retirement as it did in the first youthful burst of enthusiasm. Seventeen years on, my seed list is only a fraction of what it was in 1970, but the fun I get in producing fresh, wholesome food is every bit as great as then.

GARDENING AIDS

As a gardening writer I am on the receiving end of countless bits of good news from enthusiastic public relations practitioners. Their client company is introducing a new electric-powered cultivator that takes all the back-ache out of soil preparation – providing you are within handy distance of a power point. Firm X announces with great pride that their range of mowers has been re-styled by an Italian designer of great distinction. A household-name seed firm says it is offering in its catalogue 'the most important new food in the history of this planet'. And so on.

Unhappily, too often these publicists are economical with the truth and that makes recommendations to one's readers a mite difficult, so in this section I am not going to mention anything that I haven't tried myself.

If one takes for granted that a good-quality spade, fork, hoe, rake, trowel, dibber, secateurs, garden line and watering can are the basic kit for the amateur gardener, a cold frame, greenhouse and a range of cloches should be given serious consideration, particularly by someone wanting to grow as much as possible of their own fresh fruit and vegetables.

The Romans used a type of frame – a pit covered by mica or glass – with heat provided by fermenting manure. Garden frames, similar to those in use today, together with cloches were very widely used throughout Europe in the seventeenth century, so it seems strange that there are so many British gardeners who don't take advantage of a frame or cloches to make raising their own plants a practical proposition as well as giving

The Roselea power hoe is an excellent tool for the large vegetable garden or smallholding

You can make a garden frame from old railway sleepers, scrap timber, breeze blocks or even bales of straw. Factory-made frames of

aluminium are inexpensive and become an important extension to the greenhouse

their crops some degree of protection from the vagaries of the climate.

Cloche protection gives an earlier start to the growing season for such crops as peas, carrots, broad beans, lettuce, turnips, beetroot and French beans, and enables crop production to be extended into late autumn and early winter. I've owned numerous cold frames over the past forty years, but have never bought one. They've all been home-made jobs, ranging from brick and breeze blocks, railway sleeper and secondhand timber construction to the cheapest made from four bales of straw with a sheet of clear plastic as a light.

Frames are used in partnership with a greenhouse to harden off the plants before finally setting them out. But at times when we've been without a greenhouse because of moving home a frame to raise brassica plants, leeks and lettuce has been invaluable.

Greenhouse management is a book in itself and there are any number of titles to choose from. Nowadays because of the high

cost of heating a greenhouse in winter, nine out of ten amateur greenhouses are probably cold houses with maybe just a small electrically-heated propagator to raise early stock. If you have a lean-to greenhouse, conservatory or glazed home extension it might be practicable to extend the central heating into it for use over the worst winter weeks. But even with an unheated greenhouse there's a new dimension to one's gardening efforts.

Cloches are still the most popular form of protection for the amateur's garden, although they are probably less intensively used now than they were three or four hundred years ago. Today, of course, plastic sheeting and rigid plastic have ousted glass as cloche materials and there is a very wide range of types to suit most budgets. The least expensive is the continuous tunnel cloche of polythene with wire hoops, the most expensive are individual cloches of PVC over galvanised tubing.

Whatever the type, one should remember that cloches retain less heat than frames but, being readily mobile, are far more versatile. If you possibly can, try to use cloches and a cold frame. Plants can be raised in the frame and the cloches used for getting earlier crops and extending the growing season.

LACEY'S LORE

FLAME GUN SAFETY

When using a flame gun, follow these safety rules:
● Use only paraffin as the fuel.
● Do not allow other people, especially children or animals, near you while using the gun.
● Keep the can of paraffin well away from the area being burned.
● If the flames goes out before the tank is empty, close the control valve and relight with care.

LACEY'S LORE

THE DEADLY WIND

In early spring the great boon of cloches is that they protect young plants from the effects of east winds which can be far more damaging than frost. Biting winds can tear the tender leaves of seedlings and scorch the plants so badly that yield is severely reduced or the crop may be a total loss.

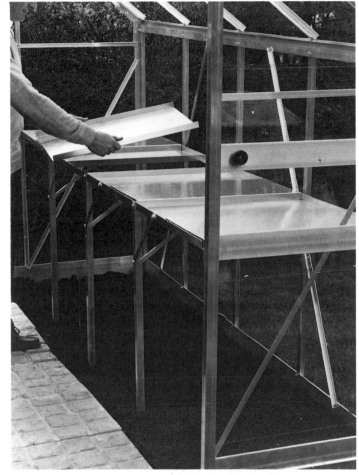

CLOCHE MANAGEMENT

Here are a few further points about cloche management:

● Don't put your cloches in shade, always site them in an open position where there is easy access.

● If the site is an exposed one, make sure the cloches are well anchored.

● Never put cloches tightly together. With individual cloches allow a little space between them for ventilation. In the case of the polythene tunnel cloche ensure there is adequate ventilation at each end.

● Cloches should be used in the normal rotation for vegetables.

● Place cloches in position for at least two weeks before sowing to allow the soil to warm up.

● If you have a piped water supply, lay a perforated pipe under the cloches for frequent, gentle watering. Otherwise remove cloches for thorough watering: do not rely on the rain. Always use a watering can with a fine rose.

● When crops have been sown or planted under cloches for an early start remove the protection gradually, not in one fell swoop.

● Remember that at the end of the season your cloches can be used to prolong the life of a crop, or to help the ripening of onions, tomatoes and seed-producing crops.

● Keep glass and rigid plastic cloches free from grime. Always clean the surfaces before storing the cloches.

THE ART OF TRANSPLANTING

A few years ago there was a television programme about American research into plant behaviour. It was on a basic level that managed to dramatise by over-simplification and I can vaguely remember one of the scientists saying that if you grabbed hold of a plant and pulled it out of the soil, roots and

Two useful accessories for the greenhouse are: above, lightweight but strong aluminium staging, below, an automatic vent opener also suitable for controlling ventilation of some metal cold frames

When buying gardening tools, choose the best you can afford. They should feel comfortable and balanced in use and, in the case of small hand tools such as these *lightweight Gardena secateurs, should have a brightly-coloured finish. They are then less likely to be mislaid among the greenery*

all, the poor plant screamed in protest. They had audio equipment to prove that plants and trees are highly tuned to possible threats and when, for example, one pruned a rose bush there was a response uncannily like a cat hissing. Heaven alone knows what sound would be heard through their equipment when a lawn is cut. For over-sensitive souls, gardening after that TV programme was never quite the same again. Even weeding took on a new, sinister significance.

On the positive side, however, the research did support a gardening folklore that all plants respond better when treated with kindness and consideration. For many plants, flowers, vegetables, shrubs and trees alike, the most traumatic happening, apart from death, is the transition from seedbed to permanent site. This act of transplanting, with the high amount of stress involved, has been the subject of much study by plant physiologists because it is a major cause of the plant's subsequent poor performance.

If the stress of transplanting is further aggravated by rough handling, poor soil conditions or adverse weather, then the result is inferior plant quality and lower yield. So always ease the plant through the transition from nursery to adult quarters as smoothly and considerately as you can. Disturb the roots as little as possible by keeping a good amount of soil as a root ball. Choose the most favourable weather and ensure adequate watering and protection from both wind and frost.

Because of the vital importance of plant stress to gardeners and commercial growers, it was inevitable that the scientists

(cont on page 69)

LACEY'S LORE

LOST ENERGY

Britain's lawns produce about 1,200,000 tonnes of grass cuttings a year with enough energy content to feed about 1,500,000 people.

But here's a sobering fact – we spend five times as much energy in cutting our lawns, mostly in petrol for the mower.

The Wilkinson Swoe, a beautifully balanced well-designed hoe, makes light work of weed suppression, cutting through the soil just below the surface

The crome has been in use for centuries for ditching and dunging, but now is used primarily for breaking down the rough-dug soil of winter into a fine *tilth for spring sowing. This one was made by a blacksmith from an old four-tine fork set at right angles to an ash shaft*

This is a cloche designed to fit over a growing bag so you can, for example, put your outdoor tomatoes in growing bags then give them protection for a few weeks with these Croptex cloches. Later the cloche converts to a taller wind *shelter or can be used elsewhere in the garden as a traditional cloche. It is made from twin-skin polypropylene sheeting and incorporates ventilation and watering panels*

LAWN CARE THE ORGANIC WAY

Everybody loves a lawn, but no-one loves a lawnmower. Or put another way, while Britain is the home of the beautiful lawn, admired by foreigners for centuries, creating a velvety turf is one of the most time-consuming tasks in the garden.

It seems that the more one cares about the condition of the lawn, the more numerous the problems become. Like a friend of mine and his hi-fi. Over the years he's spent a small fortune on his disc and tape-playing equipment, constantly seeking perfection. Now most of the enjoyment has gone out of listening to his Brahms and Bartok because he's actually listening for a hint of hiss and the merest murmur of muffle and what he calls 'muddying intermodulation'.

So perhaps the dedicated lawn lover never actually lounges back in a deck-chair and admires how the perfectly-trimmed greensward sets off the house, the herbaceous border and the rockery. His eyes are scanning the turf for trouble: a plantain here, a black medick there.

Another friend has the near-impossible combination of a much-prized lawn and a pair of prize-winning dachshund bitches. Dogs cock their legs, bitches squat. Dogs are selective about where they leave their mark and can sometimes be trained to use a particular post in the garden rather than a favoured shrub. But bitches are indiscriminate and their urine is sudden death to

grass. So when the dachs are let out to function on the lawn, Henry follows closely with a watering can to try to dilute the lethal liquid. Dogs on lawns don't make for a contented gardener.

To keep a lawn looking good you only need four things: a garden fork for aeration, a mower, a lawn rake and your own man or womanpower. There's no need for chemicals, such as weedkillers or fertilisers, and in terms of the end product of a close-carpet lawn there's little difference between the least expensive hand mower and a ride-on model that can cost nearly as much as a Mini.

The most common fault with all lawn-mowers is to cut the grass too short. For the run-of-the-mill family lawn never cut the grass shorter than 2.5cm (1in), while for a lawn of fine grasses 1.25cm (½in) is about right. Remember that grass grows outwards as well as upwards. If you cut too close, you cut off some of the side shoots or tillers and so allow quicker drying out with consequent bare patches and invasion by weeds and moss. The rule about mowing is 'little and often'. Once a week should be the norm, but during periods of rapid growth, twice a week is preferable. Whatever type of mower you use, ensure that the blades are kept sharp.

Experts argue over whether you should leave the clippings on the lawn or collect

them. However, trials for the Consumer Association carried out by Reading University's Department of Agriculture and Horticulture demonstrated quite clearly that leaving the clippings on the lawn is best. Clippings do not lead to a build up of thatch or an increase in the weeds. In fact, the clippings eventually break down to recycle the nutrients taken from the soil. In only about a fortnight the nitrogen taken from the soil is returned in this way.

If you have children or pets, it is especially important to avoid using chemicals on your lawn. An annual top dressing with sifted compost or peat and sand will aid fertility. You can use the contents of used growing bags, but do make sure it is dry and work it well into the surface with a stiff broom. Don't use spent mushroom compost because the chalk content would encourage coarse grasses and clover rather than the fine grasses which do better in moderately acid soil.

To prevent thatch building up give the lawn a light raking once a month from June onwards using a lawn rake.

Use your garden fork to aerate the lawn. This is especially important if your soil is on the heavy side. Forking systematically about 7.5cm (3in) deep over the entire lawn in spring and again in the autumn allows air to get to the grass roots and assists in the dispersion of moisture.

FACT FILE Cloches – a year's programme

January
Sow radishes French Breakfast, Cherry Belle. Harvest lettuce, parsley, spinach.

February
Sow Boltardy beetroot; The Sutton broad beans; Early Nantes, Mokum, Amsterdam Forcing early carrots; Kelvedon Wonder, Little Marvel, Titania early peas; White Lisbon spring onions; Tokyo Cross turnips; Gladiator parsnip.
Harvest lettuce, parsley, spinach.

March
Sow summer cabbage Hispi, Quickstep, Minicole; Brussels sprouts Peer Gynt, Achilles, Ormavon, Monitor; parsley; lettuce Little Gem.

April
Sow French beans Masterpiece, The Prince, Sprite; runner beans Desiree, Butler, Enorma; celeriac; sweetcorn Candle; swedes.
Harvest radishes.

May
Sow ridge cucumber Burpee Hybrid; marrow Gourmet Globe, Twickers. Cover bush tomatoes, melons.
Harvest lettuce, turnips, carrots, spring onions.

June
Harvest broad beans, peas, beetroot, French beans.

September
Sow lettuce, spinach, early carrots. Cover lettuce, land cress, watercress, harvested onions.
Harvest melons.

October
Sow winter-hardy lettuce.
Cover spinach, herbs.

November and December
Harvest lettuce, parsley, spinach.

NB Cloches will be removed from the crops in succession. The exceptions are melons, where the cloches will remain throughout the life of the crop, and crops covered during the late autumn and winter months.

A neat solution to the problem of seed sowing at the right time. This box has the seed packets filed in alphabetical order while on the underside of the lid is a month-by-month guide to sowing times

This capillary matting by Early's of Witney is a simple way of watering pot plants in the greenhouse automatically. It is made of highly absorbent polyester which retains more than eight times its own weight of water. It is fed from a trough of water, bottom left, which in turn can be fed automatically from a cistern

Aluminium-framed greenhouses that are robust, economically-priced and virtually maintenance free are available in sizes to suit even the small town garden. This is the Europa Manor Viscount, measuring 2.4m by 3.6m (8ft by 12ft) and featuring a 7.5cm (3in) high galvanised steel base as an integral part of the design

LACEY'S LORE

TAKE THE PLUNGE

House plants spending the summer outside need shelter from strong winds and the sun. Sudden rises and falls in temperature can be very hard on roots that are only protected by the thickness of the wall of the pot.

If you cannot provide a shady place, try to give your pot plants protection by making a plunge. This is a hole filled with peat, sand or soil large enough to accommodate all your pot plants up to the rim.

You can also use the plunge for bowls of spring-flowering bulbs (see page 62).

would be looking long and hard at the problem. In Rumania Professor Soeriv found a key to the way plants themselves fight stress while he was studying ways of improving plant uptake of organic nutrients.

Just as the human body at times of stress increases its intake of oxygen and speeds up production of adrenalin, so a plant under stress or suffering damage increases its production of certain amino acids, notably cysteine and proline. Unfortunately, the plant cannot produce enough of these natural stimulants to prevent stress causing permanent harm to some degree.

The agro-chemists set about synthesising the amino acids so that they could be used as a foliar spray to give the plants' own protective stimulants a boost. They called the new product a biostimulant and, after extensive trials, it is now marketed in the UK as Ergovit. The plants are sprayed immediately after lifting from the seedbed and are watered in after transplanting.

LACEY'S LORE

PLEASE DON'T TRIM

Clipping off half the leaves when transplanting seedling brassicas, leeks and other plants is said to be beneficial because it prevents water loss. There is no evidence to support this theory, so the sooner the practice is abandoned the better.

Young seedlings transplanted in early spring benefit from a little protection. This sweet pea seedling has shelter from the wind and protection from slugs with a Somerford Startaveg sleeve made of translucent plastic. It is available in several sizes, including sleeves for use with saplings

*French marigold (*Tagetes patula) *companion planted with dwarf French beans*

This biostimulant is no substitute for good husbandry. But if you have to buy in bare-rooted plants or cannot for some reason give your young plants the full care treatment at transplanting, Ergovit might well prove a boon. It is neither poisonous nor persistent, neither pesticide nor herbicide, but one of the more environmentally acceptable products from the agrochemical industry.

COMPANION PLANTS

It may be unwise to invest animals with human instincts, although anyone who has lived with dogs knows that their instincts are uncannily human. We had two crossbred border collies. They were litter sisters, rescued at eight weeks old. At nine years old Floss developed a chest tumour and that autumn the sadness of a dying year was made more melancholy for having to have her put down. We were desperately miserable, but Candy, her sister, was inconsolable, her misery deeper than anything we had seen before in animal or human. The brightness gradually returned to her eyes, although the vet had said it was touch and go whether she would survive her heartbreak. Don't tell me animals don't grieve.

So if a plant expert on television says that plants also have feelings, don't scoff, although for most of the time it may suit us not to dwell on it, especially when cutting a cabbage or hoeing the weeds.

I've been reading Gertrud Franck's book *Companion Planting* to try to unravel some of the mystery about this aspect of plant behaviour, an interest that was fuelled by Anthony Huxley's brilliant *Plant and Planet*. Far more work needs to be done on symbiosis and plant associations, on why it is that some plants thrive in each other's company while others hate each other to death. Using Mrs Franck's technique of companion planting, orthodox crop rotation is avoided, but I find her instructions very difficult to follow. These are her recommendations for plants which make good bed fellows:

- Brassicas with beans, peas, cucumbers, potatoes, beetroot, tomatoes.
- Tomatoes with onions, parsley, French beans, celeriac and brassicas.

Companion planting in a deep bed results in far less pest damage because predators are active before the harmful insect numbers build up. Here Tropaeolum *(nasturtium) has kale for company*

FACT FILE Some dos and don'ts of organic gardening

● Do try to learn the limits of what you can do in terms of your soil, the weather conditions of your district, your family commitments.
● Do all you can to improve soil structure.
● Do start a compost heap.
● Don't dig in raw vegetable waste. Try trench composting.
● Don't be in a hurry to sow, but do steal a march on the weather with cloches and a cold frame.
● Don't ignore the good old varieties, they are often more suitable for organic gardening.
● Don't buy in brassica plants. Clubroot is deadly.
● Do use great care in transplanting.
● Don't trim off the leaves of leeks or brassicas when planting out.
● Don't forget that every pest has a predator, and that soapy water is one of the best insecticides.
● Do shorten the distance between the vegetable plot and the kitchen. The fresher the food, the better.
● Do keep records of crop rotation, plant performance, quality, the weather.
● Do try deep-bed growing for many of your crops.
● Don't throw away cooked kitchen scraps. Start a worm farm.
● Don't expect miracles. Converting to organic growing is like giving up smoking: difficult at first but tremendously satisfying in the end.

● Parsnips with onions.
● Potatoes with broad beans, peas and brassicas.
● Peas with celery, potatoes and brassicas.
● Lettuce with beans, radishes, cucumbers, French beans and beetroot.
● Carrots with onions.
　But avoid planting these crops together:
● Beans and onions.
● Cabbages and onions.
● Red cabbages and tomatoes.
● Parsley and cabbage lettuce.
● Beetroot and tomatoes.
● Potatoes and onions.

A widely-held belief, although not one quoted by Mrs Franck, is that the onion family, particularly garlic, planted among the roses reduces black spot and aphids.

Chamomile was called the plants' physician because it was said to have the ability to help ailing plants back to good health, while foxglove was generally regarded by herbalists as a friend to all other plants. Mexican marigold, when planted thickly enough, is said to kill ground ivy, ground elder and bindweed, and possibly plantain, groundsel, ragwort, docks and creeping buttercup.

7

ORGANIC VEGETABLES

Growing your vegetables organically is not markedly different from growing them with the use of chemical fertilisers and pesticides: it just calls for a little more skill, and the innate understanding of the soil and the crops that we call good husbandry.

The following list of vegetables is not exhaustive either in the types you can grow or in the methods of growing. What I have tried to do is to give the salient points together with a guide on how much to grow. Bearing in mind that it is better to grow a little too much of a crop rather than too little, because the surplus can always be given to a friend, my self-sufficiency guide on page 101 is for a family of two adults and three youngsters, all with healthy appetites. You can scale down or up to suit your personal circumstances.

Each of the rows is 4.5m (15ft) long.

ARTICHOKE, GLOBE

Site and soil: Strictly a luxury vegetable that requires a lot of space for comparatively little return. Because of its handsome foliage and flowers, it is not out of place in the herbaceous border. It is unfussy about soil, but prefers an open, humus-rich site in full sun. It hails from the coast of North Africa and the best crops are grown using plenty of seaweed and compost in preparing the site.

Sowing/propagation and management: The globe artichoke can be grown from seed initially. It is a perennial, so subsequent crops can be had by taking suckers from the parent plants.

Green Globe Improved is a recommended variety to grow from seed. Sow in late March about 1.5cm (½in) deep in rows 1m (3ft) apart and thin out the plants to 60cm (2ft) apart. Crop in the second year and continue until the fifth year when suckers should be set out when they are about 22cm (9in) high. They are re-planted with about 5cm (2in) of stem buried, firmed and well watered.

The head or large flower bud is the edible part and to encourage maximum size the lateral buds around the main heads are removed. The heads will be ready to harvest in July and August. Cut the main head first, then the secondary ones. Feed the plants with a mulch of rotted farmyard manure or liquid manure after harvesting. In very exposed locations protect the plants from severe frost.

The mature plants will grow to about 1.2m (4ft) tall and produce about ten edible heads per plant, so one row is quite enough.

Troubles: Aphids and blackfly sometimes are troublesome, but can be controlled by spraying with insecticidal soap. Slugs may damage the suckers, so use the preventives given on page 152.

ARTICHOKE, JERUSALEM

Site and soil: Not strictly speaking an artichoke and it certainly doesn't hail from Jerusalem, but is becoming increasingly popular with slimmers as an alternative to good old potatoes.

Tubers are sold by seed firms or can be be bought from greengrocers and planted in February or March. They will grow virtually anywhere that is not too wet and should be set out 30cm (1ft) apart, 15cm (6in) deep. When fully grown the plants will be up to 3m (10ft) tall, so always locate them as a living windbreak or hedge where they will not overshadow other crops.

Management: Water the young plants regularly if there are dry spells in spring and early summer. From July onwards they will need support with stakes and wire. Lift the knobbly tubers as required from October onwards – each plant will yield about four pounds of tubers. Any left in the ground will become rogue plants and eventually you'll have an artichoke jungle.

One row will produce about 32kg (70lb) of edible tubers.

Troubles: The grey root aphid is the only serious pest and will be evident on the tubers when lifted. The remedy is drastic. Cut down and compost the plants; lift all the tubers and select those you want for re-planting. Find a fresh site and wash the tubers in detergent solution.

ASPARAGUS

Site and soil: Not the easiest crop to grow organically because it is a semi-permanent crop, occupying a site for anything up to twenty years and throughout that time it must be hand-weeded. Use the deep-bed method for preparing and managing the site (see page 53). Good drainage is vital to success and the site should be open but with shelter from strong winds. Aim for a pH value of 6.2 to 6.6 and be prepared to give calcified sea-weed or lime to correct every few years.

Planting and management: Recommended varieties are the oldies Connovers Colossal and Giant Mammoth, while from France we have the excellent Minerve and Lorella. Two British newcomers are Regal and Sutton's Perfection. It is easy to grow some varieties from seed, but it will be three years before a crop can be taken. The preferred method is to buy one-year-old crowns which require careful handling and planting in April. Just a few spears are cut in the following year, but thereafter each plant should yield fifteen to twenty edible spears from early May until mid-June. The remaining spears are then allowed to grow on to become ferns which are cut down to ground level in late autumn.

For a family of five to have several feasts of asparagus you will need two beds each about 1.2m (4ft) wide by 4.5m (15ft) long planted with about fifty crowns.

Troubles: Asparagus beetle eats stems and leaves and is controlled by spraying with derris. Frost can severely damage the young shoots. If hard frosts are forecast in May cover the crop with Agryl P17 or sacks. Strong winds can also harm the plants by rocking the stems in summer and autumn causing rain to penetrate and set in rotting. Provide a windbreak or give support to the stems.

AUBERGINE

Site and soil: Easy enough to grow in the cool greenhouse, but a bit tricky outdoors where cloche protection is a must. The aubergine likes a sunny site with well-drained, compost-rich soil, while in the greenhouse you can grow in pots or growing bags. Raise the plants indoors at a temperature of 18–21°C (60–70°F) in early March, move the seedlings to a cold frame or cool greenhouse in late April and plant out under cloches in late May, allowing 60cm (2ft) between each plant.

Management: Keep the plants well watered and now and then give a misting to ward off red spider mite and encourage a good set of fruit. Pinch out the growing point of each plant when there's about 30 to 37.5cm (12–15in) of growth.

Only allow five fruits to each plant and, once the fruit have started to swell, feed weekly with a liquid seaweed extract, such as SM3.

One 4.5m (15ft) row of cloches with six plants will give about thirty fruit.

Troubles: Control aphid attack with insecticidal soap spray which, with the regular misting, will also help to deter the red spider mite.

BEANS, BROAD

Site and soil: A superb crop for the amateur gardener because it is tolerant of almost all soil conditions, is easy to cultivate, yet will give a fairly long succession of fresh succulent beans. When all the beans have been picked, the plants can be chopped and dug in as a valuable green manure.

For best results rotate the crop each year and prepare the site by working in plenty of compost followed by a dressing of calcified seaweed. Aim for a pH value of 5.8 to 6.4. You will need space for three 4.5m (15ft) rows with the rows 45cm (18in) apart and the plants about 30cm (1ft) apart. Tender, young broad beans freeze particularly well, so if you want extra for your freezer, put in another row of seed.

Sowing and management: Many gardeners in favoured parts of the country like to make a November sowing outdoors of a variety such as Aquadulce or Express. The seed germinates in about ten days and the plants are expected to stand through the winter with only minor frost damage. Temperatures below −3°C (26°F) will cause fatal damage, however, and as that happens quite regularly in my part of the UK, I have given up autumn sowing of this crop.

My technique is to raise plants of The Sutton in the cool greenhouse or cold frame in February and these are planted out, when large enough to handle, to fill a couple of rows. A further sowing is made direct into the site in late March to give the second two rows and so extend the cropping period. The Sutton is a dwarf variety, never growing more than about 37.5cm (15in) tall and so is less liable to wind damage on my exposed site than the taller Aquadulce, Claudia Express, Relon, Hylon, Bunyard's Exhibition Green Windsor or Masterpiece Longpod. Windsor varieties are claimed by some experts to have a superior flavour to the quicker-growing longpod varieties, but I've found no significant difference.

When you see the first small beans, pinch out the growing point of each plant just above the top cluster of flowers. This helps the beans to swell and gives some control over blackfly. The tops are tender and delicious if popped in the pressure cooker for minimum cooking time. Don't allow any of your beans to grow old. They develop skins as tough as old boots although, strangely, an elderly Suffolk countryman friend likes nothing better for his supper than a large plateful of old broad beans, boiled until soft, served hot with a generous sprinkling of vinegar and plenty of home-made bread. For eating and freezing pick the beans when they have just begun to show through the pods as slight swellings. When you open the pod the beans should have a white scar between the segments, not a brown or black one.

If you want to save your own seed, select three or four of the best plants and don't pick any of the beans. Allow them to ripen on the plants and harvest them in August.

Troubles: Blackfly is the worst problem, with the young shoots and immature pods becoming covered in a dense, sticky mess of them. Autumn sown crops are said to escape the worst attacks, but I have never found this to be so. Pinching out the tops certainly helps to contain the pest, but spraying with liquid derris is the only safe and sure remedy.

Chocolate spot affects leaves and pods with small brown

DEEP-BED CROPPING GUIDE

	Recommended varieties	Sow or plant	Depth and spacing	Successional sowings	Cultivation	Harvest	Feeding and special care
Beetroot	Avonearly Boltardy	April	1.25cm (½in) deep in bands, 7.5cm (3in) apart	May, June	Pull alternate roots when golfball size	July to November	Appreciates mulch of seaweed or seaweed meal
Broad beans	The Sutton Bonny Lad	March	5cm (2in) deep, 37cm (15in) apart each way	Mid April	Pinch out growing tips to thwart blackfly	Late June to August	Support with string and canes
French beans	The Prince Tendergreen	March indoors	Plant out in May, 25cm (10in) apart each way	May, direct 5cm (2in) deep	Twiggy supports are helpful	July to late August	Watch out for slugs on the young plants
Runner beans, bush type	Gulliver	May	5cm (2in) deep, 37cm (15in) apart each way	June	Mulch with lawn mowings before plants flower. Water well	August to November	Pick crop from pathways
Brussels sprouts	Peer Gynt, Monitor Rampart	March in seed bed	Plant out 45cm (18in) apart each way	—	Stake each plant in exposed places to prevent windrock	September to March	Gather buttons from pathways
Cabbage, spring	April Avoncrest	August	Plant out late September, 22.5cm (9in) apart each way	—	Cut alternate plants as greens	As required from February	Rotate this and the other brassicas
summer	Minicole Hispi	March	Plant out late May, 37cm (15in) apart each way	—	Water well after planting	July to November	Use collars to protect young plants from cabbage root fly
winter	January King, Celtic, Jupiter	May	Plant late June, 37cm (15in) apart each way	—	Protect against pigeons	November to April	Felt collars
Carrots	Mokum, Jurawot Autumn King	March and May	1.25cm (½in) deep in bands	May, June July	Cover early crop with cloches or Agryl P17	June onwards. Store maincrop	Provide barrier against carrot fly
Cauliflowers	All the Year Round	April in seedbed	Plant 60cm (24in) apart each way in late June	May, June	Use Australian varieties for succession	September to January	Felt collars
Celery	Self-blanching	February indoors	Plant out 25cm (10in) apart each way in May	—	Must never be short of water	September to January	Doesn't like long, hot summers
Leeks	Argenta, Titan Musselburgh Impr.	March in seedbed	Plant 15cm (6in) apart each way with dibber	—	Can be blanched with collars	October onwards	Appreciates liquid feeding
Lettuce	Lettle Gem, Salad Bowl, Avondefiance	March in seedbed	Plant 15cm (6in) apart each way in April	May, June	Water well at all times	Late June onwards	Good subject for cloches
Marrows and courgettes	Bush varieties	April indoors	Plant out in June 60cm (24in) apart each way	—	Always keep well watered	Late July onwards	Appreciates liquid feeding
Melons	Sweetheart	Early May in heat	Plant out late May under cloches	—	Hand pollinate female flowers, pinch out to control growth	August to September	Water and liquid feed frequently
Onions, sets	Sturon Stuttgart Giant	March or April	Plant 10cm (4in) apart each way	—	Increase spacing to increase bulb size	September	Ripen thoroughly before storing
Parsnips	White Gem Gladiator	April	Station sow 3 seeds, thin to one plant 15cm (6in) apart	May	Slow to germinate so be patient	October onwards better after frost	Recommended varieties are canker resistant
Potatoes, early	Arran Pilot, Maris Bard, Concorde	Early April	Plant with trowel 12.5cm (5in) deep, 30cm (12in) apart	—	Don't earth up	Late June onwards	Mulch with lawn mowings
Radishes	Cherry Belle, French breakfast	April	Broadcast seed in wide bands, lightly cover with soil	May, June	Good under cloches	June onwards	Grow quickly to avoid woodiness
Shallots	Dutch Red, Long Keeping Yellow	Early February	Plant 15cm (6in) apart each way	—	Keep weed free	July onwards	Early planting is important
Spinach or Swiss chard	Perpetual	March or April	Station sow 15cm (6in) apart each way	August, September	Keep well watered	July to December	Crop can be overwintered under cloches
Sweetcorn	Earli King North Star	April indoors	Plant out late May, 45cm (18in) apart each way	—	Water when tassels appear	Mid-August to mid-September	Do not damage roots when transplanting
Tomatoes	Bush sorts or Gardener's Delight	Late March indoors	Plant out in June 45cm (18in) to 60cm (24in) apart each way	—	Mulch with peat or straw to protect fruit	August to October	Liquid feed fortnightly
Turnips	Early Snowball Golden Ball	March and August	Broadcast seed in broad bands	April June	Thin seedlings to 15cm (6in) apart for late sowings	Early crop – June Maincrop September	Lift and store maincrop for winter use

All these vegetables prefer a pH level of 6.5 to 7.0. Prior to sowing or planting apply a dressing of blood, fish and bone fertiliser plus rock potash at about 85g (3oz) per yard/metre run.

LACEY'S LORE

MAKE YOUR OWN POTS

Paper pots are excellent for raising broad, French and runner bean plants, as well as sweet peas.

For the beans use a wine bottle and two sheets of newspaper (tabloid size) to make three pots. Spread out the paper and roll the short side round the bottle to form a tube. Gum the edge thoroughly and, when dry, slide off the bottle and cut across the tube to make three paper pots, each about 12.5cm (5in) tall.

For the sweet pea tubes, mould the paper round kitchen rolling-pin or paper towel holder.

Fill the pots with peat-based compost, stand in a seed tray and sow the seeds as required.

When ready for planting out, simply trowel a hole and plant, pot and all. Keep moist and the plant roots penetrate the paper which eventually rots.

and this will last for about five years and benefit all the crops in the rotation.

BEANS, FRENCH

Site and soil: These are sometimes called dwarf or kidney beans. They are not particularly fussy about site but do best where plenty of compost or well-rotted farmyard manure has been dug in during the autumn or winter to give a humus-rich bed containing a good supply of the main plant foods. The French bean is a half-hardy annual, so frost is the main danger along with biting easterly and northerly winds. It crops after the main flush of broad beans and before the runner beans come on stream. For self-sufficiency and allowing for a good supply for freezing you will need space for five rows, about a foot apart with plants 25cm (10in) apart in the rows.

Sowing and management: Whatever type of French bean or variety you choose, the aim should be to keep the crop picked while the pods are young, tender and stringless. If too many pods come at once to eat fresh, freeze them because they retain

spots that spread quite rapidly. This is a symptom of a shortage of potassium. The short-term answer is to lift and destroy affected plants. In the long term, ensure the broad beans are rotated and that each site gets a good feed of your home-made compost. An extra and worthwhile precaution is to apply rock potash at the rate of 450g (1lb) to the sq m/yd over the winter

THE ORGANIC ALLOTMENT

It is more difficult to run an organic allotment than to have an organic garden. Unless, that is, you are a genius at persuasion and succeed in converting the other allotmenteers to the organic way.

A major problem is that allotment sites are like large highly intensive market gardens, and crop pests and diseases don't stick to the boundaries of individual plots. My own allotment on the Cowpasture site at Felixstowe has been organic certainly for half a century and, because the land was once within the boundaries of a monastery, it may well have been tended without chemical aid for several centuries. But several of the people with plots at Cowpasture tend to be trigger-happy with the spray gun. If only they would allow the natural balance of pest and predator to continue to achieve the reasonable harmony of many years, all would be well.

If there is a local allotment association, so much the better, because your type of gardening will be readily understood by the committee and office holders and any problems can be taken to them or aired at the meetings. You may even find enough kindred souls on the site to persuade the association to lay in stocks of organic fertilisers and the safe pesticides. But you can do yourself and the organic cause harm by being self-righteous. The smoker who's just kicked the habit can be a bigoted bore. So, too, can the new convert to organic gardening, particularly among the older tenants who, quite instinctively, have been organic growers all their lives without shouting about it or even, maybe, being aware of it.

Cost is often a major factor in their allotment gardening, so for that reason alone you won't find bottles of increasingly expensive insecticides and herbicides in their sheds. Their compost heaps are seldom aerobic, but their intentions are entirely correct.

Many of my older Cowpasture colleagues save their own seed, especially peas, beans, potatoes, onions and shallots. Most rely on annual loads of pig manure to maintain soil fertility with compost as a bonus. All fear those scourges of the vegetable grower – clubroot of brassicas and white rot of the onion family – and they know that disease can be walked from one plot to another on the gardener's boots.

It is inevitable that as newer generations take on allotments, so the organic way of doing things will become commonplace, provided we protect our allotment sites from poaching politicians.

A well-tended productive allotment is the best asset for a family, offering not only better-flavoured, fresher, cheaper vegetables and fruit but also a safety valve from the pressures of this over-materialistic society. Working an allotment gives everyone the opportunity to get back to the fundamentals of the soil, fresh air, the sun on your back, welcome rain and the sweat of the brow. As an allotment tenant you can make a small but important protest at this plastic age of take-away tastelessness and junk food.

But when the profit-seeking politicians and their Whitehall servants turn the screw yet tighter on local councils to realise their assets, allotment sites are highly vulnerable targets for handing over – at a price – to the property developers and speculators. We must fight hard and constantly to protect our allotments and hope that organisations such as the Soil Association and Henry Doubleday Research Association will add their weight to that of the National Society of Allotment and Leisure Gardeners and the local organisations in the battle to retain allotments.

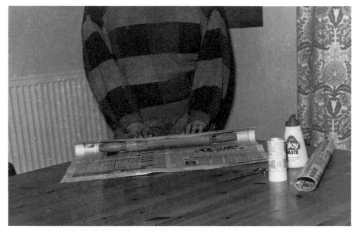

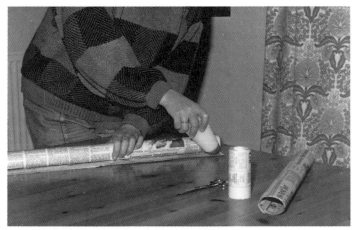

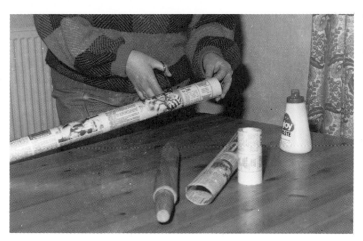

Paper pots are easy to make and are good for raising beans and sweet peas. Mould two sheets of newspaper round a rolling pin for sweet peas or a wine bottle for beans. Gum the edge. When dry, *slide off the mould and cut across the tube to make bottomless pots. Fill with peat-based compost and stand in a seed tray before sowing one seed to a pot*

their flavour and texture remarkably well.

The bush type of French bean has been a popular subject for the hybridists so you'll find most seed firms offering 'new, improved' varieties alongside the old faithfuls. As a general rule, the flat-pod or English varieties have the best flavour although they quite quickly become stringy. Most of the Continental varieties are pencil-pod types and more fleshy than the flat-pods. There are two coloured sorts – the purple and the yellow waxpod – and a few climbing varieties, such as Blue Lake and Garrafaloro, which can be grown up south-facing fences to give an early crop. Among the flat-pod varieties to look out for are The Prince, Canadian Wonder, Limelight, Masterpiece and Jumbo. Pencil or round-pod recommendations are Tendergreen, Cordon, Remus, Phoenix, Claudia, Royal Burgundy, Rodolfo, Cyrus and Pros Gitana.

French beans of whatever type require a minimum soil temperature of 10°C (50°F) to germinate. Sowing in cold, wet soil is a total waste. For an early June crop sow under cloches from mid-March onwards as soon as the soil temperature is right, remove the cloches during the day from mid-May, and completely remove them at the end of May.

Unprotected sowings can be made at any time from mid-May to July. Keep the plants free from weeds by hoeing or hand-weeding and ensure they never want for moisture. Twiggy branches placed among the plants will stop them from toppling over and a mulch of compost or lawn mowings is much appreciated.

Start picking the crop when the pods are about 10cm (4in) long.

Troubles: Too much nitrogen in the soil is to be avoided. It causes sappy growth and a shortage of flowers and, therefore, of the edible crop.

BEANS, RUNNER

Site and soil: This is deservedly one of the most popular of all vegetables and even the smallest back garden in Britain will have a few plants climbing up fences, poles or wigwams. Given a modicum of care and attention, this vegetable will go on yielding an almost daily supply for the kitchen from August right through to the first frosts of late autumn. Given that rewarding prospect, it is wise to prepare the site with thoroughness. Use the trench composting technique described on page 30 or failing that, dig the site one spit deep in the autumn and put in as much compost or farmyard manure or both as you can manage. Then give a top dressing of calcified seaweed or, in February, a sprinkling of hydrated lime. The pH reading should be, ideally, 6.4.

Sowing and management: Sow the seeds whan all danger of frost has passed, but a couple of weeks beforehand give the site a top dressing of seaweed meal or other balanced organic fertiliser.

Never sow when the soil is cold and wet – the seed will simply rot. For self-sufficiency you will need a double row, 4.5m (15ft) wide. This will give 45 to 68kg (100 to 150lb) of beans.

If you are growing up a support of some kind, the young seedlings will need tying as soon as they reach about 30cm (1ft) tall.

On my exposed Suffolk allotment I grow runner beans on the flat, sowing four rows, 60cm (2ft) apart with the seeds 30cm (1ft) apart. When the plants have made about 45cm (18in) of growth I pinch out the growing tips to encourage lateral growth and go on doing this every so often so that the bushy plants eventually give fairly dense ground cover. You can't grow exhibition beans this way because many of them are sickle-shaped, but the yield is often far more than from crops grown up supports. I never have a problem over fertilisation of the flowers, the bed is weed-free and holds moisture well.

Two ways to grow runner beans: upwards, as on the right, and on the flat, left. In exposed areas growing the beans without support often gives a heavier crop over a longer period

Runner beans lose much of their fine flavour when frozen and I much prefer to keep surplus beans in the old way by salting down. For this you should try to get hold of an earthenware pot, glazed on the inside, of the type that was used for pickling eggs. The surplus beans are sliced and washed and put in layers in the container. Between each layer give a generous sprinkling of coarse cooking or sea salt. When you have added all the beans that are surplus to your immediate needs, place a muslin cloth over the pot. They will keep for up to about three months, retaining that just-picked flavour. Just take as many as you want at a time from the pot, rinse them thoroughly and cook in the usual way.

There are so many good varieties of runner bean available that it is difficult to make a recommendation. The white- and pink-flowered varieties are a good choice if you've run into problems over flowers that failed to produce pods because those varieties, such as Desiree, Mergoles, Painted Lady, Sunset and Erecta, are all self-pollinating. Among the trustworthy old varieties are Scarlet Emperor, Streamline, Kelvedon Marvel, Crusader and Prizewinner, while some excellent newcomers are Pickwick (a bush type), Butler, Polestar, White Achievement, Romano, and Goliath.

Troubles: Too early sowing or when the soil is cold and wet may cause the seed to rot. Blackfly can be controlled with insecticidal soap.

BEETROOT

Site and soil: It is easy to be self-sufficient in this vegetable. Baby beet are a delicious salad crop and are very suitable for pickling, while the maincrop roots can be lifted in late autumn and stored for use throughout the winter and spring. So you

A runner-bean trial at Otley College with the beans sown in a cold greenhouse then planted through Hortopaper and the pathways mulched with straw. It gave a ten-day start over a crop sown in situ without the paper mulch

should allow for three rows, each 30cm (1ft) apart. This crop wants a humus-rich soil with a pH value of 6.2 to 6.6.

Sowing and management: Too early sowing can result in the crop bolting. Mid-April is early enough, with just half the row sown. The second half is sown about four weeks later. Sow the rows for autumn and winter use in late May or early June.

If the crop dries out at any time, the roots become woody with characteristic pale rings in the flesh. I use a mulch of sea-weed along the rows. It does wonders to the flavour and helps to conserve moisture. You can achieve the same effect by sprinkling seaweed meal along the rows, lightly hoe it into the soil, give the rows a good watering, then mulch with compost, lawn mowings or even shredded, soaked newspaper.

Beetroot seeds are actually a cluster of several seeds with a cork-like casing, so thin the seedlings to one per station as soon as possible. Single seeded or monogerm sorts are available, if you prefer.

Pull the baby beet for salads and pickling when they are no bigger than golf balls – that will be about twelve weeks after sowing. Some folk like to eat the young leaves as an alternative to spinach.

The maincrop beet should not be allowed to become too big and woody, so lift and store them in September.

Troubles: Birds love the seedlings. Use pea guards or black cotton over the rows to deter them. Drought, as well as too early sowing, can cause bolting, so water and mulch the rows. Rabbits and rats will often eat their way through a crop that has been left in the ground after about mid-October.

BROCCOLI, PURPLE SPROUTING

Site and soil: A site that is open and with plenty of air move-ment and soil that has been well manured for the previous crop are requirements for all the brassica family. Purple sprouting broccoli is a superb vegetable for the amateur grower. It is highly nutritious, relatively easy to grow well, matures at a time when other green vegetables are in short supply, and gives an excellent return for very little outlay. Aim for a pH of 6.2 to 6.6.

Sowing and management: Self-sufficiency is achieved with just one 4.5m (15ft) row of six plants. The average seed packet gives about 500 seeds, while the seed has a life expectancy of about five years, so one almost inevitably raises too many plants for one's own use. However, providing there is abso-lutely no risk of passing on clubroot, your friends and neighbours can benefit from surplus plants.

Sow in late April or early May, very sparingly, so that the seedlings aren't crowded. Transplant to the permanent site when they are about 7.5 to 10cm (3 to 4in) tall. On exposed sites it is advisable to stake the plants in late autumn to prevent wind rock. Christmas Purple Sprouting is ready to eat in late January or February; Early Purple Sprouting in late February and March, while Late Purple Sprouting can be cut from late March through April.

Cut the tender shoots, beginning with the central one, while the flower buds are still in a tight bunch. Cut or break off the shoots or spears with about 12.5cm (5in) of stem because this is what gives this crop its delicious asparagus-like flavour. You can usually continue taking the shoots for about six or seven weeks after which they become too tough and straggly.

Troubles: In harsh weather pigeons will strip this crop to the leaf stalks and stem, so cover with netting or Agryl P17. Cabbage white butterflies and the cabbage moth seldom seem interested in this crop. Protect the young plants after transplanting against the cabbage root fly by placing a collar round the stem (see page 145). In some areas brassica whitefly is troublesome and difficult to control, but spraying once a fortnight with soapy water is a pretty good remedy. If you suspect clubroot, consult page 147 before doing anything else.

BRUSSELS SPROUTS

Site and soil: Well-grown, properly cooked sprouts are one of the joys of wintertime meals, having a crisp texture and nutty flavour that is lost when a commercially-grown crop reappears in frozen food packs. When the amateur's crop fails it is almost always due to lack of organic material in the soil and failure to ensure the plants are thoroughly firm after transplanting. This may mean drawing soil up the stems and staking.

This is a brassica, so rotation of the crop is recommended and give a good dressing of calcified seaweed a couple of weeks before transplanting. The pH should be 6.2 to 6.6.

Sowing and management: Because this is a mainstay British vegetable the hybridists have done a lot of work on it and there are scores of varieties that enable the grower to span the cropping period September to March, although many people swear that you shouldn't pick any of the buttons until they have had a frost.

Sow an early variety in a cold frame or seedbed in March and transplant in May: mid-season and late varieties should be sown in April and planted in late May or early June. Use netting or wire guards to protect the seedlings from bird damage. Water the young plants before transplanting and water them into their permanent site then place a collar round the stem to deter the cabbage root flies from laying their eggs.

Pull off yellowed leaves, and collect any fallen ones, as the crop matures and remove only a few buttons from each stem at one time, taking the lowest ones first and working upward. The sprout tops should be cut when all the buttons have been taken and cooked like spring greens.

Modern F¹ varieties give good yields of uniform sized buttons, although they tend to mature over a much shorter period than the old open-pollinated varieties. Two of the best of the old types are Cambridge No 5 and Roodnerf Seven Hills, while among the F¹ hybrids I can recommend Peer Gynt (mid-season), Citadel (a bit later than Peer Gynt), Achilles (late), Ormavon (late), Rampart (late) and Fortress (late).

Troubles: Whitefly are a particular nuisance because the honeydew they secrete can cover the buttons and cause a sooty mould. Pest control is the same as for purple sprouting broccoli.

CABBAGE

Site and soil: A firm soil well supplied with humus is necessary for this member of the brassica tribe which has been a popular vegetable in Britain since the Romans introduced it. Boiled cabbage is reckoned by some people to be synonymous with the bleaker side of our national cookery, but we are rapidly learning that boiling is just about the worst treatment to give this all-the-year round vegetable.

For all except the spring cabbage which have to be over-wintered, apply a dressing of balanced organic fertiliser or seaweed meal a week or so before moving the plants from the seedbed or cold frame. Use the same transplanting technique as for Brussels sprouts. For self-sufficiency you will need a fair bit of space – a total of about 4.5m (15ft) each way (see page 101), but if space is restricted, you could concentrate on growing a crop for late autumn and winter use; try, nevertheless, to rotate the cabbages along with the other brassica crops.

Sowing and management: It is best to raise the plants in a seedbed and transplant when the seedlings have made four or five leaves. Thin the seedlings, if necessary, to prevent them becoming drawn and spindly, and protect them from birds.

Summer cabbage is sown from March to May for transplanting May to July. Winter cabbage is sown in April or early May and planted about mid-July. Spring cabbage is sown in late July or early August and set out from mid-September to mid-October. Red cabbage, which is grown for pickling, is sown in March and cut in September or October.

Some varieties of winter cabbage, notably Celtic F¹ and Dutch Winter White or Holland Late Winter, once they are mature, are capable of standing fresh and hard for several

Cut squares or discs from felt, carpet underlay or thick wrapping paper to protect brassica seedlings from cabbage root fly damage. Cut a slit to the centre and three or four nicks radiating from it. Then place round the stems when transplanting and leave in position for the life of the plant

months – my record is five months with a Celtic. The winter white varieties can be used fresh for cooking or raw for coleslaw or they can be cut and the outer leaves trimmed off, placed in boxes of peat or straw and will stay in good condition from late November until early March.

Recommended varieties are: Summer – Hispi, Primo, Greyhound, Quickstep, Minicole, Hornspi. Winter – Celtic, January King, Christmas Drumhead, Greensleaves. Spring – April, Durham Early, Avoncrest, Offenham Flower of Spring, Spring Hero.

Troubles: Nothing special to mention other than those described for the other brassicas. Caterpillars, especially those of the cabbage white butterflies, can cause considerable damage to the summer crops. Pinch the eggs between thumb and forefinger, hand pick the caterpillars or use the biological control *Bacillus thuringiensis* (see page 137).

CALABRESE

Site and soil: A very nutritious crop that follows on from the purple sprouting broccoli. Good for the small garden because it is ready about sixteen weeks after sowing and requires very little space compared with its big brothers in the brassica world. It will also give a good account of itself in soil that wouldn't be suitable for hungry feeders such as cauliflowers.

A row of fifteen plants, 30cm (1ft) apart, will yield nearly 7kg (about 15lb) of broccoli spears.

Sowing and management: Sow in April in situ or in soil blocks in the cold frame or cool greenhouse. Never allow the plants to want for water. After cutting the main shoot in July give a feed of SM3 liquid seaweed fertiliser to encourage production of fat side shoots.

Troubles: Generally free from brassica problems.

CARROTS

Site and soil: Back in the eighteenth century the Secretary to the Board of Agriculture wrote about my part of Suffolk: 'This corner of Suffolk is to be recommended for practising much better husbandry than any other tract of country with which I am acquainted. Their culture of carrots . . . does them honour.'

At that time farm horses ate a bushel (36 litres) a day of carrots and Suffolk-grown carrots were sent by barge to London for dray horses and the barges returned loaded with horse and human excreta to spread on the fields after composting with the calcium-rich crag. The Suffolk Sandlings still

LACEY'S LORE

PICKLED CABBAGE

Red cabbage for pickling should be given the same cultivation and husbandry as the autumn green crop. But harvest the red crop in sequence because the whole point of the pickle is that it should be nuttily crisp. So cut the red cabbage heads and make fresh jars of pickle with them at three or four week intervals from September through to January.

grow excellent crops of carrots and at Kate Mares' organic smallholding at Westleton, near Dunwich, customers come from as far away as London to buy her superbly grown fine-flavoured carrots.

Carrots grow best in a light, rich soil and if the site is within sound of the sea, so much the better. Don't sow them in land that has been freshly manured. Root vegetables, especially carrots and parsnips, will fork if they encounter pockets of plant foods, so try to save compost for the carrot rows.

Sowing and management: Carrots contain more vitamin A than any other vegetable, so don't be stingy with this crop. By careful planning it is quite easy to have a supply of your own home-grown carrots for most of the year. Sow the seeds 1.25cm (½in) deep with the early crop in rows 15cm (6in) apart, and the maincrop 20cm (8in) apart.

If your soil is too heavy or too full of stones to grow carrots well, you can grow a variety like Suko in window boxes, tubs or other containers filled with peat and fed with liquid manure. Suko grows fast to a maximum length of about 10cm (4in) and can be grown in succession from late spring to November.

The only effective way of preventing damage by carrot fly to the maincrop carrots is by erecting a physical barrier, such as this, made from polythene sheeting stapled to scrap-wood frames. It protects two rows of carrots

Another method, often used by peopie who grow to show, is to make cone-shaped holes in the soil with a crowbar. Fill up the holes with a mixture of peat and compost and station sow three seeds at each hole.

Start the carrot succession by sowing an early-maturing variety under cloches in early March or in a shelted spot in the open in early April. Recommended varieties for this are Amsterdam Forcing, Early Nantes, Nantes Frubund, Early French Frame, Early Horn, Tiana and Kundulus. The first sowing should be ready to pull in about twelve weeks. Make a second sowing of an early variety about three to four weeks after the first.

The maincrop sowings of two rows should be made in late April for the first row and about three weeks later for the second row. There's a wide choice of both open-pollinated varieties as well as F¹ hybrids to choose from. One of the very best is Juwarot which has double the vitamin A of any other sort. Autumn King is another excellent maincrop, along with Mokum, James Scarlet Intermediate. Berlicum Berjo, Redca and Giant Flak Improved.

Autumn King and Giant Flak have exceptionally large roots. A 4.5m (15ft) row of each will give a harvest of 27 to 36kg (60 to 80lb) which can be stored in moist peat or sand in layers in any suitable container in a cool, dry place.

Many commercial growers leave the maincrop carrots in the ground with a mulch of straw to prevent the soil becoming frozen rock-hard. The roots are dug as required for market.

Troubles: Enemy No 1 of the carrot grower is the carrot fly. The female fly is attracted by the smell of the carrots and comes in low like a cruise missile to lay her eggs alongside the plants. When they hatch, the maggots tunnel into the roots, causing the foliage to redden and the plants to wilt and, eventually, to die. Mature roots can be riddled with holes and will rot in store, so the carrot fly is understandably feared by amateur and commercial grower. Control measures are given on page 145.

Forked roots happen when the main root hits a stone or encounters a dollop of manure, while split roots are caused by heavy rain after a long, dry spell. In hot, dry weather water the rows and occasionally spray with soapy water or insecticide soap to hit the carrot aphids.

Green shouldered carrots are the result of sunlight on the exposed crown. You can prevent this by covering the crowns with soil throughout the growing period.

CAULIFLOWERS

Site and soil: Cauliflowers are something of a specialist crop that can be grown extremely well by commercial growers in Kent, Lincolnshire and parts of the West Country, but often rather badly by the amateur in his garden or on his allotment. Unfortunately, most commercial crops are produced with every imaginable sort of insecticide and herbicide, as well as the usual bags of chemical fertiliser, to make the heads visually attractive but nutritionally suspect.

Cauliflowers can be produced at almost any time of the year, thanks to the work of hybridists, but the crop is very fussy over soil and location. For a start, all but the mini cauliflowers need a fair bit of space – at least 75cm (2½ft) each way for the winter varieties, and 60cm (2ft) for the summer and autumn-heading ones. Secondly, the soil must have meticulous preparation. That means working in generous amounts of well-rotted manure and/or compost in the autumn, followed by lime or calcified seaweed if needed to get the pH reading 6.2 to 6.6. After that it should be kept weed free but allowed to consolidate. Thirdly, the crop must never be allowed to go short of water.

Sowing and management: For a late June early July crop, sow indoors in January and transplant in early April. Suitable varieties for this are All the Year, Abuntia, Snowball, Snow King, Alpha and Dominant.

Earthing up the trench celery needs to be done in stages. Start in mid-August by removing all side shoots and weeds, then drench the soil and tie a collar of thick brown paper, newspaper or black

polythene round each plant. Draw a little soil at a time into the trench until by about mid-September it reaches to the top of the collars, but don't let soil fall into the heart of the plants

Autumn varieties are sown outdoors in late April or early May and transplanted in late June. Recommended varieties are Dok Elgon, Flora Bianca, Canberra, Veitch's Self Protecting.

Winter varieties are sown outdoors in May and transplanted mid- to late July. Good varieties are Snow's Winter White, Early March, English Winter and Walcheren Winter.

Sow the seed very thinly 1.25cm (½in) deep, and thin to about 7.5cm (3in) apart. Transplant when the seedlings have made five or six leaves and firm the soil very thoroughly after planting.

The summer heading sorts should be protected from the sun by bending a couple of leaves over the curd, while the winter ones will need protection from frost. A good way to do this is to cover the crop with Agryl as a floating cloche or cover the heads with a light thatch of straw held in place by Netlon netting. Another trick is to save the stalk and outer leaves of each head after cutting and invert it over its uncut neighbour – useful if you have just a few caulis to protect.

Troubles: Cauliflowers are very hungry feeders, so if the curds fail to do well it could be because the plants were kept hungry. Failure to consolidate the soil after the autumn preparation and to firm the plants after transplanting are further reasons why this crop refuses to give a good account of itself.

Acid soil can cause molybdenum deficiency and whiptail – strap-like leaves, so check the pH during winter.

Put collars round the plants when transplanting to guard against cabbage root fly (see page 145).

CELERIAC

Site and soil: This is a good substitute for celery and, in fact, is often called turnip-rooted celery. The foliage is similar to celery, but the edible bit is not the stalks but the swollen root. Its advantages over celery are it is more hardy, requires no earthing up, is less prone to pests and diseases and does not bolt. Its disadvantage is that you cannot eat it like celery, for example, as a winter afternoon tea; the crisp nutty celery being accompanied by crusty bread and a wedge of good English cheese.

Celeriac can be grated or sliced for adding to a winter salad or peeled and diced for using as a cooked vegetable.

Plenty of organic matter in the soil will give this crop the feeding it needs along with the moisture retention necessary to produce good sized, tender roots.

Sowing and management: Seedlings are sown under glass in March, hardened off, then planted out in late May at 30cm (1ft) apart in rows 45cm (18in) apart. Pinch off the side shoots as they develop and water copiously in dry weather. Regular feeding with a liquid organic manure, especially liquid seaweed, will help to promote large roots. Remove the lower leaves as the winter approaches and start lifting the crop in late October. The crop can be left in the ground covered with peat or straw and lifted as required through the winter.

Recommended varieties are Balder, Claudia, Iram, Marble Ball and Tellus.

Troubles: Nothing much to worry about. The celery fly sometimes attacks causing blistered leaves which can be removed.

CELERY

Site and soil: One of the most demanding of crops for the amateur but, in my book anyway, one well worth fussing over. Growing good celery is mostly about ensuring the soil is packed with rich organic matter, then never allowing the crop to go short of water.

Trench types of celery require a trench 30cm (1ft) deep prepared early in the year. The bottom 15cm (6in) is filled with well-rotted manure or compost followed by about 7.5cm (3in) of the topsoil. The remainder of the soil removed from the trench is used for earthing up later in the year.

Self-blanching types can be grown on the surface because earthing up is not required. However, the flavour of the self-blanching types is not a patch on the trench varieties which are also rather more able to resist damage from frost.

Sowing and management: Few nurserymen offer trench type plants nowadays, although many will have self-blanching ones for sale at the right time. If you decide to raise your own trench plants, you can choose from Giant White, Giant Pink or Giant Red types, each sold under different strain names by seed firms. On the whole, Giant White types are more tender but less hardy than the Giant Red ones, while Giant Pink strains are an excellent compromise, coming rather later than the whites and rather easier to blanch than the reds.

Popular self-blanching types are Golden Self-Blanching, Celebrity and American Green. If you intend to raise either these or the trench types, the seed should be sown indoors towards the end of March with transplanting, after hardening off, in late May or early June.

The plants are set out in the trench in a double staggered row, while the self-blanching ones are put about 22.5cm (9in) apart in rows 30cm (1ft) apart.

Blanching by using paper or plastic collars followed by earthing up the stems not only whitens the stems, it also increases the length of them and improves the flavour.

Troubles: Slugs love celery and, once the earthing up starts, can severely damage the stems. Water thoroughly with Fertosan or Nobble, the safe slug killers. Celery fly causes blistering of the leaves, so pinch off affected leaves. Blight or celery leaf spot can be serious in a wet summer and autumn. It is a seed-borne disease, so always buy hot-water treated seeds. Dryness round the roots, particularly after earthing up, will often cause splitting of the stalks. Meticulous watering and a fortnightly feed with liquid manure, such as SM3, should prevent this sort of damage.

Bolting is a result of a cold spring or too little water. The plants may appear to be fine, but when they are lifted the heart of the stick will be found to be a tough flower stalk that makes the whole business of raising the plants a waste of time. Similarly, slug damage to the stalks can introduce bacteria which turn the heart of the celery stick into a gungy mess, only discovered when you lift the crop.

CUCUMBER, OUTDOORS

Site and soil: You can grow a couple of ridge cucumber plants in a grow bag outdoors or in a sunny, though sheltered, spot in the garden provided the soil is well drained and thoroughly enriched with organic material. Organically-grown ridge cucumbers have a far superior flavour to the commercial greenhouse ones and, though there are numerous varieties to choose from, you can't go far wrong with Burpee Hybrid. One never knows if the summer is going to be a wet one, of course, unless you live in a place where that is a norm. If so, the newer Japanese varieties, such as Kyoto, Burpless Tasty Green and Tokyo Slicer, are more suitable.

A soil on the acid side is preferred – aim for a pH of 5.8 to 6.4.

Sowing and management: Sow the seeds on edge in pots in gentle heat in mid-April, harden off for planting out in early June, or sow in situ in May with protection from late frosts and cold winds, using jars or cloches.

Keep the plants well watered and, once they are established, mulch with compost, Hortopaper or black polythene. Encourage the fruiting side shoots by pinching out the growing point of the plant. Feed with liquid organic fertiliser when the fruits have started to swell.

Troubles: Poor pollination is not usually a problem with outdoor cucumbers, but if the plants are under cloches it is advisable to hand pollinate the female flowers by brushing them with a male one.

Under cloches red spider mite can be a problem – spray with derris if it is – but a twice weekly syringing with water should prevent the trouble from starting. In a wet season grey mould (botrytis) can decimate the crop. Spraying with 2g of ordinary bicarbonate of soda in a litre of water is said to offer some control.

Mosaic virus is spread by greenfly. Once it has got a grip on the plant there is no remedy. Dig up the plant and destroy it.

ENDIVE

Site and soil: A seven-month salad crop that is especially welcome during the depths of winter, but the plants must be blanched for those who dislike the bitter flavour. There are two basic types: curled-leaved for late summer and autumn use, and the broad-leaved or Batavian type for winter salads.

A light, but rich soil is best for this crop which also needs a lot of moisture. Aim for a pH of 5.5 to 6.4.

Sowing and management: Sow Green Curled or Moss Curled seed thinly at fortnightly intervals from April to August in rows about 22.5cm (9in) apart. Thin the plants to 30cm (1ft) apart.

Sow Batavian Green or Winter Lettuce-Leaved seeds from July to September in rows 30cm (1ft) apart, thinning the plants to 30cm (1ft) apart.

Blanching takes about three weeks to complete and should begin about twelve weeks after sowing. With the autumn crop simply tie up the leaves and cover the plant with a flower pot, having first blocked the drainage hole.

With the winter crop the traditional way of blanching is to dig up the heads and transplant them into a cold frame or into boxes of peat or soil and cover with a thick layer of straw. The boxes can go under the staging in the greenhouse or in the garage or shed.

Troubles: Slugs can be a nuisance once blanching has started, so water with Fertosan. Otherwise this is a problem-free crop.

FENNEL

Site and soil: This is Florence or sweet fennel with feathery foliage and a swollen bulb at the base of the stem. It is an annual that must be grown quickly, so it needs a rich, moisture retentive soil with plenty of organic matter.

Sowing and management: If you sow in the spring, as recommended by many seed merchants, your fennel will bolt when it comes to the first hot, dry spell instead of producing the succulent bulb which is what you want to eat. Sow in soil blocks or peat pots in June to crop in September. Sowing this way avoids the need to transplant, a practice disliked by this plant.

The bulb has a distinct aniseed flavour and is used raw in salads or braised. The fern-like foliage can be cut for decoration or used as a herb for flavouring.

Recommended varieties are Perfection, Sirio and Zefa Fino, although you may find some seedsmen list this simply as Sweet Fennel or Florence Fennel.

Troubles: Apart from bolting, you should have no problems, but keep the plants nicely moist.

GARLIC

Site and soil: Since so many of us have discovered the delights of Continental cuisine, garlic, once despised as vulgar and French, has become popular, but still an expensive item in Britain. So it is surprising that more gardeners don't have a crack at growing it. Treat it very much as you would shallots and you won't go far wrong. An open, sunny site and an organically-rich soil are needed for best results, prepared in summer so that you can plant in late autumn.

Sowing and management: The pink or red garlic is perfectly hardy and this is the one you want for planting in late October. Buy the cloves from a delicatessen, Indian shop or greengrocers because you are unlikely to find any but white garlic on offer from garden centres and other suppliers.

Plant the cloves of garlic as you would onion sets or shallots by pushing them into the soil until just the tip is showing, then firming thoroughly. Birds will pull them out and frost will lift them, so keep a check on them.

Alternatively, you can place the cloves on moist peat in trays in a shed or garage until they have made some roots and

Kale – an easy crop for most soils and one of the hardiest of all winter vegetables

then plant them out. They should be 15cm (6in) apart in rows about 30cm (1ft) apart.

Garlic should be left in the ground until the tops die down naturally. Gently lift them with a fork and place them on a wire rack to dry off and ripen in the sun for at least a week. The cloves can be stored by hanging them in a net or old tights, somewhere cool but well ventilated.

Troubles: On the whole, this crop is a trouble-free one and makes an excellent companion plant for carrots, helping to deter the carrot fly. But don't allow the developing clove or bulbs to become crowded by weeds.

KALE

This is a group that includes types grown solely for cattle feed and those intended for human consumption, such as Thousand Head or asparagus kale, borecole, Hungry Gap or rape kale and Scotch kale.

Site and soil: A very easy crop to grow on almost any type of soil but with a preference for one with a pH of neutral 7.0. The kales are very hardy and will pull through a winter that kills off the spring greens and sprouting broccoli, but some folk find the flavour is insipid and any but the very young leaves can be as tough as old boots.

To get them through a hard winter the plants should not be given a site that is too well stocked with nutrients, so they could follow the early potatoes.

Sowing and management: Sow in early May 1.25cm (½in)

deep, with the rows 15cm (6in) apart. Thin the seedlings to 7.5cm (3in) apart. With rape kale sow where the plants will mature.

Transplant when the seedlings are about 12.5cm (5in) high and water in thoroughly. The plants should be about 45cm (18in) apart and should be firmed and, as they develop, may well need staking for support in exposed areas.

In early spring a feed with liquid dried blood will encourage the production of side shoots. Cutting out the crown of the plant in early December also helps to produce plenty of shoots which are pulled off or cut from the plant like purple sprouting broccoli spears.

The best variety of all is Pentland Brig, bred by the Scottish Plant Breeding Station. It has leaves that are fringed, but not curled like parsley. For the small garden, Frosty is a good choice, growing only about 30cm (1ft) tall, while Westland Autumn is a little taller.

Troubles: Kales are fairly resistant to most brassica problems, but not aphids, whitefly and cabbage white caterpillars. Use the same controls as for purple sprouting broccoli.

KOHL RABI

Site and soil: We grew this and thoroughly enjoyed it as an alternative to turnips when we lived in the north Midlands, but in the drier, hotter East Anglia it has never done so well for me, although the experts tell me it should do far better than the turnip in Suffolk.

It needs light land with a neutral pH of 7.0 and because it is a brassica should be part of the rotation for this group.

Fekara is a new kohl rabi introduced by Suttons Seeds

Sowing and management: Sow the summer-maturing crop in late March or April for pulling in July and August. Sow thinly, 1.25cm (½in) deep, in rows 30cm (1ft) apart. For the winter crop, sow a purple variety in late July. The edible part is the swollen stem, although the young leaves can be used as a spinach substitute.

The bulb should be taken to the cook when it is about the size of a tennis ball. It should not be peeled, but cooked whole or sliced. This crop cannot be stored, so leave the late-maturing bulbs in the ground, covered by straw, until needed.

Recommended varieties are White Vienna, Green Vienna, Purple Vienna, Fekara, Lanro and Rowel.

Troubles: Protect the seedlings from bird damage and watch out for aphids, otherwise the crop is usually free from brassica problems.

LAND CRESS

This is also known as American cress and has a flavour and appearance similar to watercress. It is one of the few salad plants that go on growing quite happily through our British winters.

Site and soil: A good organic loam with optimum moisture retention capability and a site that gives some shade are ideal for this crop.

Sowing and management: Sow in April for summer cropping and in August for winter use. Sow 1.25cm (½in) deep in rows 22.5cm (9in) apart and thin plants to about 20cm (8in) apart.

Let some plants run to seed the year after the initial sowing and you will have continuity of supply.

You can start harvesting about eight weeks after sowing, taking only the young leaves, and from November onwards it's a good plan to cover some or all of the plants with cloches or straw.

LEEKS

Site and soil: If I had to make a choice between growing onions or leeks, I'd go for leeks every time, but sneak in a few shallots as well. Although it is the national emblem of Wales, the north of England probably grows the best leeks in the word and the secret is to give the crop as much well-rotted farmyard manure or compost as you can in land that was deeply dug the previous autumn.

During the winter check the pH level of the site because leeks dislike an acid environment – aim for 7.0 to 7.5.

Sowing and management: This is primarily an exceedingly good winter vegetable, capable of being cropped from just before Christmas right through to mid-April and it needs a correspondingly long growing season. North of Birmingham it is probably wise to make a sowing under glass in February. In the south, west and east a sowing outdoors towards the end of March should give nice-sized plants for setting out in June or early July.

Sow very thinly, about 1.25cm (½in) deep in a seedbed and thin the seedlings to 5cm (2in) apart. Before lifting the seedlings for planting out, thoroughly water the seedbed and the site they are to occupy.

The easiest way of planting is to make 15–20cm (6–8in) holes with a dibber and drop the plants in at about 15cm (6in) apart each way. Don't trim the leaves and roots as many books recommend, but do fill the planting hole with water, using a watering can with a fine spout.

About three weeks after planting out give the plants a top dressing of dried poultry manure. If you can't get this, a dressing of fish, blood and bone is an excellent alternative. Give a second dressing about three weeks after the first. From mid-August to mid-October a fortnightly feed of liquid sea-weed fertiliser will help the crop along; at the same time trim the tips off any leaves that are touching the ground or the earth-worms will pull them in, and keep the rows well hoed.

From September onwards a little earth can be drawn up the stems to increase the length of blanched stem, but before doing this it is advisable to slip a cardboard collar round the stem to prevent soil getting in between the leaves.

When lifting plants for the kitchen, ease them out with a fork and cut off the roots in situ. Then take the plants to the compost heap and trim the leaves. The roots that have been cut from the leeks make an excellent food for the early lettuce crop – a tip I picked up from my friend Ramsay Shewell-Cooper, chairman of the Good Gardeners' Association.

There are many good varieties of leek. In general the Musselburgh or Scotch flag types are the hardiest. Among recommended early varieties are The Lyon, short and fat; Early Market, a good flavour but not winter hardy; Walton Mammoth, Titan, a very tall variety; St Victor, with purple foliage.

Mid and late season varieties to go for are Musselburgh, capable of producing very large stems; Monstrueux de Carentan, a very old French variety re-introduced by Henry Doubleday Research Association and available from Heritage Seeds; Giant Winter, offered in a number of strains, including Catalina, Royal Favourite and Snowster; Winter Crop, especially recommended for the bleakest northern sites; and Yates Empire which, once fully grown, stands in good condition right through to May.

Troubles: The leek is a member of the onion family, but is generally reckoned not to suffer from onion problems. However, if you've had onion white rot, your leeks will be infected if grown on the same site. Leek rust is becoming commonplace among commercial growers and is symptomatic of land heavily dosed with nitrogenous fertiliser, but is countered by organic potash. To avoid other troubles, always include leeks in your crop rotation.

In East Anglia in recent years the leek moth has proved a major pest. The larvae tunnel through the leaves and into the heart of the plants and I haven't found any remedy.

LETTUCE

There are four main types of this most popular vegetable – cos, cabbage butterhead, cabbage crisphead, and cut-and-come-again or loose leaf. Which ones you decide to grow is a matter of taste, although they all taste better grown the organic way.

Site and soil: Land that is on the light side but well manured for a previous crop and about a neutral pH of 7.0 suits this crop. The cabbage types are more tolerant of poor soil and all the groups are happy if there is some shade from the hottest summer sun. One important requirement, other than the organic manure, is for adequate water throughout the life of the crop.

Sowing and management: With cloche protection and the right choice of varieties, it is possible to grow lettuce all the year round. This calls for extra skill and advice and I would recommend Joy Larkcom's superb book *The Salad Garden* as required reading.

For a summer crop, successional sowings are made, beginning in late March outdoors or earlier indoors using soil blocks or peat pots and transplanting. Cabbage and cos varieties are ready to eat ten to twelve weeks after sowing, while the loose leaf sorts are ready to start cropping about seven weeks after sowing.

In my self-sufficiency guide on page 101 I've suggested you will want two 4.5m (15ft) rows, sown half a row at a time, for the cabbage and cos types. You can take thinnings and use as sandwich fillings.

If you grow a half row of leaf lettuce as well, then this will give you the sandwich fillings, while the other cabbage or cos lettuces can be allowed to heart up for salads.

For successional sowings seed packets often suggest fortnightly intervals, but all lettuce matures more rapidly from June onwards so that a sowing made, say, in the last week of March, and one made at mid-April will often reach maturity together. Thompson and Morgan, the Ipswich-based seed

*Newspaper and peat mulching of
this Salad Bowl lettuce proved an
effective deterrent against slugs*

firm, was the first of the major companies to try to rectify this by offering packets of mixed lettuce varieties that matured at different intervals though sown together.

Whatever sort you grow, sow the seed thinly and only about 6mm (¼in) deep. Thin the seedlings progressively so that the maturing plants do not touch each other.

Lettuce will germinate at very low soil temperatures, but some sorts refuse to germinate if the soil temperature goes above 24°C (75°F), a phenomenon called high temperature dormancy. You are unlikely to encounter such a high until well into June but when you do, the dormancy can be overcome by sowing in the early evening, having first watered the drill, and then cover the row with Agryl P17 sheeting or newspaper to reflect some of the sunshine.

In dry spells lettuce needs a lot of water – anything up to 18 litres (4gal) to the sq m/yd in summer, but watering the winter crop should be avoided to prevent problems from mildew.

There are so many good varieties in each of the four groups to choose from it is difficult to make comparisons. Our family has always voted Little Gem, a baby cos-type, as top of the

pops, while for a full cos the self-folding Romance and the earlier Erthel are newish varieties that will supersede the older Paris White and Lobjoit's Green. For the show bench I've seen nothing to beat Barcarolle and for the earliest spring crop Winter Density is supreme.

Salad Bowl and Red Salad Bowl are the recommended loose leaf sorts, although you can use Avoncrisp and Valmaine as cut-and-come-again varieties. In a technique developed by the National Vegetable Research Station at Wellesbourne the equivalent of four or five hearted lettuce per week from May to mid-October are taken from sowing an area of under one square metre/yard on each of ten dates. The method and sowing dates are given in *Know and Grow Vegetables* by P. J. Salter and J. K. A. Bleasdale of the NVRS.

Among the good butterhead varieties are Avoncrisp and Avondefiance. The prefix Avon denotes that they have been bred by the NVRS. Both are especially suitable for summer sowing being resistant to mildew, slow to bolt and resistant to root aphids. For light soils Continuity and Dolly are appropriate, while the American variety Buttercrunch has a rather different flavour that is much improved when grown organically.

Good crisphead sorts are the new Marmer, Webb's Wonderful, Iceberg, Great Lakes and Windermere.

Troubles: Unfortunately this most popular vegetable is highly regarded also by a fair number of pests. You must give the seedlings protection from birds and slugs. Overcrowded plants and hot, dry weather cause bolting, while cool, wet weather can bring the major problems of grey mould and downy mildew. No satisfactory remedy is available. Greenfly like lettuce but can be readily controlled with derris. If root aphids become persistent, the answer is to grow a resistant variety such as Avoncrisp or Salad Bowl.

MARROWS, COURGETTES

These are grouped together because courgettes are just the immature fruit of the long marrows. Unfortunately, because of EEC regulations, one of the best of all marrows for those who like small fruit – the round Gourmet Globe – is now called a squash and seeds are no longer available in Europe; you can, however, buy them in the USA.

Site and soil: A sunny, open site with humus-rich soil that is never allowed to dry out will serve this crop well. Six plants, a metre (3ft) apart each way, will give self-sufficiency in courgettes, while four bush marrow plants, a metre (3ft) apart, will give an adequate supply of mature fruits.

Sowing and management: Sow the seed indoors in April. One seed to each 7.5cm (3in) pot with the seed placed edgeways about 1.25cm (½in) deep and placed somewhere warm 24°C (65°F) will produce plants in double-quick time. They can be hardened off for planting out in late May or early June. Sowings outdoors in late May should be given a cloche or jar over the site to hasten germination.

Once the plants have started to fruit try to avoid water lodging in the crown of the plant. For courgettes the fruit are cut when they are about 10–15cm (4–6in) long, depending on variety. Don't allow the marrows to become old. They are best when the skin can be readily marked by a thumbnail.

FACT FILE Mineral content of some vegetables in mg per 100g

Vegetable	Calcium	Phosphorus	Iron	Copper
Potato	4	33	0.46	0.15
Artichoke	30	33	0.41	0.12
Beetroot	30	36	0.70	0.14
Carrot	46	38	0.60	0.11
Parsnip	59	76	0.45	0.10
Radish (raw)	30	31	1.36	0.16
Salsify	60	53	1.23	0.12
Turnip	55	19	0.35	0.04
Broccoli	160	54	1.52	–
Cabbage	27	45	0.63	–
Lettuce	43	42	0.56	–
Spinach	593	93	4.0	–

Note The high content of calcium, phosphorus and iron in spinach is misleading, because the oxalic acid content of spinach locks up these minerals.

A weekly feed with liquid manure or seaweed extract should ensure a steady supply of young fruits. Towards the end of the season, say late August, a few marrows can be left on the plants to mature for storage in a cool, dry place and use up to late December, but they aren't a patch on the young fruits of early summer.

For courgettes Zucchini and Eldorado are good varieties, while three new F¹ hybrids – Aristocrat, Onyx and Diamond, look very promising. A dual-purpose variety is Green Bush. You can take the young fruits as courgettes and allow others to grow on.

Some other promising newcomers are Clarita, Emerald Cross, Zebra Cross and Early Gem. Suttons Seeds introduced me in 1986 to Twickers with fruit shaped like a rugby ball – hence the name.

For those with space to spare Long Green Trailing and Long White Trailing produce lots of very large marrows, but apart from putting them in to flower shows and harvest festivals, who wants giant marrows?

Troubles: Young fruit sometimes wither and rot. Avoid over-watering and splashing the fruit. When fruit fails to set the cause is poor pollination and it is necessary to give nature a helping hand. Dust a male flower across the female flowers – that is, those with the small marrow shape behind the petals.

ONIONS

This covers onions grown from sets and seed for storage, and spring onions for immediate use. Shallots are dealt with on page 96.

Site and soil: All the onion family like an open, well-drained but well-manured soil which should have been prepared the previous autumn. Don't stick to the same site but rotate this crop among the roots. A dressing of calcified seaweed in December or January is helpful especially if the pH is on the acid side – aim for 6.7–7.0, and a top dressing of a balanced organic fertiliser before planting the sets or transplanting the seedlings is recommended.

Sowing and management: For cooking, rather than salad onions, sets have several advantages over growing from seed. Sets are far more tolerant of adverse soil conditions, are less prone to attack by pests and diseases, and require a shorter growing period. However, there are only a few varieties offered as onion sets, while onion seed is available in many varieties, including the new Japanese varieties.

For spring onions choose seed of a salad variety, such as White Lisbon or the new Ishikura, and sow a third of a row at a time for succession. Start in March for a June crop when the bulbs have just begun to swell. The seed is sown very thinly, 1.25cm (½in) deep, where the crop is to be harvested.

The craze for growing giant onions seems to be abating, thank heavens. There's little point in all that effort to produce bulbs of 2.7 to 3kg (6–7lb) each that are too big for the average household to use without waste and which tend not to keep anything like as long as the small and medium size bulbs. Spacing has a lot to do with the finished size of the crop: close spacing in the row gives a larger yield of smaller bulbs than wide spacing.

Onion sets are small, immature onions that have been lifted and then put through a long heat treatment. This turns the

The yellow courgette Eldorado has an excellent flavour when picked at this stage

skins golden brown and causes considerable loss of moisture. It is pointless to plant them in dry, cold soil; to get off to a good start they need warmth and moisture. Because of this it is a good plan to put the sets on to a tray of moist peat somewhere warm until the roots have grown about an inch. They can then be planted out with a trowel and there's less likelihood of the birds pulling them out again. Wait for the soil to warm up and plant when it is moist, any time from March to late April.

Seed onions, apart from the Japanese varieties, are sown outdoors at about the same time as the sets, that's to say, as soon as the soil has warmed up a bit. Prepare a seedbed with a fine tilth and sow thinly, about 1.25cm (½in) deep. Transplant when the seedlings have straightened up. Put them 10cm (4in) apart in rows 30cm (1ft) apart. Japanese varieties are sown in mid- to late August for overwintering and harvesting the following June.

Careful attention to weeding is important with onions, whether they are sets or seeds. This means hoeing between the rows, but hand-weeding between the bulbs.

When the foliage starts to turn straw-coloured and the tops bend over, the crop is almost ready to harvest. It used to be standard practice to bend over the tops to speed ripening, but this is now frowned on by the onion experts.

LACEY'S LORE

EXCESS NITROGEN

Some old gardening books recommend that to get a good crop of long-keeping onions the best plan is to allow weeds to develop in the onion bed from about the first week of July. The weeds poach excess nitrogen from the soil and deny it to the onions and this makes for a far longer life in store. The weeds are turned into the soil when the onions have been harvested.

You can pay a fair dollop of your hard-earned cash for onion sets that will give you a sporting chance of a prize in your local flower show or a tilt at the biggest onion record – it stands at 3.34kg (7lb 6oz). For my money, though, you can't beat Stuttgarter Giant sets because they produce a handy average 170g (6oz) onion, have excellent keeping qualities and are slow to bolt. Sturon is another popular one, with good bolt resistance and a rather larger bulb than Stuttgarter. Rijnsburger is similar to Giant Fen Globe – it may be identical, in fact – and is probably the longest keeping onion, while a very old favourite, Ailsa Craig, is still a fine all-rounder. For late planting Golden Ball is ideal, while the Dutch-breed Turbo is said to rival Sturon for yield.

Among the onion seed varieties you'll find Ailsa Craig, of course, and Bedfordshire Champion, with Reliance beating both for good- and long-keeping qualities.

Hygro and Buffalo are two newcomers, both F¹ hybrids, and another is Sweet Sandwich, a large bulb that after a couple of months in store becomes low in the volatile oils that cause the hotness in raw onions, the sort of pungency that could shut a five-barred gate at twenty yards.

A pink-fleshed Dutch variety that has come through UK trials very well is Noordhollandse Bloedrode or North Holland Blood Red, but it is only available outside the EEC.

Troubles: The major one is onion white rot both with amateur and commercial growers, organic and inorganic alike. Professor John Coley-Smith, of Hull University's department of biology and plant genetics, said in 1986: 'White rot is now a major threat to bulb onion production in this country, one which farmers should take very seriously. The danger is that the disease could get out of control, which would be a disaster. Chemical fungicides are not very effective, so we are busy developing other means of overcoming the fungus.'

Professor Coley-Smith has been working on the problem of white rot for thirty years and his most promising technique for control of the disease is a biological one using friendly fungi and parasites to fight the white rot enemy, a fungus that can remain dormant in the soil for at least fifteen years, to be triggered into life when a host crop of onions, leeks or garlic are grown.

If you find the foliage of your onions turning yellow prematurely, lift a bulb. If you find a fluffy white mould on the base of the bulb, you must lift and burn all the infected bulbs and give up growing any of the onion family on that bit of land for at least eight years or, any rate, until the biological control method is perfected.

Bulbs that are split at the base with bulblets forming are due to heavy rain after a long dry spell, so during a drought try to keep the onions watered.

The onion fly also causes yellowing and wilting of the foliage. Its eggs hatch into maggots which eat into the base of the bulb. Affected bulbs must be dug up and burned. The organic remedy is to stop growing onions from seed and grow them only from sets which the fly doesn't bother with.

In a wet season it is sometimes a problem getting the onion crop dried off sufficiently well for storage. It is worth taking the trouble of putting a straw mulch under the bulbs and covering them with cloches or you could bring them under cover in a cool airy place until the foliage is brittle dry. They can then be hung up in nets or tights or the traditional strings.

Too much nitrogen in the soil makes for poor keeping quality in onion bulbs. Bull neck is a symptom of this and bulbs showing a thick neck should be used as soon as possible because they will not store for long. You should do the same with any onions that have bolted, having first cut off the thick flower stem.

PARSNIPS

Site and soil: Choose a variety to suit your soil: short and fat for heavy and shallow soils, the long tapering sorts for deep, open soil.

The site should not have been freshly manured because that will cause forking of the roots. Any acidity should be corrected with lime or calcified seaweed to get to a pH of 6.5 to 6.8.

Sowing and management: The best variety for flavour, canker resistance and shallow soil is Avonresister, bred by the National Vegetable Research Station at Wellesbourne, although Offenham and The Student are also very good short types. White Gem is often offered nowadays as the successor to Offenham. I've had great success with Gladiator, the world's first F^1 hybrid parsnip. It has a medium length of root, some resistance to canker and a very good flavour, improved as with all parsnips, by a touch of frost.

The two big names among the long varieties are Tender and True, with excellent resistance to canker, and Hollow Crown Improved which is popular with exhibitors.

Parsnip seed is very slow to germinate and has one of the lowest germination rates for any vegetable. This makes it an excellent candidate for pre-germination and fluid sowing, a technique developed by the NVRS. The idea is that the seeds are germinated indoors at just the right temperature for success and the seedlings are then sown into the soil in a jelly to protect them from damage.

This is the method adapted for the home gardener, using kitchen utensils. Line a sandwich box or empty margarine carton with a thick layer of absorbent kitchen paper and cover

this with a sheet of wet-strong paper. Sprinkle on water until it is wet, then sprinkle the seeds evenly over the surface, about six seeds to 2.5sq cm (1sq in). Put the lid on the container and

keep it at a temperature of about 21°C (70°F), in the airing cupboard, for example. In about seven days the seed should have germinated, but remember that you cannot expect much more than three or four out of ten to come through.

At this stage the seeds can be sown, if the soil and weather are right, or they can be put in the refrigerator for a few days.

The jelly for sowing the pre-germinated seeds is made from ordinary wallpaper paste of the cellulose kind but not one containing fungicide. Mix it at half strength and stir in the seeds using your fingers. The jelly and the seeds are sown using an icing syringe with a 6mm (¼in) diameter nozzle or a polythene bag with a similar sized hole cut in one corner. The mixture should be extruded into a previously moistened seed drill at the rate of about 150ml to 3m (10ft). After sowing cover the seeds with soil in the usual way or use a water-retaining covering, such as peat or vermiculite, which must be kept moist in dry weather.

You should keep the crop free from weeds, but hoe with care to avoid damage to the shoulders of the parsnips. When the crop is mature you can leave it in the ground and lift as required or lift the entire crop in, say, November and store in layers in moist peat or sand.

PEAS

Peas are the most popular of all tinned and frozen vegetables, yet it is becoming increasingly difficult to buy them fresh. They are at their very best picked young from your own plants and eaten within an hour.

Site and soil: This is a crop that repays careful attention to the soil well in advance of sowing. Give it an open, sunny site and a deep soil organically manured and well drained. If your soil is light get the preparations done as soon after Christmas as possible. If it is heavy, get the work done by mid-November. Either way, reckon on putting in a good two bucketsful of manure or compost to each metre/yard run of the trench, dug a spit deep and a spade's width, and before sowing give the soil a top dressing of a balanced organic fertiliser. Aim for a pH of 5.8 to 6.4.

Sowing and management: Make a flat-bottomed drill where you prepared the trench. It wants to be about 15cm (6in) wide and 6.75cm (3in) deep while the space between each trench should be approximately the height of the crop, that's to say from about 45cm to 1.5m (18in to 5ft).

Sow the seeds in three rows in the drill, putting them 5cm (2in) apart each way, then cover with about 5cm (2in) of the soil. Immediately the peas start to germinate mice will find them and feast on them, while once the shoot has broken the surface of the soil, birds find them irresistible.

I haven't discovered a foolproof way to beat the mice. Thorny prunings, then covering the rows with cloches until the seedlings are about 7.5cm (3in) tall works quite well. Fellow allotmenteers use tarred string stretched round the rows, soot and lime sprinkled on the surface, and the seed soaked in paraffin before sowing among techniques to beat the mice, while my neighbour Frank sets traps.

Birds are easier to deal with. You can cover the rows with wire pea guards, which is the expensive way of doing it, or stretch several strands of black cotton along the rows, which deters the small birds, such as sparrows, but not the pigeons. Nylon netting, stretched over wire hoops and secured firmly at the sides and ends, will keep off even the most determined birds.

When the seedlings are 7.5 to 10cm (3 to 4in) tall, put supports in position. Nothing can beat twiggy branches, cut to the expected height of the mature plants, but they are difficult to get nowadays. You can use wire netting supported by stakes or three or four strands of wire or twine attached to canes and run round the entire row. Another method is to use nylon netting, specially sold for the purpose, and made into a tent shape bridging the row. Sowing times vary according to the region and the ability of the skilled amateur grower to have fresh-picked peas from May right through to October.

The golden rule is not to sow too early when the soil is cold and wet: use cloches and a sheltered site if you want to make a February sowing of a first early variety. The same variety could then be used to make a final sowing in late June or early July for harvesting in late September and early October.

With the cost of seed being an important consideration, many gardeners stick with just one or two pea varieties. Our typical family of two adults and three children would have all the peas they want from three rows of an early variety, such as Kelvedon Wonder, and three rows of a second early or maincrop, such as Hurst Green Shaft or Lord Chancellor. If the early peas are sown during the first week of April, the first picking would be taken in the last week of June or first few days of July. The maincrop would go in during the latter part of April or first week of May and be ready from the first week of August.

But don't take these times as gospel. As I've said, sowing times are flexible according to the weather and the area. Similarly, it is unwise to make too strong a recommendation over choice of variety; what does well for me in East Anglia might be hopeless in the cooler north. When people write to me from other parts of the UK for advice on vegetable varieties, I always preface my comments by suggesting they have a chat with other gardeners in the district to find out what has done well with them.

Both Kelvedon Wonder and Hurst Green Shaft were raised by Hurst's, the long-established seed firm based in north Essex, and those two varieties have always given me outstanding results on my plot only about thirty miles away. However, over the years I have tried many other sorts with equal success, including the new 'leafless' or self-supporting variety sold as Bikini or Markana or Eaton, depending on which seed catalogue you see it in. In 1985 and 1986 I trialled a new early pea from Thompson and Morgan called Titania, which has Hurst Green Shaft in its pedigree, and it gave a fulsome harvest of long, slender pods filled with up to eleven very sweet peas.

So the following suggestions as to varieties are an arbitrary selection with the height of each one given in brackets.

Early: Early Onward (60cm/2ft), Hurst Beagle (45cm/18in), Kelvedon Wonder (45cm/18in), Gradus (1.2m/4ft), Little Marvel (60cm/2ft), Meteor (45cm/18in), Pioneer (45cm/18in), Sweetness, from Suttons (1m/3ft), Titania, from Thompson and Morgan (75cm/2½ft).
Second early: Achievement, from Suttons (1.5m/5ft), Hurst Green Shaft (75cm/2½ft), Miracle (1.2m/4ft), Onward (75cm/2½ft), Show Perfection (1.3m/4½ft).
Maincrop: Alderman (1.5m/5ft), Lord Chancellor (1m/3ft), Recette (60cm/2ft), Senator (90cm/3ft).
Other varieties: Mangetout, sugar peas or eat-all – Oregon Sugar Pod (1m/3ft), Sugarbon (60cm/2ft), Sugar Dwarf Sweet Green (1m/3ft), Sugar Snap (1.5m/5ft). Petit Pois – Gullivert (90cm/3ft), Cobri (60cm/2ft), Waverex (60cm/2ft). Pick these sorts before the peas have started to swell.

When the crop has finished don't pull up the plants, leave the roots in the soil where they will slowly release nitrogen for the benefit of a following crop. The haulms should, of course, go on to the compost heap.

Troubles: Downy mildew can be a problem in a wet season. Spray with Burgundy mixture at fortnightly intervals. The pea moth lays its eggs on the stems and pods and when they hatch they enter the pods and, as black-headed caterpillars, eat the peas. Spray with soft soap and quassia a week after the first

In Britain peas are still sold by volume, but how many seeds do you get in a 142ml (¼pt) packet? With this pack of Kelvedon Wonder, the answer is 430. Sown in a double row, 5cm (2in) apart each way, that's sufficient to sow two 4.5m (15ft) rows, with some spares

LACEY'S LORE

PRUNINGS FOR PEAS

Save prunings from the rose-and gooseberry bushes and allow them to dry brittle hard over the winter, having first cut them into 15cm (6in) lengths. In spring when sowing the peas, place the prunings on either side of the rows to serve as a deterrent to mice.

flowers open and repeat for successive sowings. The pea weevil eats the edges of the leaves and causes scalloping. Dust with derris if you feel control is necessary.

POTATO

This is our basic vegetable and, when grown organically supplies the greatest value in terms of nutrition from the least space. So it has a chapter to itself, starting on page 104.

RADISH

Site and soil: A very unfussy subject, but the best crops of this popular salad vegetable are grown in a humus-rich soil, dressed with a balanced organic fertiliser, with some shade from the hottest sun.

Sowing and management: Make the first sowing 1.25cm (½in) deep in a cold frame in February or early March. Successional sowings are made without cover every three weeks or so until the end of May.

Vegetarian friends say that winter varieties of radish are well worth growing. They are sown in early August for use from October onwards. For spring and summer use there are two main groups of radish: the globe and the long (or inter-mediate). Globe varieties worth considering are Cherry Belle, crisp and very mild; Red Prince or Prinz Rotin, mild and long standing; Inca, another variety that doesn't go woody too quickly; Saxa Short Top, Ribella and Robino, all very suitable for the first sowing in cold frame or under cloches; Scarlet Globe, a favourite fast grower. Long varieties worth trying are: French Breakfast, probably the most popular of all the radishes; Large White Icicle, an unusual flavoured sort; Rave d'Amiens, a slow-maturing sort; April Cross, an F[1] hybrid that grows to about 37cm (15in) long.

Troubles: Although the radish is a brassica, the only major problem you are likely to encounter is the flea beetle. The first sign that it is active is the appearance of small holes in the leaves of the young plants. In no time at all, however, the tiny beetles will virtually strip the foliage. The control is to dust with derris at the first sign of damage. A fair degree of control has been reported by HDRA members who used an old dodge of coating a length of plywood or cardboard with a sticky substance, such as treacle or wet paint. You then hold it an inch or so above the crop and tap it. The flea beetles hop into the air and become trapped on the board. It may sound a bit far-fetched but it does work.

RHUBARB

Maybe not strictly speaking a vegetable, more a fruit, but a popular crop nevertheless.

Site and soil: A rich organic soil will suit this undemanding subject very well and if the site is without shade, so much the better.

Management: You buy the plants as crowns or sets, each having a stalk-bearing bud. Plant just below the surface and do not pull any sticks until at least eighteen months after planting, and then only take a few sticks.

Rhubarb is more tender and less bitter when forced. This is done by covering the crop with buckets, bins or boxes lightly stuffed with straw, placing them in position in January and pulling the sticks in March. Don't force the same crowns year after year or you will exhaust them.

Glaskin's Perpetual is the variety with the lowest oxalic acid content; Hawke's Champagne is a very old but reliable sort; Early Victoria and Timperley Early are excellent for forcing; The Sutton has extra large stems.

During the winter months cover the crowns with leaf-mould, compost or well-rotted manure. Remove any flower stems during the growing season.

SALSIFY AND SCORZONERA

Salsify is the long white-skinned root vegetable sometimes called the oyster plant, while its opposite number is the black-skinned scorzonera.

Site and soil: Both require an open, rich though light soil to give of their best. They do not want manure or compost in the site and do not need including in the rotation.

Sowing and management: Sow as you would parsnips, that is, three seeds at each station, 15cm (6in) apart, or fluid sow, 1.25cm (½in) deep in rows 30cm (1ft) apart. Sow in late April or early May and as soon as the seedlings are large enough thin to one every 15cm (6in).

The roots are ready to lift, with care because they are brittle and about 30cm (1ft) long, from October onwards. They are hardy and can be left in the ground and covered with straw or bracken or they can be lifted and stored in moist peat or sand along with the carrots, beetroot and parsnips.

Salsify and scorzonera are used as you would parsnips. In my book they have a superior flavour but require twice the space for an equivalent yield. One 4.5m (15ft) row should produce about 2.7kg (6lb) of edible roots.

There are one or two different varieties of these vegetables, but there's little to choose between them. The crop is remarkably trouble-free.

SHALLOTS

The tradition was to plant the shallot bulbs on the shortest day, 22 December, and harvest them on the longest, 21 June, but I don't imagine many people stick to that today. When cooking for just one or two people, the shallot is more times than not a more useful size than an onion and, of course, shallots are used

as pickled onions. In general, shallots keep better than onions and you can to save your own bulbs for planting year after year.

Site and soil: A light soil manured for a previous crop in full sun suits the shallot but try to rotate it as frequently as possible.

Management: Plant the bulbs as early in the year as possible – follow the old tradition if you live in a mild-winter area. Push the bulbs half into the soil, 15cm (6in) apart in rows 22.5cm (9in) apart, and for three or four weeks until the bulbs have made roots protect against birds either with wire pea guards or strands of black cotton. Alternatively, you can start the bulbs in trays of moist peat and plant them with a trowel

Frost will also lift the bulbs from the ground, so keep a check. Each bulb produces a cluster of up to ten new bulbs and, once the foliage has turned yellow, the clump can be eased from the soil with a fork. Allow the foliage to become brittle dry enough to fall away from the bulbs which can then be stored in nets, tights or on trays somewhere cool and dry. Save as many of the bulbs as necessary for the next crop.

Start off with virus-free stock from a reputable supplier. There are only three sorts generally available: Hative de Niort is the show shallot, normally producing four bulbs from each 'seed' shallot; Giant Long Keeping Yellow and Giant Long Keeping Red are both larger and more prolific, excellent for long storage and for pickling.

Troubles: Mostly free of problems, but not unfortunately immune to onion white rot.

Start shallots into growth in a tray of moist peat, then plant them with a trowel so that they are just buried. This will overcome the problem of birds pulling them out before the roots give anchorage

Shallots and onions should be left to ripen where they are growing. They are ready to harvest and store when the foliage turns straw *coloured and brittle dry. If the weather turns unkind, you can complete the ripening by covering with cloches minus the end pieces,* *or by placing on a home-made wire-netting rack which can be moved under cover at night or when it rains*

Swiss chard is preferred by many people to spinach and thrives in an organic soil. The thick stalks can be cooked like asparagus

SPINACH AND SWISS CHARD

Spinach, whether perpetual, New Zealand or ordinary, is a much overrated vegetable in my view. Its virtues are that it is dead easy to grow, and with perpetual spinach you can pull it fresh through most of the year. It used to be a health-fad food because of its iron content, but now we know that Popeye had got it all wrong. The iron content is no higher than in other leafy vegetables. What many people dislike about it is the flavour – best described as earthy – and the oxalic acid content which is high enough to make it a most unsuitable food for children. It is rich in calcium and phosphorus, but the oxalic acid locks up those minerals in much the same way that alcohol locks up the B vitamins. However, a variety called Monnopa is available which has a greatly improved flavour and a low oxalic acid content.

Far superior to spinach is Swiss chard also known as seakale beet and silver chard, and a variant called ruby chard.

Site, soil and management: All of the spinach family prefer a well-manured organic soil in partial shade during high summer, so inter-cropping between rows of potatoes, for example, is feasible.

A sowing of perpetual spinach in April, 1.8cm (¾in) deep, 15cm (6in) apart, in rows 45cm (18in) apart, will crop throughout the summer and autumn and, if picked regularly and given some protection over the winter, will go on yielding right through to next spring. In hot, dry summers it will certainly bolt unless given masses of water.

New Zealand spinach is a summer vegetable, sown in May with the seeds 30cm (1ft) apart and the rows 1m (3ft) apart, while ordinary spinach, sown in March or April, will crop through to November.

Swiss chard has very fleshy leaves and thick stalks that make it a dual-purpose vegetable. The leaves are cooked like

(cont on page 99)

HERBS

It is a fair supposition that food tasted better 500 years ago than it does today. Tougher, maybe, particularly the meat, but tastier. The reason is that those first Elizabethans were wizards in the use of herbs, both as medicines, because there was no alternative, and in cooking when the need often enough was to mask rather less-than-fresh food.

So, a well-stocked herb garden was important with, perhaps, up to sixty different herbs. They were introduced into Britain by the Romans and, apart from their use in the kitchen and for scenting the home, they remained the stock-in-trade of physicians until well into the eighteenth century. The great herbal chronicler was John Gerard of London who, in 1597, published his *Herball*, a 1,000-page treatise with illustrations of some 3,000 plants.

But the use of herbs for medicinal purposes and for flavouring food declined throughout the nineteenth century and well into the second half of this century. Herbs commonly in use were down to four: mint, parsley, sage and thyme, the latter three being used mostly in stuffings for meat and poultry. When the freedom to travel abroad returned after World War II, staid Britain rediscovered the delights of Continental cuisine with its extensive use of herbs. At the same time, at home we assaulted our palates with more and more processed flavours, junk food and some of America's unremarkable fast food lines. Highly-flavoured foods are now back in fashion and herbs enjoy a popularity only exceeded in the time of the first Elizabeth. Fresh herbs are far superior to the dried versions, so every organic gardener should try to make space available for a few plants.

For those with the space and the wish to be adventurous, the basis for a modern herb garden would be bay, borage, chervil, chives, coriander, dill, fennel, garlic, horse radish, marjoram, mint, parsley, rosemary, sage, sorrel, tarragon and thyme. These are all for use in flavouring and garnishing dishes. To them I would add lavender as the best of all herbs for scenting linen, while pennyroyal, dwarf chamomile and one of the creeping thymes could be planted where they would be trodden on occasionally to release their heady aromas at high summer.

Choosing the site for the herb garden should not be difficult. Most herbs thrive in an organic environment, preferring a light, well-drained soil with a pH of 7.0 or slightly above. The site should be open to the full sun and, of course, be as near to the kitchen as possible so that to gather fresh-picked herbs doesn't involve a long trek. As to the layout, obviously the taller subjects should not be allowed to overshadow the dwarf ones and I would have a strategically placed bench so that one could sit on warm days and savour the sweet pungency of the site.

Because most herbs have attractive foliage as well as a strong scent, they merit selection for the garden whether one is a culinary buff or not. Pennyroyal has glossy aromatic foliage which looks especially attractive when the plants are set in the gaps between crazy paving. The rich perfume of the leaves is released when the plants are walked on.

Prepare the site for the herb garden in early spring. Dig a full spade's depth and work in compost or peat all over the site, then rake to a fine tilth. Next, mark out a pattern for planting, using squares, diamonds or circles for planted and unplanted areas. The unplanted parts can be covered with gravel, forest bark or crazy paving and one can use lawn-edging strips, old bricks or tiles as retaining walls for the gravel or bark.

The hardy annuals, such as borage, chervil and dill, can be sown in late March, while the half-hardy sorts should be sown later in the spring. The hardy perennials, the largest group of herbs, can be raised from seed in a nursery bed, bought as plants from a herb nursery or increased from a friend's stock by division or by taking cuttings in the spring.

Basil, parsley, savory and thyme can be grown successfully in pots on a sunny windowsill, while for patios and small gardens a space-saving way to raise herbs is to use earthenware parsley pots. These are urn-shaped with openings in the side for the plants.

Parsley is one of the most useful herbs for year-round production. You can let a few plants run to seed and then transplant the seedlings. It is worth giving the crop winter protection with cloches

Set out sweetcorn plants in blocks, not rows, to help pollination. Tapping the top of the stem helps to transfer pollen from the male tassels to the female flowers below

spinach, while the stalks are treated like asparagus. The seed is sown in May, 22.5cm (9in) apart in rows 45cm (18in) apart, and will crop right through to next spring providing some protection is given over the winter.

Troubles: Mostly trouble-free.

SWEDES

This is a very hardy root vegetable – the name is an abbreviation for Swedish turnip – and as well as being a major ingredient of home-made winter stews is also an excellent dish in its own right or mashed with carrot. It is a brassica so must be rotated.

Site and soil: An open site is essential and a light organic soil that was manured for a previous crop with a neutral pH is preferred.

Sowing and management: Swedes require a long growing period, so a sowing made in the first week of June will not be ready to lift until early November but will then go on yielding right through the winter either left in the ground or lifted and stored as for carrots.

Seed is sown about 1.25cm (½in) deep in rows 45cm (18in) apart and the seedlings thinned to 15cm (6in) apart. Keep the plants well watered during dry spells. The best variety for the amateur grower is Marian, resistant to clubroot and mildew, while the old favourite Purple Top gives consistently good results. For its long storage capability Mancunian Brown Top is an excellent variety, and for northern areas Pandur or Wilhelmsburger Gelbe is a good choice. Another quick-growing variety I've heard good reports of but have never grown myself is Suttons Western Perfection, which can be sown in mid-May and lifted from mid-September onwards.

Troubles: Brown heart is a fairly common condition. It is the result of boron deficiency, but the regular use of seaweed meal prevents this. Soft rot of the roots in the ground or in store is deceptive because outwardly they appear in good condition – the rot is internal. Waterlogging and over-manuring can spark this rot.

Although swedes are a brassica, cabbage root fly seldom bothers with the crop.

SWEETCORN

This is a half-hardy form of maize that has become a popular crop with pick-your-own places in the south and east of England, as well as with amateur growers, but doesn't do very well in the West Country, the north of England, Wales and Scotland.

Site and soil: A sunny but sheltered site where the soil has been organically manured for a previous crop is the requirement. A pH preference of 5.5–6.0 and adequate water throughout the fourteen-week growing period are also necessary.

Sowing and management: Sow in peat pots or soil blocks in April in a minimum heat of 10°C (50°F), harden off and plant outside in early May under cloches or in late May without protection.

In July mulch with compost or lawn mowings, peat or forest bark, having first given the crop a thorough soaking. On exposed sites give the plants support with canes and wire.

The plants are set out in blocks, rather than rows, to help pollination and another aid is to tap the top of the stems. The tassels at the top are the male flowers while the silky threads above the cobs are the female flowers, so tapping the top of the stems helps to transfer pollen from the male to the female flowers.

LACEY'S LORE

PUT FEVER TO FLIGHT

Spectacular success has been claimed for the herb feverfew in the treatment of migraine headaches. Feverfew comes from the medieval Latin *febrifugia*, meaning 'that which puts fever to flight' and was used as widely and frequently as today we use aspirin in relieving headaches and the pain of arthritis and rheumatism.

Feverfew is a white daisy-flowered perennial (*Tanacetum parthenium* or *Chrysanthemum parthenium*,

depending on which reference book you use). The leaves can be dried and crushed and used, a pinch a day, as a homeopathic medicine or eaten fresh.

Thompson and Morgan, the seed firm, says in its catalogue, 'Eat three or four leaves a day in a salad sandwich. Do not expect reduction in frequency of pain before four to six weeks and not a complete cure in less than about twelve months.'

Most plants will produce two cobs, the first being a good deal larger than the following one. It is important to pick the cob at just the right stage of ripeness: too soon and the flavour is insipid, too late and the grains become tough.

Test for ripeness after the tassels have turned dark brown.

Draw back the sheath covering the cob and press a grain with a finger nail. If the juice is milky it is just right, if watery it is not ready, while if it is floury it is past its prime.

The cobs should be cooked within an hour of picking, but if this is impossible, they will keep fresh for three or four days in the fridge. Boil the cobs briskly for about six minutes, never longer than eight.

There are some excellent F^1 hybrid varieties available, including First of All, John Innes, Kelvedon Glory, Earliking, Polar Vee, Early Arctic, and Earlibelle. Two newcomers that are reckoned to be 'super sweet' are How Sweet It Is and Candle, but to prevent cross-pollination and loss of sweetness these varieties should not be grown near any others.

Troubles: Galls appear as black growths on the developing cobs and stems, particularly in hot, dry weather. Cut them off and burn them.

LACEY'S LORE

ORGANIC GROWING BAGS

Conventional growing bags contain slow-release artificial fertilisers which make them unacceptable to the dedicated organic gardener, but thanks to pressure from the market-place, one British firm is offering an entirely organic grow bag.

Stimgro Ltd has introduced this bag with a chemical-free, half-and-half mixture of farmyard manure and peat, composted together for two years. This basic compost

gives young plants an excellent start because there is no risk of young roots being scorched by powerful chemical fertilisers. But regular feeding with an organic liquid fertiliser is necessary from six weeks after planting.

Suitable feeds for this purpose would be Maxicrop or SM3, both seaweed based liquid extracts, or Farmura or Rite Feed, both based on farmyard manure.

TOMATO

Nothing is quite so bland as the commercially-grown greenhouse tomato. It may look good, is certainly uniform, and travels well, because that's what the supermarket buyer decrees. What it lacks is the true, tangy flavour of tomato. You can re-discover that by choosing a flavourful outdoor variety and growing it organically.

Site and soil: A warm site is essential, preferably so that the plants have their backs to a wall or fence and face south. Tomatoes relish the company of cabbages, carrots, onions and marigolds, but are best kept away from potatoes because of the danger of infection from blight. The herb basil is also reckoned to be a good companion plant to have with the tomatoes.

Outdoor tomatoes can be grown very successfully in grow-

FACT FILE Self-sufficiency guide

This summarises the information given in this chapter on how much to grow to feed a family of two adults and three children. Each of the rows is 4.5m (15ft) long. Also included is advice on how much to harvest for each meal. Remember that it is always better to pick your crops fresh for each meal and eat them as soon as possible after harvesting. Leaf vegetable, in particular, begin to lose some of their nutritional value immediately they are harvested. If you have a surplus of a particular crop, don't allow it to get old and tough: gather it and freeze it while it is still young and tender or give it to friends.

BEANS
Broad: 3 rows (plus one for the freezer, if needed), 45cm (18in) apart, seeds 30cm (1ft) apart. Pick 340g (¾lb) of pods when young for each adult, 226g (½lb) for each child. When pods have filled out, pick 226g (½lb) for each person.
French: 5 rows, 30cm (1ft) apart, seeds 25cm (10in) apart. This should also give you a surplus for freezing. Allow 170g–226g (6–8oz) per person.
Runner: 1 double row, 60cm (2ft) apart when grown up a support. On the flat, 4 single rows, 60cm (2ft) apart. Seeds 30cm (1ft) apart. Pick 226g (½lb) per person.
BEETROOT: One row for summer salads gives 30–40 small beet; 2 rows, 30cm (1ft) apart, for autumn and winter use.
BROCCOLI, PURPLE SPROUTING: 1 row of 6 plants. Pick without any large leaves, allowing 170g (6oz) per person.
BRUSSELS SPROUTS: 6 rows, 45cm (18in) apart, plants about 60cm (2ft) apart, but distance varies according to variety. Aim for 20 early, 20 mid-season and 20 late-maturing plants. Pick 226g (½lb) per person.
CABBAGES
Spring: 3 rows, 45cm (18in) apart each way, some to eat as spring greens, allowing others to heart up. Allow 226g (½lb) per person of greens.

Summer, autumn: 2–3 rows (giving 20–25 heads, depending on size), 45cm (18in) apart each way on average. For the family of five you will need a cabbage trimmed of coarse outer leaves weighing 1.10–1.36kg (2½–3lb).
Winter: 3 rows, plants 45cm (18in) apart each way to give about 30 heads, each with a finished weight of 1.36–1.80kg (3–4lb).
CARROTS
Early: 2 rows, 15cm (6in) apart, do not thin. Pull 6–9 carrots per person for earliest feeds, 4 to 5 when larger.
Maincrop: 2 rows, 20cm (8in) apart. Allow 170g (6oz) per person.
CAULIFLOWERS: Spring and summer – 15 heads; autumn – 12 heads; winter – 12 heads. Winter 75cm (2½ft) apart each way, others 60cm (2ft) apart each way, except for mini caulis. A 1kg (2lb) head with leaves trimmed will serve five people.
CELERY: 1 row, 1m (3ft) wide with about 25 plants staggered and 15–22.5cm (6–9in) apart. For braising you will need 3 heads for 6 people.
COURGETTES: 6 plants, 1m (3ft) apart each way. Allow 226g (½lb) per person.
KALE: 2 rows, 60cm (2ft) apart each way. Pick while young, allowing 171g (6oz) per person.
LEEKS: 3 rows, 30cm (1ft) apart, 25cm (10in) between plants. Allow one well-grown leek per person.
LETTUCE: Cos or cabbage types, 2 rows 30cm (1ft) apart, sown half a row at a time for succession, thinned 15–22.5cm (6–9in) apart, depending on variety. Pick as required for salad or sandwich use.
MARROWS: 4 plants of bush type, 1m (3ft) apart. A 1.3kg (3lb) marrow is sufficient for the family.
ONIONS
Spring: 1 row, sown a third at a time for succession.
Maincrop: 450g (1lb) of onion sets consists of about 100 bulbs. Place 10cm (4in) apart

in rows 30cm (1ft) apart to give a finished crop totalling 22.7–36.3kg (50–80lb) which will see you through the winter and spring.
PARSNIPS: 2 rows, 20cm (8in) apart, 7.5cm (3in) between plants. Allow about 340g (¾lb) of untrimmed roots per person when used as a main vegetable.
PEAS: 6 rows (3 early, 3 maincrop), 1m (3ft) between rows, 7.5cm (3in) between seeds. This should give a decent surplus for freezing. For early varieties picked young allow 450g (1lb) of pods per adult. For maincrop, picked with full pods, allow 280g (10oz) per person.
POTATOES: 3kg (6.6lb) of seed potatoes for every 3 rows produces 22.7–31.7kg (50–70lb) of earlies and up to 45kg (100lb) of second early and maincrop varieties, but a lot depends on the variety and season. Allow 170g (6oz) of earlies, and 226g (½lb) maincrop (unpeeled) per person.
RADISHES: 2 rows, sown thinly, half a row at a time for succession, 15cm (6in) between rows.
SHALLOTS: Pickling, 1 row, bulbs 30cm (1ft); apart. Cooking, 2 rows, bulbs 30cm (1ft) apart each way.
SPINACH: Summer, 3 rows, 30cm (1ft) between plants, 37.5cm (15in) between rows. Winter, 2 rows, spacing as for summer. Allow about 141g (5oz) of leaves, picked young with a minimum of stalk.
SWEDES: 2 rows, seeds 15cm (6in) apart, 45cm (18in) between rows. Allow 280g (10oz) of untrimmed roots per person when used as a main vegetable.
TOMATOES: Outdoor bush type, 6 plants, 1m (3ft) apart each way. Outdoor standard type, 6 plants, 45cm (18in) apart in row.
TURNIPS: Summer, 2 rows, 25cm (10in) apart, seedlings thinned to 10cm (4in) apart. Winter, 2 rows, 30 cm (1ft) apart, seedlings thinned to 15cm (6in) apart. Allow 226–280g (8–10oz) of untrimmed root per person.

ing bags or large pots – not smaller than 22.5cm (9in) – placed in a suitable sun trap.

Sowing and management: If you buy tomato plants from a garden centre or nursery, the choice is so often limited to just a few varieties – Moneymaker, Eurocross and Alicante, maybe – so it's a good plan to raise your own plants and it's not all that difficult. The fact file on page 103 will help you to decide which variety to buy as seed.

Sow in early March in a seed tray and keep moist at a temp-

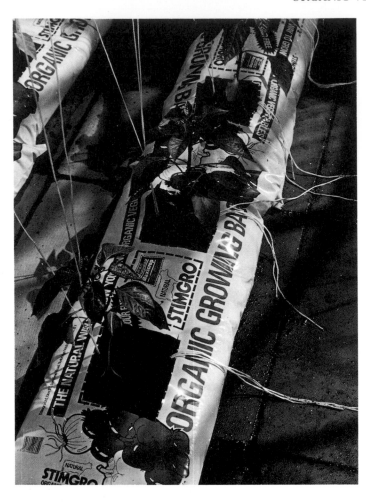

LACEY'S LORE

SUMMER SAVORY

The herb summer savory, grown among the broad beans, can help to deter the blackfly and a few of its leaves added to the beans when cooking heightens the flavour.

Savory is raised annually from seed sown in April. When the stems are in flower they should be cut, dried and stored for the winter. The dried leaves, with a mild sage flavour, are used in stuffings for pork, duck and goose.

Troubles: Outdoor tomato plants are much less liable to attack by pests and diseases than the greenhouse crops. If blight hits the potatoes, preventive spraying of the tomatoes with Bordeaux or Burgundy mixture is important.

If the soil or compost is allowed to dry out once the fruit has started to swell, the fruit are likely to split or a condition called blossom end rot develop with hard leathery patches on the bottom of the fruit.

TURNIP

Site and soil: A member of the brassica family, so rotate, but unlikely to be affected by cabbage root fly. An open, fertile soil, preferably manured for a previous crop and with a pH of 6.5–6.8 is preferred.

Sowing and management: Early turnips are a treat, while the maincrop roots are essential elements of winter stews and the tops can be used as an acceptable and nourishing alternative to spinach.

Sow an early variety outdoors about 1.25cm (½in) deep where the crop is to mature in late March or early April when the roots will be ready to eat a little smaller than tennis-ball size in July. For self-sufficiency sow two rows 25cm (10in) apart and thin the seedlings to 15cm (6in) apart. Another two rows sown in mid-July will give all the roots you need over the winter.

For the early crop choose a fast-growing variety such as Tokyo Cross, Early Snowball, Milan White, Early Six Week, Sprinter, Red Globe or Purple Top Milan. There's a good

erature of 18 to 21°C (65 to 70°F) – in the airing cupboard or above the boiler will do fine, but remove as soon as the seeds have germinated. When the seeds have made two pairs of true leaves, prick them out into 7.5cm (3in) peat or clay pots and place them in a cool greenhouse or on a warm, sunny window-sill. When the seedlings have the first flowers showing they can be planted out. The cordon or standard plants will need tying to a cane and placed about 60cm (2ft) apart in the row, while the bush varieties need about 1m (3ft) each way but no support.

At planting out and at ten-day intervals thereafter give the plants a feed of liquid seaweed, while plants in growing bags and pots will need watering as often as once a day in high summer.

Cordon-grown plants will also need side shoots removing and frequent tying in to the cane support. Bush plants need no attention other than a mulch of straw or black polythene in July to keep the fruit from being splashed and to speed ripening. Bush plants can also be grown with cloche protection, of course, especially in northern districts where the season is not long enough to ripen a worthwhile amount of fruit.

Cloches can also be used to ripen off cordon-grown plants towards the end of the season simply by cutting the ties on the canes and laying the plants on a mulch of straw or clean, dry newspaper and then covering with cloches.

LACEY'S LORE

NETTLE BOX

Green tomatoes will ripen if they are placed in a box of freshly-gathered nettles. It's a technique used to colour early fruit for shows and to ripen late trusses in a wet, cool summer. It will also hasten the ripening of trusses on greenhouse plants. Put the nettles in a large paper bag, place over the truss and tie.

Tigerella, the striped tomato for greenhouse and outdoor cultivation, has an excellent flavour

FACT FILE Outdoor tomato varieties

The star rating is my personal one based on flavour, yield and disease resistance.

BUSH TYPES

Alfresco: high-yielding, good disease resistance. ★ ★

The Amateur: an old variety, but still first rate for yield and flavour. ★ ★ ★ ★

Florida Petit: not commonly listed, but highly suitable for pot cultivation. ★ ★

French Cross: larger fruit than most bush types. ★ ★

Pipo: moderate flavour, good yield. ★ ★

Pixie: good flavour, small fruits and yield. ★ ★

Red Alert: small fruits, excellent flavour. ★ ★ ★

Sigmabush: useful in Midland and Northern districts because of its early ripening. ★ ★

Sleaford Abundance: big yield, moderate flavour. ★ ★

Sub-Arctic Plenty: very early, moderate flavour. ★ ★

Tornado: early, sweet flavour, reliable. ★ ★ ★

CORDON TYPES

Ailsa Craig: good flavour, early ripening. ★ ★ ★

Alicante: moderate flavour, reliable. ★ ★

Gardener's Delight: top for flavour, cherry-size fruits, good yield. ★ ★ ★ ★

Golden Sunrise: yellow fruits, good flavour. ★ ★

Harbinger: good yield, indifferent flavour. ★ ★

Marmande: large, fleshy fruits, very good flavour. ★ ★ ★

Outdoor Girl: early, high yielder with good flavour. ★ ★ ★

Red Ensign: heavy cropper, moderate flavour. ★ ★

Sweet 100: similar to Gardener's Delight, but poorer flavour. ★ ★

Tigerella: striped fruit, good yield and flavour. ★ ★ ★

choice of maincrop sorts, including Green Globe, Greentop White (recommended for use as a spinach substitute), Arca, Golden Ball, Veitch's Red Globe and Manchester Market

Troubles: Flea beetle can be a problem on the young seedlings, but dusting with derris is effective or the use of a sticky board as recommended for radishes (see page 95).

8

CHOOSING AND GROWING
THE BEST POTATOES

Once upon a time if you wanted a crop of potatoes, you planted seed tubers. Now there are several ways to achieve the same end.

You could, for example, sow a few rows of tissue-culture produced plantlets, the result of a new technique called micro-propagation. Or you could sow seeds, not the tubers but the true seed that is contained in the green tomato-like fruits, the so-called potato apples, that appear on the potato plants when the flowers have been fertilised. Thirdly, you could revive a wartime idea and plant just the eyes of the seed tubers.

Some of the largest, cleanest and most flavourful potatoes I've grown have been an unintentional crop from the compost heap potato peelings, and this gives a clue to what the potato likes as a growing medium: a slightly acid, humus-rich, open yet warm environment.

During World War II and for some years afterwards, when seed potatoes were in short supply, growers in Scotland and Northern Ireland sent a bag of potato eyes through the post rather than a sack of tubers by freight train. I've been told that this was highly successful, giving heavier crops because of the rapid emergence of shoots from the eyes. For some reason the practice was dropped once the supply of seed potatoes returned to normal, but now that transport costs are such a major element in the final price to the customer, I would have thought that was a big incentive to bring the technique back.

Growing from seed is very much cheaper than growing from tubers. Thompson and Morgan, the Ipswich seedsmen who offered for 1983 the first true potato seed grown from Ministry-approved tubers, reckon it is one-tenth of the cost.

Seed-raised potato plants are planted out at the same time as tomatoes, that is, when all danger of frost has passed, and the crop is said to mature later than tuber-grown crops.

The second major innovation is propagation by tissue culture which produces plants that are healthier, stronger and more uniform than propagation by any other method. Tissue culture has something of the aura of sci-fi cloning and demands sterile laboratory conditions for success. The plantlets are raised as cultures in the laboratory and sent to the customer in transparent plastic tubes containing the sterile jelly in which they have been raised. They then require careful handling at each subsequent stage of pricking out, hardening off and transplanting. Tissue culture is expensive, too costly to make it viable for the commercial potato grower. But these are early days and, no doubt, the technique will be commonplace a few years from now.

Another important development in this single most important vegetable is the work being undertaken by the National Vegetable Research Station at Wellesbourne, to try to use just one variety for both early and late crops. Under normal circumstances an early variety, such as Arran Pilot will be chitted or sprouted early in the year and planted from late March onwards for harvesting from late June. The maincrop, having been similarly chitted, will be planted in late April or early May for lifting from September onwards. NVRS scientists found that physiologically young tubers give lower yields of maincrop than 'middle-aged' tubers, while 'old' tubers give the best early yield.

Seed potatoes are harvested and sold in a dormant condition and it is the object of chitting to encourage sprouts to appear. The warmer the conditions, the quicker the sprouts appear. The longer the sprouts, when properly chitted in daylight, the 'older' the tuber. At temperatures below 4°C (39°F) sprout growth stops, so at this temperature the tubers can be kept young. 'Any temperature above 39°F,' say the researchers, 'causes growth of the sprouts, and experiments have shown that the length of the longest sprout is directly related to the number of day-degrees above 39°F.'

For calculation of day-degrees the base line is 4°C and each day with one degree Centigrade rise above 4°C is a day degree, so that a day at 8°C (46°F) counts as four day-degrees. A day at 6°C (43°F), followed by a day at 10°C (50°F), followed by a day at 4°C (39°F) gives a total of eight day-degrees.

With the old variety Home Guard harvested on 15 June, the highest yields were obtained with 'old' seed that had encountered 1,000 day-degrees since harvest and had sprouts 8cm (3¼in) long, said the NVRS. These yields were about thirty per cent more than those obtained from exactly similar seed tubers which had only encountered 100 day-degrees and had sprouts about 5mm (¼in) long.

For maximum control of physiological age you should buy your seed potatoes as early as possible and watch for the first signs of sprouts appearing as specks around the eyes.

The NVRS warned that manipulation of the age of the tubers is still experimental and it would be foolish to assume that all varieties responded in the same way as the venerable Home Guard. But the broad effects of advanced physiological age are becoming clearer, say the scientists, and are:

- Earlier emergence after planting.
- Earlier tuber formation.
- Fewer tubers per plant.
- Increased susceptibility to drought because of a less extensive root system.
- Smaller plant size and slower growth of tubers.
- More nitrogenous fertiliser needed for maximum yield.

And they conclude: 'Gardening is essentially the practical control of growth development of cherished plants by manipulating the environment. The more you know about the factors affecting growth and development, the more successful you should be.'

Freshly-dug organically-grown potatoes – a treat for those who have only eaten the commercial artificially-fed kinds

FINEST VEGETABLE

No doubt, though, about the popularity of the humble spud. Every year we in Britain eat about five and a half million tons of potatoes; more than ninety per cent are grown in this country and all but about five per cent are grown by farmers.

Although the potato is some eighty per cent water, it is the most important source of vitamin C and a major source of protein for most people. It also supplies a healthy dollop of B vitamins, eight of the essential amino acids and several of the minerals that support a person's wellbeing.

Lawrence Hills, of the Henry Doubleday Research Association says: 'The potato is the finest vegetable in terms of supplying the greatest value from the least space. Perhaps the reason why so many people give up potatoes rather than biscuits and cakes is that bought potatoes are a much less attractive food.'

He's dead right, of course. There's a world of difference between an amateur's organically-grown crop and the farmer's commercially produced crop. The farmer is concerned with maximum production to achieve maximum profit, so he chooses potato varieties with a potential maximum yield and realises that potential by applying big doses of fertiliser and completes bulking of the crop with plentiful overhead irrigation. In general, the more water the potato gets, the less flavour there is when cooked. Farm-grown potatoes are lifted and bagged in one operation and here we come across another problem: the Ministry of Agriculture found that seventy-nine per cent of commercially grown potatoes suffered damage during lifting and subsequent handling. The housewife pays for this when she comes to peel the spuds and finds bruised areas that must be cut away and even deep scars of machine damage. So the potato, labelled by some of the weight-watchers as a stodgy food, which it is not, gets a reputation for unreliable quality.

There are more than 100 varieties of potato in cultivation in Britain, but probably not more than half a dozen maincrop sorts can be bought in the High Street and all too often the choice is simply between 'reds' and 'whites'. So a further attraction for the amateur is to grow potatoes for top flavour or for particular purposes such as chipping or baking in their jackets.

For cleaning a new patch of land, potatoes are almost as good as a herd of pigs, and a favourite for this job is the old, tasty Kerr's Pink which has a dense haulm that keeps annual weeds in check and makes life difficult for perennials such as bindweed and dandelion.

Growing in popularity are the Maris and Pentland varieties. The Maris ones come from the Cambridge Plant Breeding Institute in Maris Lane, Cambridge, while those with the Pent-

FACT FILE Good potato guide

Here is my good eating – and growing – guide to potatoes with a star rating for each variety. Performance will vary, of course, with the region, the weather and the skill of the gardener. E indicates early. S/E is second early. M is maincrop.

Arran Pilot (E): A good all-rounder that crops heavily and consistently; moderate flavour, good resistance to drought and common scab. Can be allowed to grow and lifted as late as September. ★ ★ ★ ★

Arran Comet (E): Good cooking quality, boiled, baked, mashed or chipped with reasonable yield of nicely-shaped oval tubers. ★ ★

Arran Comrade (M): Raised by Donald MacKelvie on Arran, this is a round potato and is best baked in its jacket. Seed tubers are scarce in some parts of the UK. ★ ★

The Bishop (M): An indifferent cropper, which is a crying shame because this is the Cox's Orange Pippin of the potato world. Nice looking with a superb flavour. ★ ★ ★

Cara (M): A newish round tuber with cream flesh, superb cooking qualities, and some resistance to blight. When grown organically this is an aristocrat among spuds with a fine flavour. Yield is excellent even in a season of drought. Strongly recommended. ★ ★ ★ ★

Concorde (E): Good yield and flavour. Seed tubers scarce. ★ ★ ★

Craig's Alliance (S/E): White and flowery with a moderate flavour, but good for creaming and baking. Yields well except in a dry season. ★ ★

Craig's Royal (S/E): Kidney-shaped pink variety with firm flesh and shallow eyes; good flavour except when over-watered; stores as well as a maincrop. ★ ★ ★

Croft (M): A blight-resistant popular show variety with nicely-shaped tubers but a

bit of a disappointment to the discerning cook. ★ ★

Desiree (M): Often regarded as a second early rather than a maincrop because it doesn't keep very long after Christmas. It is a firm favourite with grower, supermarket and housewife alike. The skin is red, the flesh firm and creamy, and the cooking quality and flavour are superb whether roasted, chipped, boiled or baked. A very heavy yielding potato, but somewhat susceptible to scab though marginally blight resistant. ★ ★ ★ ★ ★

Drayton (M): A rising star. This is the improved version of King Edward, with the same red and white skin and superb cooking quality, but a far heavier and more consistent cropper given a good organic soil and a reasonably good season. Does better than King Edward on light land. ★ ★ ★ ★

Dr McIntosh (M): Excellent for flavour, yield and resistance to blight. Given the right conditions of organically-enriched soil and adequate moisture, the Doctor goes on growing through to October. The flavour even improves after Christmas. The snag is that the seed tubers are rather difficult to come by. ★ ★ ★ ★ ★

Duke of York (E): This one is a native of East Anglia, having been introduced by Daniels of Norwich in 1891. It has pale yellow flesh, shallow eyes and excellent flavour. Scrapes easily and can be grown on for lifting as a second early with proportionately higher yields although some loss of that new potato flavour. ★ ★ ★ ★

Dunluce (E): Bred by Mr J. Clarke in Ulster, this is one of the newcomers that I have yet to try. I'm told it has very good cooking quality, some blight resistance and good scab resistance. ★ ★ ★

Epicure (E): An old favourite and still one

of the best with the true new potato flavour. In a dry season it scrapes badly and the yield is low, but in a normal season it crops heavily. ★ ★ ★

Estima (S/E): A very handsome potato, great on the show bench but lacking in flavour when cooked. ★ ★

Golden Wonder (M): Just about the finest flavoured potato available in the UK. It is white, floury and equally good baked or boiled. Unhappily, it is a poor yielder in dry summers. ★ ★ ★ ★

Great Scot (S/E): Excellent round variety with white flesh and a superb flavour when roasted or jacket-baked. Resistant to drought and a heavy cropper, but has a tendency to hollow heart if pushed by over-irrigation. ★ ★ ★

Home Guard (E): One of the most popular and earliest of the earlies. It is tolerant of heavy soil and of drought, but tends to break up when being boiled. ★ ★

Kerr's Pink (M): An old but a good one with a dense haulm that keeps down weeds and gives some resistance to drought. It is also partly blight resistant. The excellent flavour improves after Christmas; highly regarded by the chip trade and a fine roaster as well. Regrettably, supplies of this variety are erratic, so order early. ★ ★ ★ ★

King Edward VII (M): Just about the oldest variety still in commercial production. It was renamed for the coronation of King Edward in 1902, but is now being eased from its throne by Drayton, among others. Seed tuber quality is variable, while cooking quality is moderate. It can give a good yield, has excellent storage life with the flavour improving in store. ★ ★ ★

Kingston (M): A firm, rather thin floury variety, but handsome enough for the show

land prefix have been raised at the Scottish Plant Breeding Station at Pentlandfields, near Edinburgh.

Seed potatoes start arriving in the nurseries and gardening shops in January, but if you want any of the more unusual varieties, it's as well to place an order with a specialist supplier.

CULTIVATION

For every three 4.5m (15ft) rows of earlies you will need 3kg (6.6lb) of seed tubers, planted 30cm (1ft) apart in rows 45cm (18in) apart. Three rows will produce about 22.7–31.7kg (50–70lb) of earlies, up to 36.3kg (80lb) of second early or up to 45kg (100lb) of maincrop when the planting distance is 60cm (2ft) each way.

Probably no other crop is so tolerant of soil types as the potato, but there's no question that the ideal growing medium is a light, open loam, well manured in the autumn or early spring and dressed with blood, fish and bone in March at the rate of 56g (2oz) to the square m/yd for early and second early, and 113g (4oz) for maincrop. The pH should be 6 to 6.5. Planting times vary depending on region and weather conditions. In my part of East Anglia commercial growers put out their early bench. Good cooking quality but only moderate flavour. ★ ★

Manna (E): An excellent salad potato, especially eaten cold, but unsuitable for chipping. ★ ★ ★

Majestic (M): Born in the early days of the 1914–18 War, this is still widely grown commercially because it yields well even in a dry season. Modern varieties have gained ground over this one. The flavour is poor, although best when roasted or chipped. It stores well in clamps. ★ ★

Marfona (S/E): A newish, round yellow-fleshed variety that chips, roasts and bakes well with fair flavour. ★ ★ ★

Maris Bard (E): One of the newer varieties from Cambridge Plant Breeding Institute, it has a well-earned reputation for early cropping and a heavy yield. It is earlier than Pentland Javelin and has the merit of continuing to bulk over a month or more after lifting starts. Handsome oval tubers with creamy-white flesh. Flavour is moderate to good and it has a marked resistance to disease. It could well become the successor to Arran Pilot. ★ ★ ★ ★

Maris Peer (S/E): Oval tuber with cream flesh and good cooking quality for most purposes. A heavy cropper with some resistance to blight and scab, but no resistance to drought. Moderate flavour. ★ ★ ★

Maris Piper (M): One of the best flavoured varieties to come from the Cambridge Plant Breeding Institute. It has a creamy flesh and is good for baking, roasting and mashing, but not for chipping. A heavy yielder with strong resistance to yellow-cysted eelworm, but poor resistance to scab and drought. ★ ★ ★ ★

Pentland Beauty (E): Popular with exhibitors, this is a pink-skinned beauty and a heavy cropper. But the beauty is only

skin deep because the flavour is so insipid it wins admiration from no one. ★ ★

Pentland Crown (M): One of the highest-yielding late maincrop varieties, especially in humus-rich soil. It is a good all-rounder in the kitchen, but the flavour is only moderate. Disease resistance and storage life are above average. ★ ★ ★

Pentland Dell (M): A round potato with white flesh and above average yields, but a notable absence of flavour. ★ ★

Pentland Ivory (M): One of the best from Pentlandfields with white, floury flesh and a moderate to good flavour. It is popular with the commercial growers because it has blight resistance, yields heavily, stores well and has supermarket appeal when washed and placed in see-through packs. ★ ★ ★ ★

Pentland Javelin (E): Second only to Maris Bard in early cropping, this white-fleshed variety yields well, scrapes well and is resistant to yellow-cysted eelworm. Good flavour which declines somewhat as the crop bulks up. ★ ★ ★

Pentland Lustre (E): Not so high-yielding as Javelin or so early but also resistant to yellow-cysted eelworm. Moderate flavour and cooking quality. ★ ★

Record (M): Second to Golden Wonder for flavour. Too floury for chips, but excellent for crisps or baked, boiled or roasted. The flavour even improves in store. Seed tubers are difficult to come by possibly because the yield is only moderate and falls off badly in a dry summer. ★ ★ ★

Romano (S/E): A very pretty potato, nicely shaped with a deep red skin and firm, waxy flesh. Good cooking quality and fair flavour, but low resistance to drought. ★ ★ ★

Sharpe's Express (E): An old favourite that does reasonably well on heavy land. Often grown for the early summer shows

and popular with farmers because it looks good and yields heavily. ★ ★

Stormont Dawn (M): No prizes for guessing where this originated from. Now well over forty years old, this variety has white, floury flesh and an outstandingly long storage life. The flavour is superb when jacket baked or steamed in a pressure cooker. A heavy cropper. ★ ★ ★ ★

Stormont Enterprise: (M): Another good Ulster variety, happiest on medium loam, with good yielding capability, moderate flavour and some resistance to blight. ★ ★ ★

Ukama (E): A yellow-fleshed salad variety with a good flavour but erratic yielding performance. ★ ★

Ulster Chieftain (E): This does surprisingly well almost everywhere offering a moderate to heavy yield, good scraping and passably good flavour. ★ ★ ★

Ulster Ensign (S/E): A kidney shape and shallow eyes make this popular with the cook and the exhibitor. Yellow skin hides a creamy flesh. The flavour improves the longer it is left in the ground, but slugs find this one irresistible. ★ ★ ★

Vanessa (E): A newcomer that is destined to become a top favourite with amateur growers. Even in the intense drought of 1983 the yield was acceptable and the flavour was outstanding. The pink skin scrapes well and cooking quality is good. ★ ★ ★ ★

Wilja (S/E): Becoming a very popular variety. Given a good season without too many dry spells, it will yield a big crop of long, oval tubers with pale yellow flesh. Cooks well and the flavour is fair to middling. ★ ★ ★

seed potatoes in February under floating cloches of polythene sheeting. This gives them a harvesting time ten days to a fortnight earlier than uncovered crops.

Try to get your seed potatoes chitted from as early in January as possible, with the earlies being planted from about mid-March; the second earlies in mid-April, and the maincrop in late April. If there is danger of frost, a little earth is drawn over the shoots, although one year a late May frost burned off the young haulms of all my earlies, yet the crop was as good as normal.

When the haulm has grown 22.5cm (9in) or so, start

earthing up by using a draw hoe to bring loosened soil between the rows up to the plants to form a tent-shaped ridge. For the second early and maincrop a further earthing up is usually necessary to prevent any of the developing tubers becoming greened by exposure to the light. Harvesting the earlies can begin once the flowers begin to fall. This is about twelve to thirteen weeks after planting. Lift only as many as you need for immediate use.

With second early varieties you can start lifting as soon as the early crop is finished, while the maincrop should not be lifted until September or early October. The tubers are then

Egg containers make excellent trays for chitting seed potatoes. Scab can be a problem with potatoes grown on light, alkaline soils low in organic matter. You can remedy this by incorporating compost and well-rotted manure when preparing the site. At planting time put the seed tubers in a nest of lawn mowings. As the grass cuttings decompose the local acidity neutralises the chalk in the soil

left on the surface for a few hours to thoroughly dry off before being put into paper bags or hessian sacks for storage. When lifting potatoes make sure you retrieve every tuber, however small. Any left in the ground become next year's weeds.

Blight is the worse of the potato troubles, although it seldom appears early enough to hit the early crop. It is most common in August during a damp summer and can destroy not only all the haulm of the potatoes, but also infect the tubers when spores are washed into the soil. It is a wise precaution to start preventive spraying with Burgundy mixture or Bordeaux mixture – both approved organic sprays – from the first week of July at fortnightly intervals. Some maincrop varieties are reasonably blight-resistant (see Good Potato Guide on pages 108–9).

Leaf roll virus and mosaic virus cause stunted growth and low yields. There is no effective treatment, but buying only certified seed tubers is the best preventive.

Potato cyst eelworm also causes stunted growth and only tiny tubers. Infected plants must be dug up and burned, and neither potatoes nor outdoor tomatoes should be grown on the site for at least six years.

Slugs can be a major pest of maincrop potatoes, especially the small black keel slugs that eat into the tubers that are waiting to be lifted. Watering into the centre of the haulm with Fertosan slug killer is a preventive, and a newer idea is to use lengths of impregnated tape at planting time.

Scab can make the maincrop potatoes look a bit of a mess with corky moon craters on the surface of the tubers. It doesn't harm the eating quality, fortunately, although does mar the quality of those intended as jacket potatoes. The worst affected varieties are Desiree, Craig's Royal and Maris Piper. The condition is worse on light, alkaline soils that are low in organic matter. The remedy is to use as much organic material as possible in preparing the site for potatoes and, at planting time, put the seed potato in a nest of lawn mowings. This causes local acidity as the grass decomposes and so neutralises the chalk in the soil.

NEW POTATOES FOR CHRISTMAS

When I asked in one of my newspaper pieces for readers to tell me how to grow new potatoes for Christmas, there was no shortage of ideas. But not many were entirely practical. The Clacton reader, for example, who said he regularly planted potatoes in August, covered the haulms with cloches from October onwards and dug new potatoes for lunch on Christmas Day, must have had more than his fair share of luck.

To get the tubers to behave like seed potatoes at the wrong time of year isn't just a matter of planting them. You have to break their natural dormancy. One suggestion is that this can be done by giving them a week's heat treatment at 32 to 38°C (90 to 100°F). They can then go into a 22.5cm (9in) pot half-filled with damp peat. When the foliage reaches the rim of the pot, fill to the top with more moist peat. The pot should be kept watered, but not over-wet, in a cool greenhouse or light, frost-

When harvesting potatoes, make two piles. The main one is of good-sized blemish-free tubers, while the other is for damaged and under-sized tubers

free shed and, come Christmas, you should have enough small new potatoes for the feast.

At the Rosewarne Experimental Horticultural Station in Cornwall three years of work has shown that a crop of early potatoes for Christmas is entirely feasible if you have polythene cloches or a poly tunnel and the mild West Country climate. Planting is carried out in late August and the haulm shows through in early October.

Fred Loads, of BBC *Gardeners' Question Time* fame, had an entirely original way with new potatoes for Christmas. After he had planted out most of his seed potatoes in the spring some were kept back and strung on stiff wire with one end bent to prevent them sliding off. Each tuber was reckoned to produce between five and eight ounces of new potatoes. The string of seed potatoes was hung on a nail outside the potting shed until the prospect of frost in the autumn. By then they had made strong, purple shoots. They were then laid in a box on a bed of dry peat, covered with a 5cm (2in) layer of more dry peat and stored in a shed or garage. The small potatoes developed to the size of golf balls on the parent tubers with only a minimum growth of haulm. Fred used to say that it didn't matter whether you used early, second early or maincrop seed potatoes. They all gave good results.

LACEY'S LORE

WEEPING TREES

When planting a weeping tree, such as a weeping willow, face the bare side away from the prevailing wind. This speeds up the growth on the leeward side to give the tree a balanced umbrella shape.

LACEY'S LORE

CHITTING CONTAINERS

For chitting seed potatoes, fibre or plastic egg containers are excellent and can be used for their original purpose after the potatoes have been planted out.

9

CROP STORAGE AND SEED SAVING

When you grow your own organic fruit and vegetables you can take maximum advantage of their health-giving properties by eating them within hours, even minutes, of harvesting: not for you the limp lettuce or tired, tasteless tomato. Once again sprouts have that true nutty flavour, cabbage is crisp and fresh-picked peas have a sweetness no deep-freeze version can match.

Vegetables and soft fruit begin to lose their nutritional value from the moment they are harvested, so try to shorten the distance, as it were, between the vegetable plot and the kitchen. Don't pick stuff today that you intend to eat tomorrow, if picking can wait until tomorrow also.

Some vegetables store remarkably well – carrots, onions, parsnips and beetroot are examples, and in the winter these vegetables are a boon to have in store because weather conditions may put a temporary halt to gathering fresh produce. Even so, carrots are best eaten on the day they are pulled or dug from the ground.

In the great carrot-growing area of east Suffolk it is commonplace today to see over the winter months large fields covered in a deep layer of straw. This is the alternative to clamping the carrots. The crop is left in the ground under the insulating shelter of the straw and even in the deepest frost the soil remains unfrozen. The amateur grower can adopt the same idea, using straw, bracken, peat or forest bark as a crop cover.

The National Vegetable Research Station, in an excellent leaflet on the storage of home-grown vegetables, offers the advice summarised in the fact files with the rider that vegetables should be stored only when there is good reason for not leaving them in the ground. Emphasising that many vegetables are still growing at the time of harvest, the NVRS says growth must be rapidly reduced if the vegetable is to maintain quality during storage. This is best done by cooling to near 0°C (32°F) as soon as possible after harvesting and then keeping it in store at this temperature. Most vegetables are badly damaged at just below freezing point but, as most domestic refrigerators run at 2 to 4°C (35 to 40°F) storage in the fridge shouldn't harm them. The exceptions are French and runner beans, sweet peppers, cucumbers, courgettes, marrows and tomatoes, which should be stored outside the fridge in loosely-tied polythene bags, and potatoes which should be kept in a dark place, preferably in hessian sacks or, failing that, double-walled paper sacks.

You don't have to pop vegetables into the fridge to cool them, you can place them in the shade immediately after harvesting and then cool them by evaporation. This is particularly effective with leafy crops, such as lettuce and celery which can be kept cool if they are sprayed with water twice a day. On sunny summer days vegetables can heat up by as much as 10°C (50°F) so avoid harvesting in full sunlight. It is important also to try to minimise desiccation by storing crops in closed

Cross section of a garden shed adapted for storage of winter vegetables, from a drawing in the leaflet Storing Home-Grown Vegetables *by the National Vegetable Research Station, Wellesbourne. Air circulates through a vent at floor level and leaves through small gaps under the eaves. 1 Nets or strings of onions. 2 Boxes of small roots ready for early use. 3 Carrots, beetroot, parsnips and swedes stored in boxes of sand or peat. 4 Potatoes in double-thickness paper sacks in the warmest part of the shed with old carpet or blankets for extra protection*

polythene bags when they are cold, but not when they are being cooled.

Treat your vegetables with care after harvesting because rough handling increases the rate of deterioration and damaged produce rots more quickly. Trim off the damaged parts of leafy vegetables and with root crops use any damaged ones first. Don't try to store carrots that show signs of carrot fly attack (see page 145) or onions that have soft necks.

With soft fruit it is advisable to handle the berries as little as possible. Pick when the fruit is dry and not wet with rain or dew because damp fruit quickly rots. Strawberries are best picked when fully ripe in the evening. To bring out the full flavour crush them slightly, sprinkle with sugar if desired and leave overnight to soak.

Remember that all soft fruits are best eaten as soon as possible after picking. Neither strawberries nor raspberries will store for longer than about forty-eight hours after gathering them, while cultivated blackberries, and the hybrid berries deteriorate quite rapidly after twenty-four hours from harvesting. With apples and pears, pick and handle carefully because bruised fruits do not store well. Store only sound, undamaged

You can use sand or the peat from used growing bags to store carrots, parsnips and beetroot over the winter. Arrange them in layers so that they are not touching each other and place the container in a cool place

fruits, preferably with the stalks intact. Choose medium-size fruits which store better than oversize ones.

Ideally, apples should be wrapped individually using oiled paper, and placed in wooden fruit trays in a store where the temperature is 2 to 4°C (35 to 40°F) where it is dark and rather humid but with some air circulation. Most of us have to compromise and use a shed, garage or cellar which should be vermin-proof. Apples can also be stored in polythene bags, each holding about 1kg (2lb) of fruit. The bags should have holes punched in them and the tops turned over, not sealed.

The same general principles apply for the storage of pears, but the fruit should not be wrapped or kept in bags but placed on trays so that the fruits are not touching one another.

All fruit should be examined regularly while in store, so ease of access to the storage place is important. Plums, cherries, peaches and nectarines cannot be stored for more than a few days, so if you have a surplus the best plan is to bottle them in Kilner jars or use them for jam-making.

SAVE YOUR OWN SEEDS

The Henry Doubleday Research Association has alerted British gardeners to the dangers of EEC regulations intended to 'rationalise' member states' vegetable varieties.

In 1975 HDRA began a campaign to save our heritage of varieties by establishing a seed library from which members can get their selection of favourite or traditional varieties for a fee to cover postage and packing. They are grown by 'seed guardians', members who take on the job of raising a set of

single kinds that will not cross. HDRA says that since 1973 we have been losing vegetable varieties by the hundred every year. In one month alone back in 1978 more than 800 varieties were lost, including the Pot Leek, the darling of the North of England miners, Market King tomato, one of the most flavoursome I've ever grown, and the most famous variety of spinach – Victoria. This was in addition to about 600 varieties regarded as synonymous with other varieties.

My favourite marrow, Gourmet Globe, a marvellous variety for the small family, simply vanished from all the seedsmen's lists and when I asked why I was told it had been reclassified as a squash and it was no longer legal to sell it in any EEC country, but it was available in the United States. HDRA says:

Vegetables have qualities like flavour, disease resistance and slowness to run to seed, of value to gardeners rather than to commercial growers, who want weight, a long shelf life, thick skins for long journeys to the supermarkets and bright colour to show through polythene prepacks.

The reason for these regulations is that horticultural and agricultural seeds can now be patented, earning large royalties, but to secure a patent they must satisfy the Ministry of Agriculture department concerned (or its equivalent in any other EEC country) that the variety is uniform, stable and distinct. The smaller the national lists are, the fewer varieties there are to search through and less space in the catalogues needs to be given to those that gardeners have grown on their merits for up to a century.

Store onions in strings and shallots in nets or old tights in a cool well-ventilated place

Apples can be stored in polythene bags each holding about 1kg (2.2lb) of fruit. Punch holes in the bag and turn the top over

FACT FILE Seed saving table

Vegetable	Annual/ biennial	Pollin- ation	Storage life in years
Broad bean	Annual	Self	Up to 10
French bean	Annual	Self	Up to 10
Runner bean	Annual	Self	Up to 10
Cabbage, sprouts, cauliflower	Biennial	Insect	Up to 9
Carrot	Biennial	Insect	Up to 6
Celery, celeriac	Biennial	Insect	Up to 3
Courgette, marrow	Annual	Insect	Up to 6
Cucumber	Annual	Insect	Up to 6
Chard, Swiss	Biennial	Wind	Up to 3
Leek	Biennial	Insect	Up to 3
Lettuce	Annual	Self	Up to 3
Onion	Biennial	Insect	Up to 3
Parsley	Biennial	Insect	Up to 3
Parsnip	Biennial	Insect	Up to 3
Pea	Annual	Self	Up to 7
Pumpkin	Annual	Insect	Up to 6
Radish	Annual	Insect	Up to 10
Sweetcorn	Annual	Wind	Up to 10
Swede	Biennial	Insect	Up to 9
Tomato	Annual	Insect	Up to 10
Turnip	Biennial	Insect	Up to 9

FACT FILE Tips on storage

1 Don't store vegetables that you can grow in succession to give fresh supplies.

2 Many leafy vegetables quickly lose flavour and crispness when stored, so eat lettuce, spinach, Swiss chard and spring greens for example, as soon as possible after harvesting.

3 Most vegetables suffer chilling injury at 0°C (32°F) and below, but rapid cooling to about 4°C (40°F), then storage at 2–4°C (36–40°F) (the normal running temperature range of most domestic fridges) will minimise quality loss.

4 When storing root crops, such as carrots and parsnips, place them so that the small roots will be used first because these are the first to become shrivelled through moisture loss.

5 Never store diseased or damaged crops as these are quick to rot. Trim off damaged areas of leaf crops.

6 Avoid harvesting crops in full sunlight or with moisture on them.

7 After harvesting handle the vegetables carefully. Don't wash root crops, just lightly brush off surplus soil.

8 Store root crops in a dry, airy, frost-proof place that is easily accessible but vermin-proof.

9 Apples and pears should be free from blemish and not over-ripe. Store in shallow boxes, seed trays or in polythene bags that have been perforated. Cool, but humid conditions are preferred. Watch out for rats and mice.

10 Check all stored fruit and vegetables regularly and remove any that show signs of rot.

Nowadays most of the seed firms are owned by international corporations and those that remain outside the octopus grip of the oil companies and chemical conglomerates are tending to amalgamate. So the net effect is a very substantial reduction in the choice of varieties on offer to the gardener. One way to resist this pressure to conform to the wishes of the Eurocrats, Whitehall mandarins and the oil barons is to save one's own seed or, better still, to get together with a few friends and form a seed-saving co-operative. At Westleton, Kate Mares and a half dozen or so other organic gardeners have been doing this for years, selecting plants that do particularly well in their locality and then growing them on for seed production. One result has been an outstanding strain of carrot.

Seed saving offers these advantages:

• It saves money because home-produced seed costs virtually nothing.

• It enables one to protect and preserve a favourite variety that could be threatened by national or European 'rationalisation' of the seed lists.

• It gives you the opportunity to select and re-select a strain that best responds to your soil, your climate, your growing technique and your particular requirements in terms of yield, flavour, drought resistance and harvesting date.

• Seed production is a fascinating extension to this wonderful hobby of gardening and, though there will undoubtedly be a surplus for one's own needs, home-produced seeds make very welcome gifts for friends and relatives.

When growing vegetables for seed bear in mind that some species are biennial: carrots are an example. We harvest them halfway through the cycle of growth when we take the roots to the kitchen. To complete that cycle and produce a seed head requires a further season of growth.

When choosing vegetables for seed production select two plants of open-pollinated types to ensure cross pollination. F1

or first filial generation plants are unsuitable for seed saving as the seed does not breed true. The original cross has to be made each year under carefully controlled conditions to produce a new batch of hybrids and this is outside the scope of most amateur seed producers. Brassicas also need two years to achieve seed production, so it is usually best to transplant the selected specimens for the second season while avoiding having more than one sort of brassica in flower at the same time. Collect the brassica seed pods while they are yellow but unopened.

With root crops, either transplant the selected plants and give them protection during the winter or choose the best specimens from store and plant them out in March to grow on and produce seed heads. With marrows and outdoor cucumbers select a good specimen on a plant early in the season and don't allow the plant to produce any more fruit. Courgettes are immature marrows, so the selected fruit should be allowed to develop to full size and ripeness. By late autumn the skins will have become brittle and very hard, so use a saw to open them. One marrow will produce 300 or more seeds, more than enough for you and your friends. Remove the seeds carefully and wash to remove the fleshy pulp. Then spread them on blotting paper or kitchen towelling to dry naturally, not in the oven.

Leeks and onions need two years to seed and the selected plants should be transplanted and staked. Tie a paper bag round the seed head if the weather turns wet and windy during the final stages of ripening. With lettuce don't choose a plant that bolted prematurely because this trait might be carried through into the next generation. Harvest lettuce seed before the 'parachutes' open.

Peas and beans for seed should be allowed to ripen on the plant and then the entire plant is brought under cover to complete the process or laid flat and covered with cloches.

FACT FILE Storage conditions for vegetables

1 Lettuce, cabbage, Brussels sprouts, cauliflowers, calabrese
Store at 0°C (32°F) and 98 per cent relative humidity. Place in polythene bags, folded over or tied to restrict air.

2 Carrots, beetroot, parsnips, swedes, turnips
Store at 0°C (32°F) and 98 per cent relative humidity. Leave in ground for as long as possible. From early November onwards protect from frost by covering with a mulch of straw, bracken, peat, forest bark, soil or polythene, but remember that parsnips are

sweetened by frost. When lifted, trim off leaves. Store in polythene bags or in layers in boxes using moist peat or sand.

3 French beans, runner beans, cucumber, marrows, peppers, tomatoes
Store at 5–10°C (42–50°F) and 90 per cent relative humidity. Place in polythene bags, loosely tied.

4 Potatoes, maincrop
Store at 4–10°C (40–50°F) and 90 per cent relative humidity. Store in double thickness paper sacks or hessian sacks, but

do not use plastic ones.
Loosely tie at neck to restrict ventilation.

5 Onions and shallots
Store at 0°C (32°F) and 70 per cent relative humidity. Ensure that bulbs are thoroughly ripe with brittle dry skins. Hang onions in traditional ropes or cotton or plastic nets or discarded tights. Storage life can be extended by keeping part of the crop in the fridge, otherwise choose a cool, dry place. Shallots can be stored in shallow boxes, nets or tights.

Marrow seed is well worth collecting by the amateur gardener. Select a good specimen on a plant early in the season and allow it to develop to full size and ripeness. In late autumn cut open the marrow with a saw, remove and wash the seeds and spread them to dry on kitchen towelling. Store in a paper bag labelled with name of variety and date collected

FACT FILE Seed-saving reminders

● Choose the right plants, only open-pollinated sorts, not F[1]. Select for vigour, form, early ripening, yield, flavour, drought resistance, disease resistance, height.

● Pick the seed at the right time. This means leaving the seed on the plants for as long as possible. Some seeds are only fully ripe after shedding. When ripe the colour of the seed changes to a dark brown or black and the seed capsule texture changes.

● Dry the seed naturally in a well-ventilated atmosphere, not in the oven. Tree seeds, such as acorns and chestnuts, should not be allowed to dry out, so store in damp peat.

● While drying keep seed heads in paper bags – not polythene ones – hung up to dry. Spread large seeds, such as marrow, pea and bean, in paper-lined trays or boxes. Fleshy seeds, like marrow, cucumber and tomato, should be washed to remove pulp, then spread on blotting paper or kitchen towelling.

● Label all seeds throughout with name, variety and date of collection.

● When dry, separate seeds from the pods or rest of the plant by shaking or straining, then reject all debris and misshapen seeds.

● Store carefully in envelopes or paper bags, clearly labelled. Then place in a cool, dry place.

● Finally, test your home-produced seed for germination before making a crop-producing sowing. Place ten seeds on damp kitchen paper and keep warm and moist. After three weeks count the number that have germinated. If there are fewer than five, then it might not be worth sowing that sample. Better luck, next time.

10

TIPS FOR SHOWING
AND FLAVOUR

Visiting many fruit, flower and vegetable shows as a judge, I'm struck by the strong evidence of pride in appearance in most villages and country towns. Not all are magnets to tourists, but compared with our cities and large towns, the villages are relatively free of litter and unburdened by the more evident signs of vandalism. Village gardens today retain many of the qualities of the traditional cottage garden, and long may that continue, while the village flower show gives a spirit of friendly competition to the individual gardener's efforts.

A major cause for regret, however, is how few young people enter for the produce classes. The skill to produce fine fruit, flowers and vegetables is not the prerogative of the pensioners, although it is fair to assume that everyone who enters something in a flower show shares a degree of dedication for growing a plant, making wine or baking bread or whatever to as near to perfection as possible.

This is recognised by the organisers of shows in putting together their schedules and by the Royal Horticultural Society which provides the guidelines in *Horticultural Show Handbook*, a bible for organisers, exhibitors and judges. The RHS says there are eight vegetables that are especially meritorious if grown particularly well and this is recognised by a twenty-point award in collections – those handsome arrangements of vegetables that normally form the centrepiece of the show's vegetable classes. They are carrots, cauliflowers, celery, leeks, onions, parsnips, peas and potatoes. Close behind, with a possible eighteen points are aubergines, runner beans, cucumbers, okra and tomatoes. Earning a maximum fifteen points are a larger group which includes globe artichokes, asparagus, broad and French beans, broccoli, Brussels sprouts, cabbages, lettuces, swedes, sweet corn and turnips. Bottom of the list, earning only five possible points, are such things as watercress, salad onions, mustard, cress and herbs.

As a judge, I cross swords with the RHS over pointing of some vegetables. For example, I think it takes a lot more skill to grow a well-blanched, clean, pest-free stick of celery than it does to produce a dish of shapely, clean, clear-skinned potatoes. Yet both are in the twenty-point group. However judges have to stick to the rules whatever their personal opinions, although there are finishing touches that can make all the difference to the judge's view of an exhibit.

CELERY

It is a good plan to lift the selected sticks on the evening before the show, trim the roots but be careful not to damage the stems or foliage. Before taking them to the show, tie the sticks with raffia just below the foliage, and at the show cover the sticks with damp paper until judging is about to start. Well-grown sticks of celery dominate any collection of vegetables, so posi-

tion them first on the tray or board, and place the other items in descending order of size. That usually means that leeks, one of the most popular of show vegetables, become the second dominant part of the collection.

LEEKS

The judges will be looking for leeks that have a good length of straight, well-blanched stem without a bulbous base. Excessive stripping of the outer skin should be avoided as this will uncover ribbing and lose points. In the marking, condition and solidity gain up to eight points each, and uniformity four points. Make the display as neat as possible, but leave the roots on.

LACEY'S LORE

FROST AND FLAVOUR

There's a widely-held belief that celery, parsnips and Brussels sprouts taste better after a frost. But is it a fact?

Scientists are divided on this issue. With celery, for example, frost causes damage that can be fatal. With parsnips and sprouts there is some scientific backing to the idea that frost improves the flavour.

With most food crops the flavour improves as the crop nears maturity.

This is because changes are taking place in the acids and sugars together with a compound that has, so far, defied identification.

As the average ambient temperature falls, this signals to the crop that the ageing process is reaching a climax. It is a gradual change, although not necessarily a slow one, and it seems that flavour peaks as the first frost arrives.

POTATOES

Potatoes are often problem classes with judges, especially when the schedule-makers have failed to make class divisions crystal clear. If you plan to exhibit in these classes, read the schedule with extra care and if in any doubt about which variety belongs in which class, speak to the show organisers. Don't go for the biggest tubers. Select medium-sized ones that are well matched, free from skin blemishes and with shallow eyes. Prepare the potatoes by washing them with a soft sponge dipped in milk – never use a brush – and when dry, wrap them in paper. Always take some spare tubers with you to the show, just in case of mishaps. Arrange your potatoes on a paper plate, without any decoration, and cover with a clean, damp cloth. Make sure your entry carries the name of the variety in block letters.

PEAS

When the judge comes to the pea classes there might be very

little to choose between the exhibits. But when a pod from each entry is opened and maggoty peas are found, the sorting out has begun in earnest. Pods should retain their fresh-as-the-morning-dew look. This means cutting them with scissors so as not to damage the calyx and holding them tenderly so as not to mar the bloom on the pods. When opened the pod should be entirely filled with tender peas and it is sometimes possible to check your pods for fullness by holding them up to a strong light.

ONIONS

Onions attract intense competition at shows up and down the country and are frequently the most difficult classes to judge. I'm no lover of over-size vegetables and that includes onions. When you remember that vegetables are produced to eat, show-bench specimen onions weighing in at 2kg or so (4 to 5lb) each are rather absurd. What does the cook do with them? But given that all the contenders are hard, well-shaped and ripened with firm, thin necks, then size and presentation become the key features. A piece of black velvet over plastic foam shows off the onions which should never have the outer skins peeled off.

CAULIFLOWERS

Cauliflowers must be as white as driven snow with close, solid curds without stain or whiptail, which is the leaf in the curd. One way to assist a cauliflower to reach show standards is to tie the leaves loosely over the curd as it develops. This helps to keep the curd white and should prevent any weather damage. On show day, trim the leaves neatly, but keep them as long as possible. Wicker baskets make attractive stands for individual cauliflowers. In a collection they should be positioned on the back board with, maybe, a few sprigs of parsley.

CARROTS

Carrots come in three main types and it is essential that the schedule defines which types are required for the individual classes. The old favourites like Red Intermediate, St Valery and Autumn King still win prizes aplenty, although some of the new F¹ varieties are proving fine for show work as well as being very well thought of in the kitchen. Carrots quickly lose their crispness, so delay lifting them until the morning of the show. Wash the selected roots gently and wrap them in a damp cloth, foliage and all.

LACEY'S LORE

STICK TO SCHEDULE

If you intend to try your skill as a gardener in the local flower show, the first golden rule is to read the schedule carefully. Entries can be disqualified or down-graded for even a minor breach of the rules, so make sure your exhibit sticks to the schedule. If in doubt, ask the show secretary before the big day.

FACT FILE Vegetable varieties for top flavour when grown organically

Beans Runners: Enorma, Scarlet Emperor, Red Knight.
Broad: The Sutton
Climbing French: Blue Lake white seeded.
Dwarf French: Sprite, Remus.
Beetroot Beethoven, Burpee's Golden.
Brussels sprout Monitor, Peer Gynt, Cambridge No 5.
Cabbage Spring: Hispi, Early Market, Spring Hero.
Summer: Primo, Greyhound.
Autumn: Minicole, Sprite.
Winter: January King, Celtic.
Salad and coleslaw: Winter White.
Carrot Early: Cluseed New Model.
Mid-season: Mokum, Chantenay Red Cored.
Cauliflower Summer: Snow King.
Winter and spring: Pinnacle, Bostonian.

Celery Giant White, Giant Pink.
Cucumber Indoors: Pepinex 69.
Outdoors: Burpee Hybrid.
Leek Snowstar, Catalina, Molos.
Lettuce Little Gem or Paris White.
Marrow Gourmet Globe or, if unobtainable, Table Dainty.
Parsley French or plain-leaved, Afro.
Parsnip Gladiator, Cobham Improved, Tender and True.
Peas Early: Kelvedon Wonder, Little Marvel.
Maincrop: Hurst Green Shaft.
Potato Early: Duke of York, Vanessa, Epicure.
Second early: Craig's Royal, Ulster Ensign.
Maincrop: Cara, Desiree, Golden Wonder, Dr McIntosh, Stormont Dawn.
(Golden Wonder is about the finest

flavoured all-purpose variety, but seed potatoes are difficult to get. The flavour of Dr McIntosh improves after Christmas.)
Radish Cherry Belle, French Breakfast.
Spinach Swiss Chard is preferred, but for low oxalic acid content try Monnopa (from Thompson and Morgan).
Tomato Outdoors: The Amateur, Gardener's Delight.
Indoors: Harbinger, Gardener's Delight, Tigerella, Alicante.
Unusual vegetables Texsel Greens (could become popular); Scorzonera and salsify; Kohl rabi; Land cress; Hamburg parsley (use leaves as well as roots); Florence fennel (the bulb is delicious braised); Endive (a good winter salad); Chinese cabbage.

PARSNIPS

Finally among the twenty-point vegetables are parsnips which require much the same growing technique as carrots. On the show bench good specimens will have strong, broad shoulders and shapely, tapering white root without trace of canker with the root tip intact. Keep the roots fresh by wrapping them in a damp cloth.

FLAVOUR

No matter how well a vegetable does in a show, the final test is at the table, when flavour is the most important factor, and there is no way the show judge can award points for that.

There's an old maxim that if it looks right, it tastes right, but that doesn't hold good with the commercially-produced tomato. It is uniform in size, has a good colour and thick skin but is almost totally tasteless. Many modern commercial varieties of vegetable have been developed to respond to artificial fertilisers to produce maximum yield. In fact, it is because those plants take the soluble fertilisers as food rather than the organic wholefood diet that flavour is most seriously impaired.

Flavour is directly affected by the nutrients given to the crop together with the amount of moisture and warmth, all of which influence the dry matter and sugar content. Generally speaking, providing the crop is organically grown, the more water given, the less pronounced the flavour, especially of peas, tomatoes, onions, carrots and potatoes.

Most seasons you'll find the flavour of the crop improves as the crop nears its finish. This is particularly the case with runner beans, French beans, tomatoes and many root crops. You can enhance the flavour of many vegetables by giving a mid-growth dressing of seaweed meal at the rate of 56g (2oz) to the sq m/yd. Apply close to the plants and lightly tease it into the soil. Leafy crops and tomatoes also benefit from the high potash content of seaweed if it is given in the form of liquid extract and foliar fed.

Other factors that influence flavour are choice of variety – some have a more pronounced or untypical flavour than others – harvesting at the optimum level of maturity, minimising the time between harvesting and eating and, finally, never over-cooking the vegetable, whatever it is.

Fruits of the earth compete for honours at the village flower show, but no points are awarded for flavour which many of us believe to be more important than good looks

11

BERRIES FOR
THE BACK GARDEN

STRAWBERRY

Summer is the taste of strawberries and cream in a sun-dappled garden and the sound of someone mowing the lawn.

Fortunately there are many ways of growing strawberries and even the smallest garden should have a few plants growing in a strawberry barrel or on a strawberry wall when shortage of space excludes the traditional strawberry bed. It is the quickest fruit to crop. You can plant in September and take a picking of luscious, ripe berries in June.

Strawberries like a well-drained humus-rich home, without waterlogging, and they relish large dressings of compost or well-rotted farmyard manure. In the inter-war years commercial growers both in Britain and on the Continent gave their strawberry beds up to fifty tonnes of manure to the acre. Since then, yields have steadily declined from about six tonnes to the acre to the present average of about three tonnes. Part of the decline could be due to poorer quality strains of the main commercial varieties, but I suspect that a far lower mucking rate is the main cause.

Strawberries are never happy with inorganic fertilisers, much preferring to get their nutritional needs from organic sources. When adequate quantities of farmyard manure are not available, well-made compost is an excellent alternative, augmented with a dressing of bonemeal in the second and third years of cropping. The crop is an excellent one for deep-bed cultivation and particularly satisfying for the amateur gardener.

It is an interesting berry to grow, comes quickly into bearing and, given the little space it occupies, crops more heavily than any other fruit. And who turns up their nose at a bowl of freshly-gathered sun-warmed scarlet strawberries?

More and more commercial growers are treating strawberries as an annual crop rather than as plants that will crop for three or four years, but I don't know of any amateurs who prefer the annual technique.

The scourge of the strawberry grower has always been virus diseases and although strict certification schemes have done a lot to improve the health and vigour of stocks, virus disease and attack from soil-borne pests and diseases remain a problem. So it is advisable to rotate the strawberry crop, choosing a fresh site every three years.

When establishing a strawberry bed or growing on a wall or in a container, always buy certified healthy stock or take runners from the best parent plants. In England and Wales buy the plants from a nursery whose stock has been inspected and certified by the Ministry of Agriculture. In Scotland nurseries are not allowed to sell uncertified strawberry plants. Strawberries are shallow-rooting plants, so the aim when preparing the site is to pack the top 30cm (1ft) or so of the soil with manure or compost at the rate of up to 9kg (20lb) to the sq m/yd.

The site should be open, well-drained and at the highest point of the garden or allotment to avoid waterlogging and frost pockets. A slightly acid soil in the pH range 6.0 to 6.5 is preferred. The addition of peat, just teased into the top few inches

Ripening strawberries need protection from birds. This can be an elaborate walk-in fruit cage or simply netting draped over rope stretched between wooden posts, like this. Make sure the sides are secure, but try to check your strawberry bed daily in case a bird or hedgehog has got tangled in the net

of the soil, usually gives both that little extra acidity as well as more welcome humus, but try not to leave any organic matter on the surface because this might attract slugs and millipedes. The site must be weed-free, so do ensure that all the traces of perennial weeds are removed before planting the bed. In the old days the runners would be planted out in October and religiously disbudded the following spring to encourage strong plants that would yield heavily in their second and third years, with a gradual decline after that. Today, we set out the plants as soon as they are available, that is, from early July to about mid-September, giving them 37.5 to 45cm (15 to 18in) in rows 75 to 90cm (30 to 36in) apart with the crown made very firm in the soil and the roots well spread. After planting make frequent checks that the plants haven't lifted, particularly after frost. The crown should be at soil level.

A hard frost in May will cause the centre of the flower, the embryo fruit, to blacken and die and then it's goodbye to a good crop. Keep an eye on the weather forecasts and if frost is predicted, take evasive action by covering the plants lightly with straw or dried bracken or a plastic floating cloche such as Agryl P17 non-woven fleece. If a long, dry spell comes along once the fruit has set – and May and June are often the driest months of the year – then watering will be needed to enable the fruits to swell.

In a modestly moist spring a mulch of peat is appreciated especially if straw is to be used to tuck around the plants to prevent splashing of the ripening berries with mud and to deter slugs. Straw has the disadvantage that it harbours thistle seeds and other weeds and reflects the sunlight and so delays ripening. The alternatives to strawing are Hortopaper mulch or black polythene sheeting which can be placed in position over the bed before the plants are bought and they are then planted through slits in the material. Strawberry mats can be bought to place round the plants or you can use thick layers of well-soaked newspaper.

When the berries begin to ripen they will need protection from blackbirds and thrushes which share our human interest in these delectable berries. Far and away the most efficient protection is the fruit cage consisting of a metal or plastic framework over which bird-proof netting is secured. The framework can be tall enough to allow one to walk upright inside the cage. For my strawberry bed I use Netlon plastic netting, which is rotproof and very strong, suspended over the plants by four-foot canes surmounted by old tennis balls. These have been collected from various places over the years by our dogs. An inch-long cut is made in each ball so that it fits fairly tightly over the cane.

If watering is necessary, it should be done in the morning so that the foliage is dry by nightfall. This reduces the risk of the plants developing grey mould or botrytis.

When picking time arrives only pick berries that are fully ripe and dry, so this means the best time for harvesting is the evening. The fruit should be picked with stalk and calyx attached.

Runners should only be taken from healthy plants that have been de-blossomed so that they put all their energy into producing sturdy offspring. Allow about six runners per plant and peg them down into peat pots. They can be severed from the parents in August.

With the other plants all the foliage should be cut off at ground level as soon as picking is finished and the debris taken to the compost heap. If straw is used for the bed another way of clearing the foliage is the traditional one of setting fire to it.

The following varieties are recommended by Harry Baker, fruit officer at the RHS Garden, Wisley:

Pantagruella Very early, crops well with a good flavour, but requires a moisture retentive soil.

Tamella Large, firm fruits of good flavour. Crops well. Second early in first year, mid-season thereafter.

Cambridge Vigour Moderate sized fruits, but good yield. Good flavour.

Royal Sovereign This was introduced by Laxtons of Bedford in 1892 and was an immediate success. It is still widely grown, the berries are large, wedge-shaped and the flavour is superb. The snag is that Royal Sovereign has been around so long that it is highly susceptible to virus disease, botrytis and mildew.

Redgauntlet This one is resistant to mildew. It is a heavy cropper but the flavour is indifferent.

Cambridge Favourite This has always done me very well. The fruits are a good size and the yield is high, but the flavour is only moderate.

Hapil A widely grown variety on the light, hot soils of East Anglia. Large, handsome berries and a good flavour.

Tenira Medium fruits, good cropper and good to very good flavour.

Maxim Drought resistant with large well-flavoured berries.

Hedley A very early, heavy cropping variety of only moderate flavour.

Cambridge Late Pine One of the sweetest flavoured strawberries and a late though small cropper.

Totem Bred for freezing, but too acid for eating fresh.

Talisman Not one of Mr Baker's recommendations, but worth growing, I think, for its lateness, high quality fruit and very good flavour.

Domanil Another late variety, cropping heavily with large, good flavoured berries.

You can get a crop of strawberries from July until late autumn by planting one of the so-called perpetual fruiting (remontant) varieties. Particularly recommended are *Rapella*, *Aromel*, *Gento* and *Rabunda*.

RASPBERRY

One of the delights of boyhood was my mother's summer pudding based on fresh strawberries, raspberries and red and white currants. Since those pre-war days the raspberry's fortunes as a back garden crop have declined somewhat. That's a shame because raspberries take up little space, are fairly easy to cultivate and give a good return for a modest outlay for up to ten years.

A hundred years ago as many as fifty varieties of raspberry were listed. In England soft-fruit growing was concentrated in the Orpington-Swanley area of Kent. The partners Edward and William Vinson were then considered to be the largest strawberry and raspberry growers in the world with 650 acres of strawberries and 350 acres of raspberries in Kent, and an army of 1,000-plus pickers. Came World War II and the raspberry all but disappeared – along with the cream – from summertime England. As with the strawberry, virus disease played havoc with most strains of raspberry, and it is difficult to understand why this happened. Raymond Bush, that most erudite writer on fruit growing, thought that the gradual change from farmyard manure to chemical fertilising resulted in a lowering of the plants' resistance to disease, and modern research tends to endorse that theory. But there were other factors.

Before the war new varieties of raspberry were introduced with low resistance to disease and there was uncontrolled distribution of canes from areas of Scotland known to have endemic virus diseases. That was a scandal and a tragedy because it gave the Scottish producers a very bad name indeed. and virtually wiped out the back-garden production of this delicious fruit. Scotland's reputation as Europe's major producer of raspberry stock, which began at the turn of the century, from about 1880 to 1910, was restored with the introduction of new resistant varieties and the Ministry of Agriculture certification scheme.

Today, Scotland produces about four-fifths of the total British crop, with growing concentrated on some 6,000 acres in Perthshire and Angus. Almost all of the crop ends up in cans and jam jars. The climate in Perthshire and Angus – cool summers, light winds – and the soil – a heavy humus-rich loam – are ideal for the raspberry, and this gives a clue to success with this crop. The raspberry is fibrous rooting, so it likes plenty of moisture, but detests waterlogging. An open, sunny site that is frost-free, or at any rate, free from May frosts, but not exposed to damaging winds, is needed.

Before planting the canes from October onwards as much as possible of well-rotted farmyard manure or compost must be worked into the top 30cm (12in) of the soil. The rows need to be 1.5 to 1.8m (5 to 6ft) apart with the canes planted 45cm (18in) to 60cm (2ft) apart in the rows.

On heavy soils with a heart of clay the canes tend to die back unless the ground is opened out with mortar rubble or strawy litter. As with all soft fruit, the site for the raspberries should be meticulously cleared of perennial weeds – once the canes are planted, any couch grass, nettles or thistles that remain undetected will relish the rich soil and become almost impossible to eliminate.

Planting involves setting the canes no more than 7.6cm (3in) deep, firming thoroughly, then cutting back the canes to about 22.8cm (9in) from soil level. This is to encourage strong root growth and healthy fruiting canes during the second season when a crop will be gathered.

During the first summer after planting suckers will be produced and it is these that will bear next year's fruit. These canes will need staking and tying to prevent damage from wind. Posts about 1.98m (6ft 6in) tall are driven in 30cm (1ft) deep at intervals of 2m (7ft) in the row. The end posts are braced and three, fourteen-gauge galvanised wires are strained horizontally at equal intervals between the posts. The canes are then tied into the wires using fillis, raffia or plastic ties.

After the canes have fruited they should be cut out; up to eight of the strongest new canes per stool being allowed to ripen to bear next summer's crop. Cut out all suckers away from the rows and during late spring and summer frequent mulches of lawn mowings will help to keep the roots moist and cool while assisting in the production of strong new canes. Mulching between the rows with newspaper, straw or old carpet also discourages annual weeds. Over the winter the mulch should be drawn away from the canes to allow birds to discover any pupating raspberry beetles. I like to apply an organic mulch in February or March to boost the potash and nitrogen to the canes. In dry summers water the canes copiously in June and again in late August.

The berries should be picked when they are dry and well coloured, but not over-ripe, and should part company quite cleanly from the core or plug.

Recommended varieties no longer include two of the best from the past – Lloyd George and Norfolk Giant. The newer breeds of raspberry we owe mostly to the hybridists at East Malling Research Station in Kent. Each has the prefix Malling, and the first to appear was the outstanding Malling Promise, introduced by Norman Grubb in 1946. It is a very early variety, and therefore liable to frost damage, with large, conical fruits of good flavour. The berries part easily from the plug without undue squeezing; cane growth is vigorous and abundant. Add to that strong resistance to virus infection and you have a first-rate all-rounder.

Another early heavy cropper is Glen Clova, a favourite with exhibitors but rather susceptible to virus infection. In late frost areas Malling Jewel is a good choice because, while fruiting

early, its blooms open later than Malling Promise or Glen Clova. It is a compact grower so the canes can be planted at 37.5cm (15in) intervals. Malling Enterprise, a sister of Jewel, is a good choice for late frost areas and heavy soils, but it needs masses of humus-rich material to ensure adequate new cane production.

Moving to the mid-season varieties, Malling Orion is outstanding for berry quality and flavour. It does particularly well on my open light loam in Suffolk, growing more than 2m (6ft) tall and producing a veritable jungle of canes. Malling Delight and the later fruiting Malling Admiral have also given a very good account of themselves. The Admiral's growth is vigorous with excellent cane production and it has marked resistance to botrytis and virus infection.

Autumn-fruiting varieties give smaller yields from September to late October and there are fewer to choose from. The aptly-named September crops well, though cane production is very variable, while the heaviest cropper in this department is the American variety Heritage. Also from the United States is Fallgold which gives a rather meagre crop of yellow berries with a very distinctive flavour. Zeva ripens from early September onwards with a good weight of berries and prolific cane production, while Autumn Bliss is a couple of weeks earlier with fruit of excellent flavour and rather short in stature canes that, after fruiting, can be cut out and used as surrogate bamboo canes.

Autumn-fruiting raspberries bear their berries on canes produced during the current year, so autumn-fruiting canes planted in October or November would be cut back to near ground level in February and the canes that develop require little or no support.

For those who like to try something unusual I can recommend raising raspberries from seed, a technique that guarantees virus-free stock. The berries must be top-quality ones and fully ripe so that the seeds part company with the flesh quite readily. Wash the seed and dry in full sun, then sow in pans in John Innes seed compost. When large enough to handle, prick out the seedlings into pots and, finally, plant out into permanent positions when the plants are about 22.5cm (9in) tall.

GOOSEBERRY

Far more popular than both the strawberry and raspberry for nineteenth-century gardeners was the gooseberry; indeed, thoughout Queen Victoria's long spell on the throne the gooseberry was king of the soft fruits. Almost every town and village had its group of devoted gooseberry fanciers. In Ipswich, for example, the Ipswich and East of England Horticultural Society began life in a town pub in the early 1800s as the Gooseberry Society. We are talking about the gooseberry as a far different basket of fruit to today's green berries with tongue-curling tartness. The Victorian ideal of a gooseberry approximated in size, sweetness and desirability to the finest dessert grape, and the competition at the town and village gooseberry shows was intense, having something of the fervour – and the stake money – of the pot leek shows in the north of England today.

There's absolutely no reason why the dessert gooseberry should not make a comeback among amateur growers and I can promise anyone who hasn't tasted a large, luscious fully-ripe gooseberry that it is the biggest incentive to lead the revival. The gooseberry grows well in almost any soil, but especially likes a humus-rich free-draining gritty loam. It is relatively free from disease and its few pests are readily controlled by organic methods. It is the earliest flowering soft fruit, so some shelter is essential and frost pockets should be avoided.

A well-managed bush will go on bearing for at least fifteen years, yielding up to 4.5kg (10lb) of fruit a year, propagation is easy, and pruning doesn't require a textbook, so the gooseberry has a lot going for it. But there is one drawback to this delightful fruit. It is armed with the most fiendish spikes that make picking the berries a torment to even the toughest hands, although much of it can be avoided if the dessert

FRUIT WITHOUT RISK

Pioneering Suffolk fruit grower Gavin Cherry has achieved what many horticultural experts thought was impossible. He has turned the clock back and is growing apples and pears of the highest quality without the use of artificial fertilisers or poisonous fungicides, herbicides and insecticides.

To understand the extent of that achievement one has to appreciate that nowadays, with supermarket shopping, the eyes have it. 'The average shopper has one eye on the price tag, the other on whether the product looks nice or not,' a chain store manager told me. So the apple of her eye is rosy red, highly polished, totally free of blemish and is keenly priced. For the grower to get that sort of cosmetic finish there's a mind-boggling programme of spraying: fenitrothion or permethrin twice to control codling moth caterpillars, dimenthoate against apple sawfly caterpillars, tar oil and pirimicarb or heptenophos to check five sorts of aphids, malathion or dimenthoate for capsid bug control, grease banding and spraying permethrin or pirimiphosmethyl against winter moth caterpiller, and then dinocap and mancozeb to control red spider

mite, scab and powdery mildew, and paint containing thiophanate-methyl to check canker.

There are also carefully calculated doses of chemical fertilisers. It's more like a pharmacy than a fruit farm.

But that's not Gavin Cherry's way. At his Sweetapples Orchard at Stowupland he grows fruit entirely organically to Soil Association Symbol standard, and is one of the very few commercial growers in Europe to do so. It has been a long and difficult task because you don't just give up all the chemical aids and let the trees get on with it. He has had to rediscover many of the skills of our forefathers in the management of his orchards and, above all, he has to concentrate on providing the right conditions for predators to take over the work of controlling pests.

Fungi and bacteria problems, such as canker, are kept in check by highly-skilled pruning and the use of organic sprays, including SM3 seaweed extract and herbal mixes, but even these are kept to a very few.

The grass in the orchards has a high clover content to attract bees and there are

many wild flowers that the unitiated would regard as weeds which, in fact, encourage predator insects. Some, such as rough chervil, appear to have intrinsic insecticidal properties.

Conventionally produced fruit carries to the consumer a cocktail of chemical residues from all the sprays that have been used. You would be most unwise to eat such an apple straight from the tree. It should be thoroughly washed and, preferably, peeled before being eaten, because although the individual sprays may have had safety clearance, no one knows what the cumulative effect is likely to be.

But with Gavin Cherry's organically-grown fruit, there is no risk. His apples and pears are not only safer to eat, they really do taste better. You can eat the peel as well to provide extra dietary fibre.

On the far smaller scale of the amateur top fruit gardener, growing apples and pears organically is a far easier operation and I know of no better guide than Lawrence Hills' *Good Fruit Guide*, published by the Henry Doubleday Research Association.

Discovery apples ready for picking at Gavin Cherry's organic orchard

Cox's Orange Pippin apples, organically grown at Sweetapples Orchard in Suffolk

Organic Conference pears grown by Gavin Cherry

gooseberry is grown as a cordon rather than as a bush.

November is the best month for planting gooseberries, but if the ground is waterlogged, wait until December or even February or March. In 1872, during the heyday of the gooseberry, a catalogue listed 122 varieties. Thirty years ago the choice was down to about forty, and now most nurserymen limit their stocks to the five or six most popular varieties. The old groupings were white, green, yellow and red, the latter being mid- to late-season sorts that were thinned early when green, then allowed to grow on to become large wine-red dessert berries. There were scores of varieties in each section; today it is difficult to find even three or four in each grouping. However, worth searching for are the green Invicta, Lancer and Keepsake, with Careless or its synonym Jubilee as a poor-flavoured runner-up.

The very fine-flavoured Whinham's Industry leads the red group with the port wine red Lord Derby hot on its heels. May Duke and Lancashire Lad, both reds, are fairly widely available, while Captivator is recommended for its dark red, very sweet berries and almost thornless branches. Two white with exceptionally good flavour are the mid-season Whitesmith and Langley Gage, while the yellow Golden Drop and Leveller are also noted for their fine flavour.

For the beginner with space to spare I would recommend growing one each of Invicta, Whinham's Industry, Whitesmith and Golden Drop. This means, for bush growth, planting 1.5m (5ft) apart each way in an open, sunny but sheltered site. When buying, look for two to four year old bushes that have a clean leg or stem about 15cm (6in) long. As cordons, the young stock can be planted 60cm (2ft) apart in a row, or as double cordons 90cm (3ft) apart.

Soil preparation plays a big role in the successful raising of gooseberries for the fruit is a greedy feeder with a special liking for potash. Light land should have farmyard manure or compost added before planting at the rate of a barrowload forked into the top spit. Heavy soils should be lightened by adding crushed old mortar rubble and straw as well as the manure or compost. The roots should be carefully spread out in the prepared planting holes so that they are 10 to 15cm (4 to 6in) below the surface, then the soil is trodden down firmly. Later the hoe should be used with extreme caution between the bushes otherwise the tender root network can be damaged.

In May bushes and cordons benefit from a mulch of lawn mowings, but no more manure should be given until the following spring. Thereafter a mulch, manure or compost, should be given every other year in early spring. The gooseberry dislikes drought during the late spring. When a dry spell stretches from a week into ten days, give the bushes or cordons regular watering or the ripening berries will split and spoil.

Once the bush or cordon has become established, pruning is an important and interesting part of the management. Fruit forms on both old and new wood, so one doesn't have to bother overmuch about which bits to cut back. The aim is to keep the centre of the bush open and clear of growth to help picking and the control of pests and disease. When the main framework of branches has formed, with an inverted umbrella shape, side growths should be trimmed back to three or four buds or taken off flush with the main branch.

With cordons the main stem is first cut back to buds about 30cm (1ft) or so from the ground. Wires strained between posts are needed and, as the shoots on either side of the main stem develop, they are tied in to the wires, first at forty-five degrees, then horizontally. Buds on the upper part of the horizontal shoots are trained vertically and these bear large, easily-picked berries that can be readily protected from birds.

With bushes, Scaraweb sprayed-on plastic filament offers good protection for buds and fruit, but netting is the more attractive alternative.

CURRANT FAMILY

Sharing a demise of popularity with the gooseberry are the currant family, although there are probably ten times as many blackcurrants grown in back gardens as there are white and redcurrants.

Yields of up to 4.5 to 5.4kg (10 to 12lb) per bush make currant bushes a good proposition for the amateur and they will go on producing for twelve to fifteen years. They need well-drained fertile soil with a good potash supply and a pH level of 6.5 to 7.0. The ideal site is a sunny, open one though with some shelter from east to north winds, and frost pockets should be avoided.

As with other soft fruits, currants need plenty of well-rotted manure or compost dug into the site before planting and all traces of perennial weeds removed. Established bushes should be given a dressing of wood ash or rock potash in February. There is a certification scheme for blackcurrants, but not for white or redcurrants. Try to secure two-year-old blackcurrant bushes for planting in October while there is still warmth in the soil. They will need to be about 1.5m (5ft) apart each way for most varieties, although the small Ben Sarek is happy enough at 1.2m (4ft) apart.

The roots should be well spread out and the soil returned so that the stem is slightly deeper than the soil mark. The bush is then cut back to one bud above soil level to encourage the formation of shoots from the base. Now give the bush a mulch of organic material, preferably compost or manure, repeat this every year in early spring after the dressing of wood ash or rock potash. This not only feeds the bush, but also helps to suppress

Weed control among the currant bushes using a deep (15cm/6in) layer of straw

weeds. A deep layer of straw will also control weeds. In spells of dry weather during the fruiting period from May to late July give plenty of water to encourage the berries to swell. Water round the base of the bush, not overhead.

Prune the bushes to maintain an open goblet shape, cutting out about a quarter of the wood each year. This is best done in November when any low-lying or damaged branches should also be cut out. Cuttings of hardwood are also taken at this time: simply trim the cutting so that about 15cm (6in) goes into the prepared bed with two buds remaining above soil level. If the cutting site is on the heavy side, mix plenty of sharp sand with the soil. The cuttings will have rooted after about a year. The blackcurrants are picked when the whole strig is ripe.

Recommended varieties are Ben Sarek, a new, late variety with large berries on a small bush making it an excellent choice for the smaller garden. In contrast Boskoop Giant needs at least 1.8m (6ft) planting distance each way. It is early and the flowers are susceptible to frost damage. Another large variety is Laxton's Giant, also early and very rigorous. Tsema is also vigorous and early, but can be given 1.5m (5ft) planting

distance. An old favourite, Wellington, is still widely grown. It is a mid-season sort giving a heavy crop of well-flavoured berries.

Blacksmith, Ben Nevis and Ben Lomond are three good mid-season varieties, all giving good crops of large berries.

The late sorts are Baldwin, Ben More and Jet, the latter being a more vigorous grower than the other two and so less suitable for the small garden.

The same general needs in management are required for redcurrants and whitecurrants, although I prefer to grow the reds and the whites as cordons or fan-trained against a south-facing fence or wall. This enables one to give them protection from frost, strong winds and the attention of birds.

Recommended varieties for redcurrants, and in order of cropping, are: Jonkheer van Tets, Laxton's No 1, Red Lake, one of the best flavoured of the reds, Stanza, Rondom and Wilson's Long Bunch. Whitecurrants are White Grape, White Dutch and White Versailles.

The Medana tayberry was raised by the Scottish Crop Research Institute by crossing the Aurora blackberry with a tetraploid raspberry. The fruit is excellent for desserts, jam-making and freezing

BLACKBERRY AND THE HYBRID BERRIES

The problem with most of them is the room they need to give of their best. Blackberries, for instance, need room to stretch 4.5m (15ft) with 2m (7ft) between rows. The hybrids need 3m (10ft) at least and 1.8m (6ft) between rows. All grow best in an organically enriched soil where there is full sun. There are now many of these hybrid berries – boysenberry, marionberry, worcesterberry, youngberry, veitchberry, nectarberry, and so on, but the tayberry I reckon to be the best. It is a Scottish invention, a cross between a blackberry and raspberry and was made by the Scottish Crop Research Institute.

The tayberries are large, rather like long loganberries, have a delicious flavour, and it is extremely unlikely that you will ever see them in the greengrocer's because they are too delicate to pack and market. You train the tayberry as you would a blackberry, planting it where it can spread laterally up to 4.5m (15ft) with horizontal wires strained between posts for support. Cut back the newly-planted cane to about 45cm (18in) and thereafter cut out all the fruited wood in late autumn, as you do with raspberries, and train the new canes when they are mature to the horizontal wires.

One of the best ways of training the tayberry or any briar fruit is fan fashion. The one-year-old fruiting canes are splayed out in a fan and tied to the wires, while the new canes are allowed to grow up to the centre and are tied in at fortnightly intervals. When they reach the top wire they are tied down so that they extend horizontally. When the fruited wood is cut out, the new canes are untied from their central position and re-tied to the wires in fan fashion.

A limited certification scheme for briar fruit covers only the Ashton Cross blackberry, the tayberry and sunberry.

12

PEST AND DISEASE CONTROL

For the gardener used to reaching for a bottle of a chemical firm's wonder brew the moment greenfly or blackfly or caterpillers appear on the vegetables, flowers or shrubs, the organic way of life might seem several steps backward. Giving up dependence on poisonous sprays can seem like giving up smoking: the spirit is willing enough, but the first arrival of unfriendly insects finds the flesh very weak. But in preventing crop damage without recourse to chemicals, the organic gardener can use several techniques:

• Organically-grown plants invariably have vigour and strength to shrug off attacks by run-of-the-mill pests and in this they are aided by the natural predators of the pests which are given every encouragement.

• Soil-borne diseases can largely be controlled by rotation of the vegetable crops, while biological controls are the most promising hope for some of those diseases where rotation is ineffective.

• Knowledge of the life cycle of pests enables preventive action to be taken before damage begins.

• When necessary, timely and minimum use of biological controls, and safe pesticides and fungicides.

That organically-grown crops have an inbuilt ability to withstand attack by pests and diseases is not an opinion, it's a fact. It's like the sad fact of human life – when people are under-nourished they are more open to attack by illness and less able to make a good recovery. So a well-fed soil is a prerequisite to healthy crops which also need adequate living space with the optimum of light and moisture.

Whenever possible the organic gardener should raise his or her own brassica plants to avoid introducing the dreaded disease of clubroot, for which at present there is no cure. Brussels sprouts, cabbages, cauliflowers, kale, kohl rabi, turnips, swedes, radishes and wallflowers are all liable to attack. The only remedy, once the disease has struck, is to starve the dormant fungus spores of clubroot by ensuring that brassicas are not grown on the same patch of land more than once in three years.

The mealy cabbage aphis and cabbage white fly both overwinter among the brassicas, so when your Brussels sprouts are finished, along with the purple sprouting broccoli, the kale, and so on, dig out the stumps to use in the trench composting method described on page 30.

Good housekeeping in the garden – or hygiene, if you prefer to call it that – is another way to ward off pests and diseases. Slugs abound where there is garden debris, so don't leave piles of plant waste and leaves scattered around the garden: get the material on to the compost heap or store it in plastic sacks until you've enough to add to the compost.

Try to give all the woodwork in the garden an annual treatment with wood preservative, preferably during the winter when this will keep shed walls and the fences free of cabbage white butterfly pupae. Flea beetles, pea and bean weevils, wireworms and slugs will take up residence in patches of weeds, particularly at the foot of fences and walls and under soft fruit bushes, so always keep these areas weeded. Grease band fruit trees to protect them against apple capsids and codling moths.

Unfortunately, however careful we are to prevent pests and diseases we have no control over what our neighbours do and we may have to make use of one of the safe control measures. Potato blight, for example, is a most dangerous disease if it is allowed to go unchecked. The disease overwinters in infected tubers left in the soil, and the main source is from farms where any number of potatoes may be missed by the mechanical harvester. If you've been touched by blight, it is very important to lift every tuber of your potato crop, however small; while if you have an allotment or your garden is in a vulnerable rural area, it is prudent to spray your potato crop once a fortnight from July onwards with Bordeaux mixture.

ROTATION

Rotation prevents a build up of diseases such as clubroot, onion white rot, and pests such as potato cyst eelworm. At the same time it helps to ensure that vital plant foods are not poached by one group of vegetables to the detriment of others.

As we have already noted, pea and bean crops have the ability to put nitrogen into the soil, so if you can follow those crops with leafy ones, such as lettuce and cabbage, they will benefit from the extra nitrogen made available to them. Only you can decide the best rotation plan for your individual vegetable plot or allotment because it will depend on the size of cropping area, the scale of your growing, and the sorts of crops you grow according to your personal needs and the limitations of soil and climate in your district.

As a general rule, though, rotation involves dividing the vegetable plot into three parts. In part one will be the general group of peas, beans, onions, leeks, shallots, marrows, courgettes, cucumbers, tomatoes and sweetcorn. In the second part will be the brassicas, while the third section will carry the root crops, including, maybe, potatoes. Lettuce, parsley, spinach or Swiss chard could be fitted in with the first or third groups. With compost-fed soil you can safely sow both carrots and parsnips without fear that the roots will fork.

NATURAL CONTROLS

One of the best preventive measures against pests is to encourage natural predators. Many of the chemical control methods have gone badly wrong by ignoring this simple fact: if you kill

Encourage birds to the garden so
that they will help to keep pests
under control. A bird table, such
as this, if kept supplied daily with
food from September to March,
will attract a wide variety of birds

all the pests, then though the insecticide might have spared the predators you may have starved them to death. Early in the year, for instance, predatory beetles play an important part in controlling aphids, while in late summer and autumn ladybirds are a major natural control of aphid infestation. So any chemical control which affected the ability of these natural predators to do their work is not the boon to the grower that it's cracked up to be, but harmful.

We often forget that birds are the natural predators of most insect pests. Consider this. A pair of swallows rearing five youngsters must collect at least 8,000 insects a day for up to 20 days to feed their brood, and a patient ornithologist who carried out a survey on a pair of dunnocks with a brood in his garden found that they each fed grubs, mostly garden pests, at the rate of seventy an hour for sixteen hours a day. So each bird was eliminating about 1,120 insects a day.

You can start helping the birds to help you in January. If the soil is workable, lightly fork over the ground of your vegetable plot. This will enable the robins, blackbirds and thrushes to eat the chrysalids of cabbage, carrot and onion flies. Fork the ground also among the raspberry canes to turn up the larvae of the raspberry beetle.

Insecticidal soap, pyrethrum, derris and quassia are organic products capable of controlling a wide range of pests. They are non-persistent and non-systematic, so early spraying and repeated applications may be necessary.

With greenhouse pests biological controls, using natural predators, are now the normal technique and are an example of how the organic movement can come up with a novel idea that eventually wins acceptance by even the most stubborn inorganic growers.

Too often the manufacturers of agricultural chemicals have discovered their miracle brew, capable of killing just about every pest of every crop, leads to the emergence of resistant strains of the insect pests, so new and even more potent chemical compounds have to be devised. In contrast, the pest control methods of the organic gardener are designed to provide the safest possible way of dealing with the problem – safest for mankind, safest for wildlife, particularly the birds, bees, hedgehogs, frogs and toads, and safest also for the soil and its teeming population of gardening friends, the earthworms and micro-organisms that help to make the soil a living entity.

For everyone in the organic movement, in fact for all of us with concern for a cleaner, safer planet, the work by plant pathologists on biological weapons to fight plant diseases is both important and exciting. It uses nature's controls rather than chemical compounds. Parallel in importance is the breeding of varieties resistant to disease, a branch or research in which British scientists have made many major contributions. A good example of what the future holds in biological control

techniques is the investigation of bacteria and fungi to fight off fusarium wilt, rhizoctonia and some dangerous types of pythium. This research is being led in America by Professor Ralph Baker at Colorado State University, Fort Collins, and he told me: 'The potential for biological control of disease is absolutely incredible. We are developing new techniques as alternatives to conventional chemical fungicides to offer growers a radically different approach to controlling a wide range of diseases in horticultural crops.'

So, although the commercial growers will be the first to benefit from this work, and I don't quarrel with that, in time the techniques should be available to amateur gardeners everywhere.

Fighting wilt, a very damaging soil-borne disease, with bacteria (a strain of *Pseudomonas bacterium*) is particularly impressive because the fungi causing the disease can survive in the soil for at least nine years and so control by rotation isn't

As well as being a focal point of a garden, a pool will encourage frogs and toads to take up residence as slug control experts

feasible. It was found that where pseudomonas bacteria were present in high enough numbers – and it exists in a wide range of soils – the fusarium fungus was unable to compete. According to Professor Baker:

What we needed to discover was whether the pseudomonas bacteria had to be artificially introduced or whether the natural population could be induced to expand.

To germinate, a fusarium spore needs carbon, nitrogen and iron. As the root of a susceptible host plant grows through the soil it exudes reducing sugars and amino acids which supply the carbon and nitrogen.

Iron is not exuded. It has to come from the soil, and the amount of iron available decreases as the soil pH increases. We know that pseudomonas produces iron-requiring compounds called siderophores, so if it is put into the soil it searches for iron and so comes into direct competition with the disease-causing fungus. This is how it is starved of its iron supply.

So the professor demonstrated that by dipping the roots of

carnations, raised in a bed in a glasshouse infected with fusarium wilt, in a mixture of pseudomonas and iron chelate before planting out, the rate of infection dropped from thirty-five per cent to ten per cent.

Similar work is being done by Professor John Coley-Smith and Hull University's department of biology and plant genetics on the control of onion white rot and, I've no doubt, other significant developments in biological control are happening elsewhere in the world.

PUBLIC CONCERN

Another development that has come in the wake of the British Government's tougher legislation on the use of insecticides, fungicides and herbicides is the evident desire of some agro-chemical manufacturers to be more sympathetic to the mounting public concern over poisonous sprays.

At an Institute of Horticulture conference in 1986 on the implications of the new legislation, chaired by Professor John

Bleasedale, director of the National Vegetable Research Station, the UK's biggest manufacturer, ICI, was represented by Mr Chris Major, of the plant protection division. According to the *Grower* trade magazine, he told delegates that the market worldwide for pesticides at 1986 figures was worth 12.8 billion US dollars, of which fruit and vegetable protection accounted for nearly three billion dollars (23 per cent). Of the total, 39 per cent was represented by herbicides, 33 per cent by insecticides, and 22 per cent by fungicides.

While the market for new pesticides is undoubtedly huge, said Mr Major, so, too, are the development costs. Bringing a new pesticide to market could involve seven years work from the discovery of a new chemical and cost about £15 million or, exceptionally, as much as £30 million.

If this wasn't enough, said Mr Major, manufacturers and, to an extent, the users of pesticides, faced an increasingly hostile anti-pesticide lobby which mounted demonstrations like parading a coffin outside the headquarters of the British Agrochemicals Association to express opposition to exports of pesticides to Third World countries. Pressure groups had grown dramatically in the past twenty years and it was important 'that users did not exacerbate the protesters'.

He said ICI was collaborating with Friends of the Earth in an 'audit' of the company's pesticide operations and expected to gain as much from the exercise as the protesters. He believed that the aims of both sides were compatible and that a priority for the pesticide industry was product stewardship which meant clear labelling, explicit promotion material and a central reference service.

'What matters,' he concluded, 'is perceived public interest and safer pesticides is the industry's goal as much as anyone else's.'

That conciliatory attitude is in marked contrast to a speech made about the same time by Sir Emrys Jones. Opening a new packing station for Lincolnshire cauliflower growers in October 1986, he made a most astonishing and gratuitous attack on the organic movement.

'Avoid organic and natural food at all costs,' he said. 'You can be sure it is deficient in some essential factor. Don't turn the clock back.'

'In my youth when we had only farmyard manure and basic slag to apply to crops, we had a poor diet and constantly suffered from sore throats and other ailments,' he went on.

'I only want to eat the best and my food must be protected against pests with chemicals and given the right fertilisers. Farmyard manure is forbidden in my garden, and my wife is not allowed to buy anything labelled organic.'

I was assured by officials that this wasn't an attempt at humour, it was intended to be taken seriously. And that is ominous until one discovers Sir Emrys Jones' track record.

He was for many years head of ADAS, the agricultural advisory service of the Ministry of Agriculture, which has been so pre-occupied with chemical solutions to all agricultural and horticultural problems that advice on the organic alternatives is not available from the advisory officers. Sir Emrys was also president for a long spell of the British Crop Protection Council which is very largely devoted to pest control by pesticides although its objects are 'To promote and encourage the science and practice of pest, disease and weed control and allied subjects' which, presumably, should embrace mechanical methods and biological control.

The view of the BCPC seems to be that as pesticides do the job, there's no point in wasting time on alternative methods of control, even though biological control often can do the job more cheaply and certainly far more safely.

One of the first things to appreciate about the problem of pests and disease in plants is that it is very largely a manmade one.

Man has created a symbiotic relationship with plants that provide him with food and so we have the phenomenon of vast areas of land given over to one crop at a time, wheat for example, or a large field of nothing but cabbages. Even our gardens are expected to produce a relatively few crops very intensively. And so we have made it incredibly easy for the pests of our food crops to find their hosts, because as well as being food for man, those crops will quite naturally be a source of food for insects and other wildlife. Man, his crops and the crop pests are dependent on each other.

In *The Constant Pest* George Ordish's history of pests and their control, the author says:

The earwig is a much-maligned insect. An adult will eat up to 100 aphids a day, along with maggots and small caterpillars. To encourage earwigs in the organic garden Peter Langdon designed this earwig nest. Hung among the flowers and vegetables, it provides biological control over several insect pests, but it is probably wise to keep it away from the prize chrysanthemums and dahlias

The farmer is encouraged in the belief that if he left off using pesticides the alternatives would be worse. That they would be cheaper and better is not generally realised.

So far very little or nothing has been done on the breeding of new varieties of insects for specific pest control purposes. That insects can be bred to man's advantage in the same way as horse and hound is seen in the cases of bees, silkworms and fighting crickets, where great improvements have been made. It has not yet been tried in biological control, but no doubt soon will be.

In 1794 Erasmus Darwin, grandfather of Charles, said that the best control for aphids would be the artificial propagation of the predators – the lacewings and ladybirds.

TRADITIONAL CONTROLS

Some pest control techniques, still in use today, are very old indeed. Grease banding of trees and vines to protect them from insect pests is referred to by Cato (234–149 BC) in his great book on agriculture *De Re Rustica*. The grease was made by boiling down bitumen, sulphur and olive oil sediment, while banding to deter ants was done with a mixture of red earth and tar.

Reading George Ordish's book I was interested to learn that the value of urine, often referred to as chamber lye, has long been recognised. Alexandre Henri Tessier in 1783 described it as the cheapest and most successful way of curing wheat bunt or smut. It was used as a seed dressing and the process was called brining the seed.

Pepper dust and tobacco dust were recommended by Phillip Miller (1691–1771) in his *Gardeners Dictionary* for use against insect pests on fruit trees. His pupil William Forsyth (1757–1804) wrote *A Treatise on the Culture and Management of Fruit Trees* in 1802 in which he recommended soap and urine as a highly-effective insecticide – and it still is today, while for canker the cure was to cut away the diseased parts to healthy wood and then dress the wounds with Forsyth's Compound made from dung, lime, ashes and sand.

For many years I've used just soapy water to fight aphids on the rose bushes. It needs application with a pressure sprayer, but works extremely well. By the end of the eighteenth century spraying with garden engines was practised and plain rainwater was recommended to deal with aphids, although nicotine spray was considered the most effective insecticide.

Cordon, espalier and fan-trained fruit trees were cleared of aphid infestation by putting a tent over them and blowing in tobacco smoke from a bellows, while potted plants could be put in smoke boxes filled with tobacco smoke.

Bordeaux mixture, made from copper sulphate and lime, was 'discovered' in 1885 as a control for grape downy mildew and potato blight, but had actually been invented forty years earlier by Charles Morren at Liege University.

Lime sulphur was invented in 1852 by Monsieur Grison, head greenhouse gardener at the Palace of Versailles when the royal grapes were attacked by powdery mildew. He boiled lime and sulphur together, let the liquid cool, then diluted it with water and sprayed it on the vines with a syringe or 'garden engine'. He called his invention Eau Grison.

A little later Professor Duchatre, of Versailles, discovered that powdered sulphur, blown over the vines, controlled the disease, a simple treatment used extensively today.

James Duncan in *The Naturalists' Library* of about 1850 wrote about the voracity of the cabbage white caterpillars and recommended the use of ducks or 'a seagull with the wings cut so that it cannot fly away'. He said he had one in his garden for eight years and that 'it lived entirely all the while upon the insects, slugs and worms it found in the garden' along with cabbage white butterflies he caught in a net.

RECENT TRENDS

The two World Wars demonstrated the vulnerability of the British Isles to blockade by sea. World War II, in particular, saw the highest priority given to home production of food with farmer, allotment holder and householder all being urged to Dig for Victory. Common land, village greens and public parks in towns and cities were requisitioned for food production, mainly as allotments, and the contribution they made to wartime self-sufficiency was massive.

It was impossible to provide enough organic fertilisers and compost to sustain that magnificent war effort towards self-sufficiency, so the British Government decreed that a national fertiliser (Growmore) would be formulated and used. This was a balanced fertiliser with seven per cent each of nitrogen, phosphorus and potash. For many thousands of gardeners, until then used to traditional farmyard muck and compost for manuring their land, this was the start of the honeymoon with chemical fertilisers.

Coincidentally, World War II saw some remarkable developments in pest control by chemicals and the discovery of selective weedkillers. They were compounds of undreamt-of potency and persistence compared with everything that had gone before and the magic initials DDT, BHC and MCPA entered the language of the food producers.

'These two new classes of pesticides, the organo-chlorine compounds and selective herbicides, give an immense boost to the pest control trade,' says George Ordish. 'Chemical manufacturers welcomed them not only because they extended their business, but also because it gave them an outlet for surplus chlorine gas.'

One of the problems of applying a pesticide to a crop had been the difficulty in ensuring that every bit of a plant was covered by the control material. A German discovery overcame this difficulty, as George Ordish explains:

During the war research into new toxic gases led to the isolation of highly poisonous organo-phosphorus compounds. After the war some of these were found to be insecticidal and systemic in plants. That is, the products could be absorbed by one portion of a plant and translocated to all parts of it, without doing the plant any harm, yet making it toxic for insects. Spraying no longer had to be perfect.

Soon a whole range of organo-phosphorus insecticides was on the market and agriculture appeared to be entering the pest-free millenium.

Surprisingly, that millenium did not arrive. Strains of insects and fungi resistant to the new chemicals began to appear, and the destruction of the predators along with the pests meant that, even a few survivors of a chemical treatment could quickly build up to a damaging population, needing another treatment. The pesticide bonanza in which a pest species was destroyed led to the appearance of a hitherto harmless species as a new pest.

In 1962 Rachel Carson's book *Silent Spring* polarised public opinion about the use of pesticides into those for and those against although she, herself, only pleaded that pesticides should be used with far greater care. George Ordish says:

In my view the use of pesticides has been attacked and denigrated for the wrong reasons. Their use should be avoided not because they are an 'interference with nature', but because they are so expensive compared with biological control and pest management. Pesticides should only be used as a last resort, when no other methods will do, as is more likely to be the case in future.

That seems to me to be an eminently fair and sensible view with which only but the extremists on either side of the pro- and anti-pesticide argument will disagree. With that in mind, the following advice on pest and disease control by organic means should be read as the state of play in 1988.

The previous forty years saw more major changes in every aspect of our lives than in the previous 400 years and no doubt the years to come to the end of the twentieth century have many tremendous advances in store, including crop protection techniques.

Certain to be in the forefront will be genetically-engineered crops with built-in resistance to pests and diseases. This is bound to be bad news for those in the agro-chemical industry, and will the organic diehards, I wonder, shun it as an interference with nature?

THE SAFE CONTROLS

It is a fact of life that there are times in the garden when, despite all precautions, pest and disease become a problem. In the spring, for example, the aphid population can multiply very rapidly as the temperature rises above 10°C (50°F), but there are relatively few ladybird predators about to sort them out. Similarly, on apple and plum trees, currant and gooseberry bushes powdery mildew can gain a hold during the growing season almost by stealth.

At times like this the organic gardener brings into use the safe alternatives to the conventional agro-chemical sprays: safe because they are naturally-occurring substances that are non-systemic and non-residual.

For ease of reference the more commonly encountered pests and diseases and their controls are listed but first, a few words about the principal controls.

Biological control

Now recognised as the branch of pest control with the biggest potential for development but already showing some outstanding successes in the control of greenhouse pests, notably whitefly and red spider mite.

The biological control of whitefly utilises a parasitic chalcid wasp called *Encarsia formosa* which inserts its eggs into the whitefly eggs found on the underside of the leaves of the tomato and cucumber plants. The parasitised eggs turn black as the wasps develop and after about two weeks the wasps emerge and seek out more whitefly larvae or scales as they are sometimes called.

The wasp is only about the size of a pinhead and is absolutely harmless to anything except its whitefly prey and when it has eradicated all the whitefly in the greenhouse it dies.

The encarsia are introduced into the greenhouse as eggs on strips of card and full instructions are given by the supplying firm (see list of suppliers).

Trichoderma viride (Binab T) pellets give biological control of silver leaf disease of fruit trees, while in wettable powder form it is used to make a paste to protect tree pruning wounds from fungal attack. The pellets are placed in pre-drilled holes in the tree at any time from February to April with the holes drilled every 10cm (4in) in a spiral round the tree.

Binab T pellets and powder can be bought from HDRA and full instructions are given on the use of the products.

The naturally-occurring pathogen *Bacillus thuringiensis* formulated as Bactospeine WP or BiobiT, is today by far the best and safest way of controlling caterpillar pests in all crops, including cabbages, tomatoes and cucumbers. It is a bacterial culture made from the spores of the bacillus and is supplied in

The safe controls: liquid and powder derris, insecticidal soap, pyrethrum and Bordeaux powder

sachets each of which makes five litres of spray. The solution is sprayed on to the leaves where the caterpillars are eating. It is entirely specific to caterpillars, so will not harm insects, birds, fish, pets or humans. *Bacillus thuringiensis* is most effective on young caterpillars and should be applied as soon as they appear on the crops. To maintain control it may prove necessary to repeat the spray after about eight days.

On cabbage, Brussels sprouts and other brassica plants it is advisable to use a wetting agent with the solution because this will ensure thorough coverage of the leaves, particularly the undersides.

An important point to remember is that large caterpillars may take three to five days to die after the application of the spray, so allow that sort of interval before cutting a cabbage for the kitchen.

Red spider mite control in greenhouse crops such as tomatoes, cucumbers, roses, chrysanthemums, strawberries and pot plants is effected very readily by a predator, *Phytoseiulus persimilis* which itself is a spider mite. It is orange coloured and very fast moving and has a very healthy appetite for its prey, eating at least five red spiders a day and many eggs.

Mealy bug, another commonly encountered pest of indoor pot plants and greenhouse crops is controlled by a ladybird predator *Cryptolaemus montrouzieri*. The female lays eggs among the mealy bugs and, after about two weeks, the larvae emerge. They are white and furry and have a fearsome appetite for mealy bugs, eating up to 300 during the two to three week period before they pupate.

Leaf miners can be controlled using the parasites *Opius pallipes* and *Dacnusa sibirica* and these can be used in conjunction with encarsia for whitefly control. By the way, where the whitefly infestation is quite low, sticky yellow traps have been found very effective. Cards coated with yellow paint and non-drying glue are hung among the tomato or cucumber plants where they attract both whitefly and adult leaf miners.

Another promising development in biological control is the use of pheromones. These are the substances secreted and released by animals and insects to attract mates and can obviously be used as bait in insect traps. A good example is the pheromone developed by scientists at Rothamsted Experimental Station to combat the pea moth whose larvae penetrate the immature pea pod and cause maggoty peas.

Pea moths overwinter in the soil as larvae. They pupate in early May and the adults emerge in late May, in June and July. They mate and the eggs hatch about fourteen days later and the larvae hurry into the pea pods. There they fatten on the peas for about three weeks, emerge, fall to the ground, spin a cocoon and overwinter. Control by insecticide is, therefore, a bit tricky because you have to catch the larvae after the hatching but before they enter the pea pods. At Rothamsted they have been able to synthesise the chemical exuded by the female moths to attract the males. This pheromone is place in sticky traps set among the pea plants to catch the males. Commercial growers then spray with a short-acting insecticide to kill any larvae that have resulted from matings by males that missed the traps.

LACEY'S LORE

BETTER CONTROL

You can improve the effectiveness of biological control of whitefly in your greenhouse by putting a fine mesh net over the ventilation openings. This reduces very considerably the number of adult whitefly entering the greenhouse and so enables the *Encarsia formosa* parasites to do their job more effectively.

It should have no effect on temperature or humidity, according to trials at Naples University in Italy.

Derris

This was originally used as a fish poison in Malaya and South America, although it has been widely known and used as an insecticide for more than 100 years. It is derived from the leguminous tropical plant *Derris elliptica*. The root is ground to produce the active ingredient, a powerful alkaloid, rotenone.

It can be used as a powder or liquid and controls aphids, red spider mite, weevils and caterpillars. It is harmless to warm-blooded animals, but deadly to fish so must never be used near to garden or farm ponds, lakes or rivers. It breaks down quickly and is non-persistent.

Nicotine

Not a safe insecticide because it is a deadly poison at high concentrations. It is extracted from the dried tobacco leaf and has been used as an insecticide since the middle of the eighteenth century. It is a contact poison which penetrates the insect's cuticle and controls a wide range of pests yet spares ladybirds and hoverfly larvae. The Soil Association no longer approves of this poison, and it has been withdrawn from sale by the Henry Doubleday Research Association.

Potassium permanganate

A combined insecticide and fungicide which I have found too weak to be effective against anything other than a small colony of aphids. It is a good tool to use against powdery mildew, however, and used at the rate of 28g in 9 litres (1oz in 2gal) of water is non-tainting on food crops.

It can be bought from the High Street chemist in granule form for mixing yourself.

Pyrethrum

This insecticide is prepared from the flowers of *Chrysanthemum cinerariifolium*, grown as a commercial crop in Zimbabwe, although it has been in use for centuries. It is less long-lasting than derris so can safely be used on crops to be eaten the next day. It is devoid of phytotoxicity so it will not harm any plant, but is harmful to ladybirds, ladybird larvae and bees, so spray in the evening if crops are in flower. It gives a rapid knock-down. It paralyses the insect, but after a small dose the insect may recover, so the dose might have to be increased slightly.

Sunlight and air cause rapid loss of toxicity, though pyrethrum is more stable in an emulsifier. It is non-toxic to human beings and other warm-blooded creatures; however, there have been cases of it causing fits in cats. It is harmful also to fish so do not spray near to pools and ponds or, indoors, the fish tank.

Controls greenfly, blackfly and other aphids, including strawberry aphids, thrips and ants, sawfly, weevils, leaf hoppers, flea beetles and capsids.

Quassia

The safest of the safe insecticides because it will not harm bees, ladybirds, ladybird larvae and eggs, and Anthocoris. It is sold as chips of wood from the tropical tree *Picrasma excelsa* and can be bought from some chemists and HDRA.

The chips are made into a control against small caterpillars and all aphids by simmering 28g (1oz) in 1.1 litres (2pt) water for two hours, topping up as required. Strain off the liquid and add 28g (1oz) soft soap or soap flakes.

For aphids dilute the mixture with five parts of water, while for gooseberry and apple sawflies and small caterpillars dilute the liquid with three parts of water.

At the stronger concentration it can be sprayed on gooseberry bushes to act as a repellent to birds that take the buds, however it is easily washed off by rain, so repeated applications may be necessary.

Soap

The insecticidal properties of ordinary soapy water should be more widely known because it would undoubtedly save inorganic gardeners a small fortune in poisonous sprays and save many helpful insects into the bargain.

I've used nothing but soapy water as a spray on my roses for many years and have never had more than minor trouble with aphids. Soft soap, a pharmaceutical product used as a liquid in enemas, is a very safe and very effective insecticide to control brassica whitefly and cabbage white caterpillars. Dissolve 56g

LACEY'S LORE

ICE ON POOLS

In winter if ice persists, fish in the garden pool might die through lack of oxygen. Melt a hole by standing a saucepan of boiling water on the surface.

Float rubber balls in concrete-lined pools to prevent cracks from the pressure of the ice.

(2oz) in 4.5 litres (1gal) hot water and use diluted when cool enough. Soft soap can be bought from HDRA.

Savona insecticidal soap is a relatively new product for the control of aphids, whitefly, red spider mite and scale insects. It is perfectly safe to human beings, mammals, bees, ladybirds and other predators and is recommended for use in greenhouses before the introduction of biological controls if there are high pest levels. It is diluted with fifty parts of rainwater and is now widely available from garden shops.

DO-IT-YOURSELF SPRAYS

There are any number of recipes for home-made pesticides, many of them handed down over the centuries (and some of doubtful efficacy).

For example, an old remedy to deter snails and slugs is to collect as many as possible, morning and evening. Tip them into a bucket of boiling water and let it stand for a few days until the smell becomes fearsome, then strain off the liquid and use it to sprinkle round vulnerable plants, such as the young growth of delphiniums, lettuce and so on – but not on them. The remains of the slugs and snails can also be scattered.

What I recommend with this and the following DIY sprays is that you try them. If they work for you, that's fine. If they don't, use one of the safe insecticides.

Bracken spray

Effective against blackfly on, for example, broad beans and runner beans but not against cherry blackfly.

The bracken must be gathered when brown and brittle dry. Pulp the leaves and store in paper bags until wanted. Using a graduated jar, measure out 120cc (4fl oz) of the bracken and pour on 420cc (14fl oz) of hot water, stir and allow to soak for twenty-four hours, strain, then bottle into airtight jars and keep out of reach of children, of course.

For use as a spray, dilute 25cc (1fl oz) to 4.5 litres (1gal) of rainwater and spray each day for three days.

Elder spray

This kills aphids, small caterpillars and is useful as a fungicide for mildew and blackspot on roses. The toxic agent is hydrocyanic acid, so in preparing the spray use an old saucepan.

Gather 450g (1lb) leaves and young stems of elder preferably in spring when the sap is rising. Place in the saucepan and add 3.3 litres (6pt) water. Boil for half an hour, topping up as necessary. Strain through old tights and use the liquid cold and undiluted. It will keep for three months if bottled tightly while still hot.

Twigs of elder, cut in the spring and placed at intervals, inverted V-wise, over early turnip rows, are said to ward off attack by flea beetles.

Horsetail tea

Horsetail (*Equisetum arvense*) is a pernicious weed which spreads by underground stems which may go down as deep as ten feet, forming horizontal rhizome systems at intervals. This makes it particularly difficult to control. If you have a horsetail problem, there's a bright side to it because an infusion of the weed makes a good fungicide for control of mildew on strawberries and other crops, and checks rust on celery and celeriac.

Collect the horsetail, foliage, stems, rhizomes and all, and for each 28g (1oz) pour on 1.1 litres (2pt) hot, not boiling, water, and allow to stand for twenty-four hours. Strain off the 'tea' and use undiluted.

Nettle spray

Bio-dynamic gardeners and growers have a very high regard for the common stinging nettle, using the leaves in sprays of several kinds. As well as using nettles as an activator on the compost heap (page 27) the organic gardener can use them as a liquid manure and as an aphicide.

Gather 224g (½lb) young nettles and soak in a bucket of water for a week. Strain and use undiluted as a control of aphids on roses and celery leaf miner. Add the mushy nettles to the compost heap.

Rhubarb spray

The oxalic acid in rhubarb leaves is a safe control agent for aphids, particularly those on roses. Cut 450g (1lb) rhubarb leaves, place in an old saucepan with 1.1 litres (2pt) water and boil for half an hour, topping up as necessary. When cool, add 1dsp soap flakes dissolved in 275ml (½pt) warm water. This acts as the wetting agent when added to the strained rhubarb liquid. Stir the mixture thoroughly and use undiluted as a spray.

Soap spray

Use the recipe on page 140 as an effective weapon against aphids on many crops.

Seaweed spray

The value of seaweed as a liquid manure is described on page 43. Used as a foliar feed on a wide range of vegetable crops, it also has an insecticidal and fungicidal effect possibly because the alginates make the surface of the foliage less attractive to pests and the spores of fungi.

ORGANIC FUNGICIDES

Bordeaux mixture

This was discovered in 1845, but not used as a fungicide until 1885 when it was found to control downy mildew. It is the most important preventative of potato blight and is made from copper sulphate and lime. Applied before the fungus spores of blight settle on the leaves, the copper sulphate gradually releases small amounts of soluble copper which kills the germinating spores. It is equally effective in preventing blight attack on tomatoes outdoors.

Burgundy mixture

Substantially the same as Bordeaux mixture, but the lime is replaced by washing soda. It can be used as a prevention against mildew on roses and gooseberries by spraying the bushes in January.

Potassium permanganate

A combined pesticide and fungicide that offers some control over aphids and powdery mildew on roses, delphiniums, chrysanthemums and other plants.

Sulphur

Usually sold as flowers of sulphur or yellow sulphur, it is also available as a brand-named spray for control of black spot on roses, powdery mildew and scab on fruit vegetables and ornamentals. It can harm parasitic wasps and predatory mites.

Also available as a combined insecticide and fungicide when mixed with lime. It is used as a winter wash on fruit trees and is useful in controlling big bud and other mites.

Urine

Used neat it is an effective winter wash for soft and top fruit. For gooseberry mildew use 0.5 litre (1pt) urine to 3.9 litres (7pt) hot water into which 84g (3oz) washing soda and 28g (1oz) soap flakes have been dissolved. Spray when cool.

A–Z OF PESTS
AND DISEASES

ANTS

I may be wrong, but I believe ants are only a problem when they leave the garden and enter the house, usually in search of something sweet. If you feel that extermination is then necessary, a proprietary inorganic killer, such as Nippon ant powder, will do the deed. Alternatively, you can buy 112g (4oz) of borax from the High Street chemist, mix it with 112g (4oz) of castor sugar and sprinkle it along the ants' route.

In the garden the harm that ants do – mostly stealing newly sown seeds – is outweighed by their helpfulness in destroying pests and aerating the soil.

APHIDS

If you ask the man in the street which pest in his garden is most troublesome, his answer nine times out of ten is 'greenfly'. That's not my personal polling but one of the findings in a survey conducted by one of the chemical companies.

In fact, greenfly or aphids, are not totally destructive, some even serve quite useful purposes in the garden. The snag is there are so many of them: probably every cultivated plant in the garden is host at some time to its own species of aphid, and if you would like a fascinating and very readable insight into the life and times of this enormous family of insects, get hold of a copy of Jennifer Owen's book *Garden Life*.

Aphids multiply exceedingly quickly, so early control is

desirable. Fortunately, there are several very effective organic aphicides and it is always best to choose the safest that will do the trick without harming the predators. Ordinary soapy water is usually satisfactory, but will need to be repeated several times and is best applied through a pressure sprayer. Quassia, rhubarb spray and elder spray are also effective and safe. Do not use derris or pyrethrum because that would would be like taking a sledge-hammer to crack a nut.

APPLE CANKER

Frequently encountered disease where trees have received over-generous amounts of nitrogenous fertiliser. It also affects pear trees, poplars and hawthorn. Canker appears as lesions on small side branches and, eventually, the lesions girdle the branch causing dieback of the wood. The fungus may develop creamy pustules in the summer, while in autumn and winter there are red bodies on the lesions. The fungus may also damage the fruit while still on the tree.

Prevention of canker is difficult on wet, clay soils, although grassing between the trees is helpful. If you inherit badly-cankered trees, the best plan is to grub them out and burn all the wood. Mildly cankered branches should be cut back to clean, healthy wood and the wounds painted with Trichoderma paste, and never leave diseased fruit hanging on the trees.

Bramley's Seedling and Newton Wonder are fairly resistant to canker.

Aphids on a young shoot of a rose bush. At this stage the pest is easily controlled by spraying with soapy water

APPLE SAWFLY

This small insect resembles a flying ant, while the larvae look like caterpillars which tunnel into the fruitlets in spring and gave rise to the saying: There's only one thing worse than biting into an apple and finding a maggot, and that's finding half a maggot.

Sawfly attack causes premature dropping of the fruit, external scarring, as well as the mess the larvae make inside the fruit. Worcester Pearmain, James Grieve, Ellison's Orange and Charles Ross are varieties particularly prone to attack.

Control of sawfly is by spraying with derris a week after petal fall.

APPLE SCAB

Just about the most commonly encountered disease of apples, with some varieties, including Cox's Orange Pippin, particularly prone. Because it causes blemishes on the fruit, commercial growers go to great lengths to fight scab, but the amateur grower, less concerned to have the cosmetic finish beloved of supermarket managers, is generally not too bothered with fruit that has a slight corky skin surface.

The spores of the fungus causing scab overwinter on fallen leaves, so in the autumn and winter all fallen leaves should be collected and buried or turned into leafmould (see page 28). Some organic growers spray at bud burst to control scab, using one part urine and one part water. An alternative is to spray with Bordeaux mixture at pink bud stage and again four weeks later.

BEAN WEEVIL

These little creatures, rather like beetles with snouts, eat the leaves of broan beans, giving them scalloped edges. They don't do any significant harm, so I don't bother them and they then move on to feed on the leaves of the early peas. If you are more fussy than me, place empty tins along the rows in March. They should be sunk up to the rims and the weevils fall in. Unhappily, so do some friendly beetles which should be spared the *coup de grace*.

BIG BUD

This is caused by a mite and is the worst pest of blackcurrant bushes, because it causes reversion (see opposite). You can recognise its presence in early spring by comparing the relative sizes of the developing buds. Those with big bud mite are appreciably larger than the normal ones. Pick off the big buds carefully and destroy them. Spray with lime sulphur when the flower trusses are fully developed and at three-weekly intervals until the buds are open. If more than half of all the buds on a bush are attacked, it is probably more sensible to grub out the entire bush and burn it, then replant with clean stock.

BLACKBERRY MITE

This pest overwinters on the old canes then in spring moves to the leaves, flowers and finally the fruit. Control is by spraying or dusting with derris before the petals open.

BLACKCURRANT REVERSION

The gall mites that cause big bud are also responsible for passing on the agent that causes reversion disease in blackcurrant bushes. This virus disease severely reduces cropping and the symptoms are not easy to recognise unless you are an expert. When the disease gets a hold the leaves become smaller and have fewer of the typical lobes with five or fewer veins. There is no remedy, but before taking out the bush and burning it, have an experienced eye cast over it.

BLACKFLY

This is one of the aphid family and is a major pest of broad beans. If you live in a favourable part of the country, sow your broad beans in late autumn. This results in too tough a skin on the stems for the blackflies' enjoyment. Pinching out the growing tips of each branch is also a help. Control on spring-sown broad beans is first by soapy water, then quassia or derris.

BLACKSPOT

A fungal disease of roses that is readily recognisable by the black patches on leaves that then turn yellow and fall. Leaf buds and stems may also be affected. Some varieties are more susceptible to this disease which always seems worse in warm, wet summers. Spraying a summer dilution of lime sulphur or dusting with sulphur offers some control, and scrupulous collection of all infected leaves is necessary to avoid spores of the fungus being passed on. Some people use elder spray as a preventive.

BOTRYTIS

A fluffy, grey mould that affects many types of garden plant, including bedding plants, strawberries, raspberries, grapes and the currant family, particularly in wet and warm summers. It is especially damaging to strawberries under cloches. There is no cure so burn all infected leaves and fruit.

Cabbage root fly damage causes stunted growth, purple colouring of the leaves and, eventually, collapse, particularly in hot weather

CABBAGE ROOT FLY

Attacks all the brassica family, but cabbages and Brussels sprouts plants are most at risk immediately after planting out, from April to July. The female fly lays its eggs in the soil against the stems of the plants and sometimes actually on the stems. After about a week the eggs hatch and the larvae tunnel down and into the main roots of the plant often eating the entire root system so that the plant collapses and dies. A second generation of flies emerges in July and a third in early autumn.

A physical barrier to stop the fly laying its eggs is the surest control. You can buy special paper collars to slip round the plants when planting out or make your own. Old foam-backed carpet, carpet underlay, thick brown paper or cardboard can be used as squares or circles, 10cm (4in) diameter or 10cm (4in) square. Cut a slit to the centre and four 2.5cm (1in) slits crossing through the centre. Slide the stem of the plant to the centre after planting out and thoroughly watering the transplants. As the plant grows the stem fills the centre of the collar and the fly is unable to locate a suitable site for egg laying. Thorough winter cultivation will expose overwintering pupae in the soil to the attention of the birds.

CABBAGE WHITE CATERPILLAR

The caterpillars of the large white and the small white butterflies eat the leaves of brassicas, especially cabbages. If unchecked they will eat their way into the heart of the cabbage. The damage is most severe in summer through to October.

Preventing the butterflies from laying their eggs is the simplest control and you can cover the crop from April onwards with fine mesh plastic netting or polypropylene fibre cloth, such as Agryl P17.

Infested plants can be cleared of caterpillars by spraying with the biological control agent *Bacillus thuringiensis* (page 137).

CARROT ROOT FLY

This is the crop's number one pest and comes from the same family as the cabbage root fly. On a field scale there is no satisfactory chemical control, particularly when the pest mounts a

Cabbage white caterpillars can be cleared by spraying with the biological control Bacillus thuringiensis

large-scale attack, so carrot growers in East Anglia are now advised to grow and harvest at carefully-defined times to minimise the need for sprays which are neither entirely effective nor free from possible tainting of the crop.

Happily for the amateur grower, providing a physical barrier round the crop offers a high rate of protection. The reason is this: the carrot root fly is like a tiny house fly which feeds on hemlock and cow parsley. It homes in on carrots (with celery and parsley as alternative targets) using scent as its radar and zooming in low like a cruise missile. Nearing the target, its eyes help it to pinpoint the exact location.

The female fly lays its eggs on the surface close to the carrots. When they hatch, the maggots bore down into the soil and then up into the roots. They are voracious feeders and in maincrop carrots the damage they do makes the roots unsuitable for storage.

Varying degrees of control can be achieved by one or more of these methods:

● Avoid thinning the young carrots or bruising the foliage.
● Sow and raise early carrots under cloches or use polypropylene fibre cloth, such as Agryl P17 or Papronet.
● Dig beds thoroughly in October and turn them over again in November to allow birds to feed on the pupae.
● Try scent-jamming by the traditional technique of planting onions or garlic close to the carrots; use tarred string along the rows; spray the seedlings with garlic oil.
● Erect a barrier around the crop – this is the method that offers the highest rate of control, so I have made plastic-

covered panels as carrot fly guards. You can use opaque or clear polythene sheeting, secondhand roofing laths or other rough timber about 3.75cm (1½in) by 1.87cm (¾in).

I've made my panels 90cm (3ft) long by 37.5cm (15in) tall because my allotment beds are 4.5m (15ft) wide. The corner joints are glued and screwed and I used a staple gun to fix the sheeting to the frame. The panels are positioned round the crop without any gaps and are held in place by bamboo canes, pushed into the soil on either side.

CELERY LEAF MINER

The culprit here is a fly which lays its eggs on the leaves of the celery plants. The larvae then tunnel between the upper and lower leaf surfaces. The attacks normally take place in June and again in September. Where you see the characteristic tunnel-

Tell-tale sign of carrot fly damage is the foliage turning from green to orange and red

Celery leaf miner damage. Maggots tunnel into the leaves causing blisters and shrivelling of the tissue. Pinch out and burn the affected parts

ling lines and bumps hiding the larvae, simply squeeze between finger and thumb or remove that portion of the leaf and burn it. Some control is achieved by spraying with nettle spray or liquid manure, in June and September.

CHERRY BLACKFLY

This aphid attacks the young growing tips of all types of cherry including the ornamental ones. Control by pinching off the young shoots or spray with quassia and soft soap or Savona.

CHERRY FRUIT MOTH

The caterpillars of this moth hibernate in crevices of the bark of the trees and in spring eat their way into the developing fruit. Spray with derris in September and repeat in the spring before the blossoms open.

CLUBROOT

The most difficult vegetable disease for the gardener to deal with. It affects all crucifers, but most at risk are Brussels sprouts, cabbages, cauliflowers, sprouting broccoli, calabrese, swedes, turnips, stocks and wallflowers and it is worse on acid, badly-drained soils.

A slime fungus is responsible and, once introduced into the garden, there is no cure because the spores remain dormant in the soil and will happily latch on to any weeds that belong to the crucifer family, including shepherd's purse and charlock. Some experts believe that, in the absence of a host plant, the resting spores can survive for twenty or more years and can be transferred from infected sites to disease-free sites in the soil on plants, on the gardener's boots and on tools.

Symptoms of the disease are, above ground, somewhat similar to those of attack by the cabbage root fly. The plants become stunted, wilt during the day, and the foliage has a red to purple tint. Below ground the roots develop swellings and distortions that, when broken open, have an evil smell.

Once the disease has entered the garden, there is no cure, but you can lessen the effects by improving the drainage and liming to raise the pH to 7.5, along with strict adherence to crop rotation. Dig up all infected crops with as much root and rootball as possible and either burn completely or place in a plastic sack for the dustcart to dispose of.

Growing your brassica plants in soil blocks or peat pots, then potting on to 22.5cm (9in) clay or plastic pots and, finally, planting out, pot and all, to grow to maturity is a recommended technique. HDRA members had some success using 7.5cm (3in) lengths of rhubarb stem dropped into the planting hole when the brassica plants were set out. The decaying stem of rhubarb excreted oxalic acid which masked the cabbage root secretions to the lurking clubroot spores.

If you haven't got clubroot in your soil, give praise and take precautions by strict weed control, don't wander on to known infected land then back on to your own land, and raise all your brassica plants yourself because bought-in plants may be infected without the grower knowing.

CODLING MOTH

A very common pest of apples and, in closely-related form, of plums. Caterpillars eat into apples, feeding for a month or more, then spin cocoons under loose bark and other hiding places to emerge next season. Grease band the trees and use a pheromone codling moth trap in May. Destroy any fruit with tell-tale holes in them.

FLEA BEETLE

Many types attack cruciferous plants, but especially radishes, turnips and swedes, eating small holes in the leaves which can so badly check growth that young plants die. Although they are beetles, they jump like fleas and are active in May and June. The larvae pupate in the soil and a second generation hatches in the autumn and hibernates in the garden over the winter.

Spray the young plants with derris liquid or dust with derris powder at first sign of damage, or use a sticky board (page 95).

GOOSEBERRY SAWFLY

Larvae eat leaves of the bushes in spring and summer, stripping an entire bush in under a week unless checked. Keep a sharp watch for the little green larvae with black heads and black spots from late April onwards and spray with derris, paying particular attention to the centre of the bush. Repeat at weekly intervals if necessary. Bushes are still at risk even as late as June.

LEEK MOTH

A tiny brown moth which lays its eggs alongside the leek plants in spring. The small caterpillars eat into the leaves, causing long slits that fray. Severe attacks result in death of the plant. In some parts the moth also attacks onion plants. There is, I'm afraid, no practical control of this pest at present.

LETTUCE ROOT APHID

This can be a serious nuisance especially in a hot, dry summer. The aphids lay their eggs on Lombardy poplars for overwintering, while others actually overwinter in the soil where the previous season's lettuce have been attacked.

Control is by growing a resistant variety of lettuce, such as Avoncrisp or Avondefiance.

Other preventive measures: ensure your outdoor lettuce is given plenty of water during hot, dry weather; avoid using the same site more then once in three years; don't leave any lettuce roots in the ground to harbour the pest and give the soil a good turning over in the autumn so the birds can feed on any aphids that might still be about.

MEALY APHID

There are more than 500 species of aphid in Britain and virtually every sort of fruit, flower and vegetable plant has its own sap-sucking version of the pest. The mealy cabbage aphid can be a serious pest in a dry summer, building up vast colonies

Downy mildew on the foliage of a swede

until the predatory ladybird larvae multiply correspondingly.

Control the aphids as early as possible with Savona or soft soap spray, repeating at weekly intervals.

MILDEW, DOWNY

This is a greyish fungal mould that actually penetrates the tissue of the infected plant. Most at risk are the crucifer family of vegetables and ornamental plants (cabbages, Brussels sprouts, swedes, turnips, wallflowers, stocks), lettuce and onions.

Remove all infected plant debris and burn, then spray with solution of 112g (4oz) washing soda in 4.5 litres (1gal) of water and 56g (2oz) soft soap or soap flakes. In the greenhouse maintain a buoyant atmosphere and avoid water getting into the heart of the lettuces.

Planting bottles is said to be one way to deter moles. Sink wine bottles up to threequarters their height every 2m (6ft) or so on the boundary of the garden. The sound of the wind reverberating in the empty bottles is supposed to do the trick

MILDEW, POWDERY

A large family of fungi that attack a very wide range of garden plants but, most seriously, apple trees, gooseberry bushes and roses. Unlike downy mildews, the powdery ones remain on the surface of the leaves, stems and buds as a white coating.

The apple infection begins in spring from the overwintered fungus and may continue throughout the summer. Sulphur is the traditional control but is phytotoxic to many varieties. The organic grower should attempt to minimise the infection by cutting back infected shoots in the winter to below the limit of the visible mildew. Affected shoots and buds can be removed throughout the spring and early summer and, for good measure, spray at pink bud stage and fortnightly thereafter with a solution of 21g (¾oz) potassium permanganate in 13.5 litres (3gal) water.

American gooseberry mildew appears first in spring as a white coating on the young shoots, spreads to the stems and, eventually, to the berries. It stunts the growth and can decimate the crop. Avoid planting the bushes in a damp, sheltered site and prune them to give an open, inverted umbrella shape.

Spray with Bordeaux mixture in the winter and with a solution of 84g (3oz) washing soda and 28g (1oz) soap flakes in 4.5 litres (1 gal) hot water, used when cool.

Mildew on roses appears in early May and can spread rapidly. The best control is to plant only resistant varieties. Avoid sites that are over-protective from air movement; mulch the bushes with compost or peat and do not use nitrogous fertilisers which produce soft growth. Spray with 56g (2oz) carbolic soap in 4.5 litres (1gal) water every three weeks from May to September except in wet summers.

Albertine, introduced in 1921, is one of the great names in rambler roses with attractive foliage, very fragrant double-pink blooms and

vigorous growth. Mildew can be a problem, however, so avoid sites without air movement, and mulch with compost or peat

MINERAL DEFICIENCIES

Boron, calcium, magnesium, potassium, iron, phosphorus and manganese are essential in minute quantities for healthy plant growth, but might be denied to the plants by being locked out of reach of the feeding roots, by heavy liming or by a natural shortage in some types of soil.

Symptoms of a deficiency of one or more minerals vary from crop to crop. For example, boron deficiency in beet causes crown canker, while in turnips and swedes it causes brown heart. Potassium shortage in beans causes scorching of the leaf edge while in gooseberries there's leaf scorch and the colour changes to a blueish tint.

Iron shortage shows as anaemic foliage with pale green leaves fading to almost white among the youngest growth. Magnesium shortage occurs quite frequently with outdoor tomatoes and lettuces, when the symptoms are progressive yellowing of the lower leaves while the leaf veins remain green.

Identification of mineral shortage in crops isn't easy. The symptoms can be confused with virus disorders and vice versa. Generally speaking, if your soil is at or near a neutral pH, and is neither a too-heavy clay nor a too-light sand, mineral deficiency can be avoided by the incorporation of adequate amounts of compost.

Routine feeding with a seaweed extract used as a foliar feed is a near-100 per cent guarantee against mineral shortage.

ONION FLY

Like its close relatives the cabbage root fly and the carrot fly, the onion fly is tiny and inconspicuous, but it homes in on the host plant to lay its eggs on the soil. The resulting maggots feed in the stems and bulbs, causing young plants to wilt and the more mature bulbs to rot.

The pupae overwinter in the soil so turn it over to give the birds a chance to eliminate them. However, as the onion fly is most active after onions grown from seed have been thinned, a high degree of control is achieved by growing your onions from sets.

ONION WHITE ROT

This is a fungus disease of great significance to both the commercial and amateur grower because once it gets a grip there is no certain cure other than resting the land from onion growing for at least eight years. However, as already mentioned (page 92) there is hope that current research will produce biological control.

The first sign of attack by the white rot spores is yellowing of the leaves of the onions – although leeks, shallots, chives and garlic can also be affected. As the roots rot, so the plant loses its grip on the soil and keels over, exposing the mass of cotton-wool like threads of the fungus. This can spread to other plants in the onion patch either by contact or through the soil. Infected plants must be burnt and not put on the compost heap.

PEA MOTH

The small caterpillars of this moth feed on the peas in the pod causing considerable loss of edible peas in the July and August cropping period.

The critical period for egg-laying by the female moth is June and July, so by careful juggling with sowing times it is possible to avoid peas being vulnerable to attack. This means sowing before March and after April. See also page 139.

LACEY'S LORE

FLY A KITE

Flying a kite to ward off pigeons from one's overwintering brassicas seems effective, particularly if the kite is kestrel-shaped. One kite can keep up to 4 hectares (10 acres) clear.
Another method is to place empty wine bottles on stakes or canes about five feet tall, dotted about the vegetable garden.
Humming tape stretched around the crops is also a useful deterrent.

PEAR CANKER

See apple canker (page 143).

POTATO BLIGHT

The worst disease of potatoes especially in wet summers. It will also hit the outdoor tomatoes. Collins *Guide to Pests, Diseases*

and Disorders of Garden Plants has this to say about the biology of blight:

The fungus persists over winter in diseased potato tubers from the previous crop, either in the ground or, more usually, on dumps or in undetected seed tubers. When such tubers grow, either as seed in the ground or in large diseased heaps, they sometimes produce infected shoots. Spores may then be blown from them to infect a new crop. Tubers become infected by spores falling from the haulm on to the soil and being washed downwards by rain.

Spores are produced and dispersed only in damp conditions, and foggy weather in summer is therefore very favourable to the disease. Infection by blight spores is likely to take place when the temperature does not fall below 10°C (50°F) and the relative humidity does not fall below 75 per cent during a period of 48 hours, this being known as a Beaumont period. The Ministry of Agriculture broadcasts warnings when Beaumont or the comparable Smith periods have occurred in the main potato growing regions and these indicate that commercial growers should apply protective sprays.

The disease shows as dark brown blotches on the leaves, often with a white mould on the underside. The blotches rapidly fill out and spread until the entire haulm turns dark brown and it is pretty certain that some of the tubers in the ground will have been affected.

In damp seasons don't wait for the disease to appear, start preventive spraying with Bordeaux mixture fortnightly from July and include your outdoor tomatoes. If you are an allotment holder, preventive spraying is particularly important, because rogue tubers on a neighbour's plot can spread the blight spores far and wide very speedily.

If you live in a mild area, it is prudent to start the spraying at about mid-June.

POTATO EELWORM

This, one of the most damaging pests of potatoes, is also called yellow potato cyst eelworm or golden nematode and it also attacks outdoor tomato plants. It causes stunted growth of the haulm and when the tubers are lifted they are marble size while on the roots there will be the white or yellow cysts, although you will need a magnifying glass to see them.

Each cyst is the dead body of a female eelworm and contains up to 600 eggs which remain dormant in the soil for up to ten years. They are triggered into life when potato tubers or tomato plants are planted. The eelworm larvae then feed on the roots of the plants. With a maincrop potato the increase in the eelworm population may be as much as twenty-five times; a very large proportion of cysts – many millions, in fact – will be left behind in the soil to latch on to a subsequent crop.

This is another good reason to practise rotation and it is prudent also to grow a resistant variety of maincrop potato or, on land known to be infected, to stick to early varieties.

POTATO KEEL SLUGS

This one is my personal pet hate. Too often the full extent of the damage they do is not discovered until the potatoes are being peeled in the kitchen. They are an underground species, small in relation to most of the above-ground slugs, but their greed is only bounded by the size of the potato they eat into. I have seen a potato the size of a clenched fist completely eaten except for the skin.

A new development that offers hope of good control over this and other types of slug is Imp Slugtape, a paper-based tape incorporating a bait which attracts and kills slugs and snails, but does not attract wildlife or pets and is not affected by rain. At planting time lengths of the tape are placed in the trench alongside the tubers where it will remain toxic to the slugs for the full growing period of the crop.

Alternatively you can water the soil around the haulms with a solution of salt and potassium permanganate. For each 9 litres (2gal) water, mix in a teaspoonful of the permanganate and one of salt. Water this on the soil at the rate of 9 litres (2gal) to each 12sq m/yd.

POTATO SCAB

This is common scab, a skin-deep disease that looks unsightly with corky growths, but it neither reduces the yield nor affects the eating quality of the potatoes. It is worse on light soils and in dry summers or in ground that has recently been limed and is low in organic matter. Desiree and Maris Piper are two very popular varieties that are most susceptible to scab.

You can avoid scab by giving your land plenty of organic material, rotating the crops, and as a belt-and-braces precaution adding a generous handful of lawn mowings when setting out the seed tuber. Make the planting hole or trench, put the mowings in position, then place the chitted tuber on top, like an egg in a nest.

RASPBERRY BEETLE

This small beetle also attacks cultivated blackberries and the hybrid berries. In June and July it lays eggs in the blossom and after a couple of weeks they hatch into larvae which eat into the embryo fruit. After about four weeks of feeding, the grubs drop to the ground and pupate in the soil until the following spring.

Some control is achieved by gently forking over the soil to allow the birds to feed on the pupae. A second line of defence is to spray with soft soap or derris as soon as the flowers open with a second spray as the flowers die and a third when the berries turn pink.

RED SPIDER MITE

Two types cause gardeners problems: the glasshouse red spider mite and the fruit tree one. In the greenhouse, if an appropriate crop is being grown, regular misting to maintain high humidity is a deterrent. Full control is achieved by introducing the predatory mite *Phytosieiulus persimilis* (page 138).

The fruit tree red spider mite feeds on the leaves of apples, pears and plums and damsons, extracting the contents from the plant tissues. They are active from April onwards and can cause severe damage to the foliage with consequent reduction in yield of fruit. The leaves turn mottled, then bronze and become covered with fine silk webbing.

Fortunately, the fruit tree red spider mite has several natural predators which, if they are not killed by poisonous sprays, will normally keep the pest under control.

SILVER LEAF

A fungal disease that affects plums mainly, but also other top fruit, currants and gooseberries, and in the flower garden it is sometimes found on roses and laburnum.

It is first seen from about mid-April as a silvery sheen on a single branch which may spread to other branches. The wood of the affected branch will be found to have a brown stain in it and from August onward die-back of the branch will occur. The infected wood should be cut back and burned. Biological control is achieved by the parasitic fungus *Trichoderma viride* which is applied to the tree in pellet form (see page 137).

SLUGS AND SNAILS

A slug can eat up to forty times its own weight in a year and, as a tribe, would serve a useful purpose if they stuck to fallen leaves and decaying fruit. Unfortunately, they don't distinguish between garden debris and garden delights, such as dahlias and delphiniums and, as already mentioned, can cause chaos in the potato crop waiting to be harvested.

Snails are less of a problem. They hibernate in the winter and, come the spring, are fair game for the thrushes.

Both slugs and snails are killed by metaldehyde, a poison that is avoided by organic gardeners and others concerned for wildlife because it is highly toxic to hedgehogs, the major pre-

You can make an effective slug trap using an empty tin or carton topped up with stale beer. Place it, buried to the rim, near to *susceptible plants, such as this hosta, empty the drowned victims and remains of the beer once a week, then refill with beer*

dators of slugs, and to dogs and cats, who are attracted to the bait containing the metaldehyde.

Fertosan and Nobble are the safe alternative killers. Fertosan has been on the market for several years and is guaranteed to be harmless to humans, pets, livestock and wildlife as it kills by contact and is not a bait. Nobble is a newer product which is sprayed, or poured from a watering can, and kills slug eggs on contact.

Imp Slugtape is a paper-based tape filled with a bait that attracts and kills slugs and snails but does not attract wildlife or pets and is not washed out by the rain. The tape comes in reels and is easily applied in long or short lengths to go round individual plants at planting out, along rows of seedlings or in the seed potato trench to beat the keel slugs.

An age-old trap for slugs can be made by sinking an empty can in the ground up to its rim and half filling it with stale beer or brown sugar and water. While on page 153 is an even older technique.

SPRAING

Brown wavy marks in the flesh of maincrop potatoes is a sign of spraing, a virus disease which is common on light soils and in a wet summer. Some varieties, particularly Maris Peer and Pentland Dell are highly susceptible to attack by this virus.

Destroy infected tubers and never grow potatoes on the same site in two consecutive years.

STRAWBERRY APHID

A major pest because it transmits virus diseases and is present on the leaves of the plants throughout the year. Those growers who still use straw as a mulch should set light to it so that it burns off the leaves, aphids and all. Or spray with rhubarb spray and soap or pyrethrum or derris, making sure the underside of the leaves is covered with the spray. Do this in April and again in May in the evening when the bees are not active.

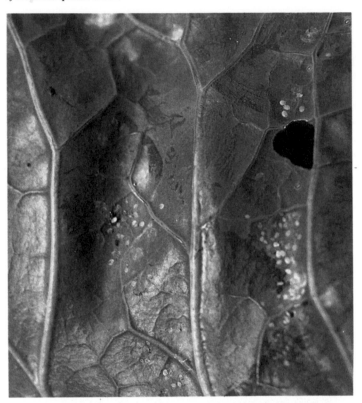

Whitefly larvae on the underside of Brussels sprouts leaves

TOMATO BLIGHT

Use the same control as for potato blight (page 151).

TORTRIX MOTHS

Three species attack apples, pears, plums and cherries, the green caterpillars feeding on fruit, leaves and buds. Spray with *Bacillus thuringiensis* as soon as the caterpillars are seen.

WASPS

On the whole, wasps do more good in the garden than harm so I don't rate them as pests. As Jennifer Owen says: 'With understanding and tolerance, it is possible to live happily with garden insects and other animals: the surest way of avoiding a wasp sting is not to interfere with a wasp . . . to me the garden is a habitat to which I must adjust rather than a territory to be conquered.'

LACEY'S LORE

MORE FRIEND THAN FOE

Wasps, like ants and earwigs, are pests only if they are in the wrong places. They are very efficient at clearing up waste fruit, but will also feed on fruit on the bough. You can protect precious apples and pears by covering them with pieces cut from old tights and stockings.

If you find a wasp nest indoors – the loft is a favourite location – don't try to remove it yourself. Consult the pest control people in the local council's environmental health department.

You can deal with a wasp nest in the garden the non-poisonous organic way by putting a pile of fresh grass cuttings over the entrance to the nest. The mowings decompose rapidly, using up all the oxygen in the underground nest, and the wasps die.

WHITEFLY

In the greenhouse this can be a major pest, but is readily controlled by *Encarsia formosa*, a tiny wasp that lays its eggs in the whitefly larvae (see page 137).

Brassica whitefly or cabbage whitefly cannot be controlled by biological means, as yet. The larvae mass on the underside of the leaves of Brussels sprouts, in particular, and excrete honeydew. This falls on the buttons and upper surfaces of leaves and gives rise to a sooty mould. The remedy is to spray weekly with 220g (8oz) of soft soap in 22.5 litres (5gal) of water.

WINTER MOTHS

This family of moths attacks all the top fruit trees and, less

Whitefly adults, such as these, can be checked by spraying with soft soap solution

frequently, currants and gooseberries. The females are wing-less and they therefore have to climb up the trunk of the tree to lay their eggs which become the destructive green caterpillars that feed on the fresh leaves from April to June.

The first line of defence is to grease band the fruit trees. If this fails to be completely effective – and, of course, it isn't possible to grease band the currants and gooseberries – spray with *Bacillus thuringiensis* as soon as the first caterpillars are sighted.

LACEY'S LORE

FRUIT TREE BANDING

Grease banding is an old but effective way of preventing the wingless females of the winter moths from climbing the trunks of fruit trees to lay their eggs on buds and leaves. Place the bands in position in late October. If the bark of the trees is rough enough to allow the moths to crawl under the band, use soft putty rubbed into the crevices to get a smooth surface.

Always use vegetable grease on the bands, not animal or mineral greases which can harm the trees.

WIREWORM

This is the slender, smooth, tough larva of the click beetle that can cause so much damage to root crops and flower bulbs. Wireworms are present throughout the year, although most active in the spring, and feed as larvae for four to five years, becoming larger and tougher all the time. Old turf is often infected with wireworm and anyone taking over a neglected garden or allotment should anticipate having to cope with a big population of the pest.

By far the best control technique is to sow a green manure crop of mustard in April at the rate of 28g (1oz) to the sq m/yd. Dig this in during July and immediately re-sow with mustard again for digging in before the first frost arrives.

Wireworm feed on the mustard so fully that they become beetles and fly away. In well-cultivated gardens wireworm shouldn't be a pest because the birds love them. If some escape the attention of your resident robins, put pieces of potato on sticks and push them about 15cm (6in) into the soil. Examine them once a week and destroy any wireworms or millipedes that have eaten into the potato.

FACT FILE Summary of major pests and diseases

Aphids Many species. Spray with insecticidal soap, elder, rhubarb or nettle spray. Do not use derris or pyrethrum which would also kill hoverfly and ladybird predators.
Apple sawfly Spray with derris a week after petal fall.
Big bud Worst pest of blackcurrants. Pick off big buds and destroy them.
Blackfly Worse on broad beans, so sow in November. Spray spring-sown crops with soft soap, quassia or derris. Pinch out growing tips.
Black spot Collect all infected leaves. Spray with lime sulphur or elder spray.
Cabbage root fly Attacks all brassicas. Put protective collar round stems when planting out.
Cabbage white butterflies Lays eggs on cabbage leaves June to September. Squash eggs by hand or kill young caterpillars with *Bacillus thuringiensis* spray.
Carrot root fly Put barrier round the crop or try scent jamming by interplanting with onions or garlic.

Celery leaf miner Spray with nettle spray in June and again in September.
Clubroot Fearsome fungus attacks brassicas, swedes, turnips, wallflowers. Lift carefully and burn all infected plants. No cure, so grow your own to avoid introducing infection.
Leek moth Caterpillars bore tunnels in leaves. No control at present.
Lettuce root aphid Grow a resistant variety.
Mildew Two-types: downy and powdery. Downy penetrates plant tissue; powdery remains on surface of leaves. For downy dissolve 112g (4oz) washing soda in 4.5 litres (1gal) water, stir in 56g (2oz) soft soap or soap flakes. For powdery stir 14g (½oz) potassium permanganate in 13.5 litres (3gal) water.
Mineral deficiency Spray foliage with seaweed liquid once a week for four weeks.
Onion fly Maggots bore into base of bulbs. Grow from sets.
Onion white rot White fluffy fungus on base of bulbs, foliage turns yellow. Spores

last up to eight years in soil. No remedy except to rest from growing onions.
Pea moth Responsible for maggots in peas. Juggle sowing dates to avoid attack.
Pea and bean weevils Eats notches in leaves. Dust with derris.
Potato blight Spray with Bordeaux mixture fortnightly from July.
Potato scab Rotate crop to avoid newly-limed land.
Potato eelworm Causes stunted growth, tiny tubers. Dig up plant and burn. Grow resistant varieties.
Potato keel slugs Water soil with teaspoonful potassium permanganate and one of salt dissolved in 9 litres (2gal) water for each 12sq m/yd or use Imp Slugtape.
Slugs Use Fertosan, Nobble or Imp Slugtape or trap with brown sugar water or stale beer.
Whitefly Brassica whitefly now a widespread pest. Causes sooty mould on leaves and sprout buttons. Spray weekly with 224g (8oz) soft soap in 22.5 litres (5gal) water.

FRUIT

Symptoms	Probable cause	Control
Maggots in mature apples	Codling moth	Grease band trees or use pheromone trap
Dark spots on apple leaves and fruit	Apple scab	See page 144
Skin and flesh of apples develop brown blotches and decay on tree or in store	Brown rot	No control. Remove infected fruit from tree and from store
Apples fail to ripen, skin has corky scars	Apple sawfly	See page 144
Sunken patches on bark of apples and pears. If lesions girdle branch or shoot, it dies back	Canker	See page 143
Leaves become mottled and yellow. Dense fine webs on underside. Apples and pears most affected	Red spider mite	See page 152
Patches of cotton-wool like insects on apple and pear shoots in late spring	Woolly aphid	Scrape off. If infestation too widespread, spray with derris after petal fall
Powdery white coating on surface of leaves, stems and buds, particularly on apple trees and gooseberry bushes	Powdery mildew	See page 149
Swollen buds on blackcurrant bushes	Big bud mite	See page 144
Buds are eaten, particularly of gooseberries. Soft fruits eaten as they ripen. Holes pecked in hard fruit	Birds	Protect all soft fruit (with netting, preferably)
Foliage of pears covered in sticky, sooty mould in spring	Pear sucker	Spray with insecticidal soap or derris
Holes in leaves of all top fruit	Winter moth	See page 154–5
Malformed fruit and grubs in raspberries	Raspberry beetle	See page 152
Silver areas on raspberry canes and hybrid briars, fruiting buds fail	Spur blight	Spray with Bordeaux mixture. See page 141

VEGETABLES

Symptoms	Probable cause	Control
Young brassica plants wilt, leaves turn purplish. Plants eventually collapse and die	Cabbage root fly	See page 145
Colonies of small white insects, some winged, on underside of brassica leaves. Sooty mould forms on sprout buttons	Brassica whitefly	See page 154
Soil-borne fungus affects all brassicas, swedes, turnips and some flowers. Plants stunted, foliage has purple tinge. Roots have evil-smelling swellings	Clubroot	See pages 147–8
Clusters of black wingless insects on growing tips of broad beans	Blackfly	See page 144
Colonies of greyish wingless insects mainly on summer cabbage	Mealy aphid	See page 148–9
Foliage of carrots changes to bronze. Roots become riddled with maggot borings	Carrot root fly	See page 145–6
Onion plants wilt. Maggots tunnel into stem and bulb	Onion fly	See page 150–1
Yellowing of onion leaves, plant wilts then keels over. Underside of bulb has mass of cotton-wool like fungus	White rot	See page 151
Rusty scars round neck of mature parsnips gradually causing flesh to rot	Canker	Grow resistant variety, such as Avonresister
Small maggots in peas, found when shelled	Pea moth	See pages 139 and 151
Brown patches on leaves of potatoes and outdoor tomatoes. Quickly spread to stems. Plant collapses	Potato blight	See pages 141 and 151
Stunted growth of potato plant. Marble size tubers	Potato eelworm	See page 151–2
Corky growths on skin of potatoes when harvested	Potato scab	See page 152
Small holes in leaves of radish, swedes and turnips	Flea beetle	See page 148
Wiry, black larvae up to 2.5cm (1in) long eat into root crops below soil. Foliage yellows	Wireworm	See page 155
Leaves and growing points of many vegetable and flower crops eaten	Slugs	See page 152–3

ROSES

Symptoms	Probable cause	Control
Young leaves and shoots covered with small green insects	Aphids	See page 143
Irregular holes in leaves	Caterpillars	Remove by hand
Black or brown spots with yellow fringes on leaves which fall prematurely	Blackspot	See page 144
White powdery mould on leaves, stems and buds in summer	Mildew	See page 149
Young shoots wither and die	Die-back through frost, waterlogging or canker	Feed in spring with liquid seaweed and mulch with compost
Froth on shoots in late spring	Froghopper or cuckoo spit	Spray with water or remove by hand
Mature stem fails to produce flower bud	Blindness	Cut back by about half to a bud
Large yellow areas on leaves	Waterlogging or mineral shortage	Improve drainage. Feed with seaweed meal, mulch with compost
Newly-planted bushes fail to make good growth	Roses on same site for 10 years or more can cause soil sickness	Rest site from roses for three years
Bronze patches on upper surface of leaves. Dense, fine cobwebs on underside	Red spider mite	Spray daily with water in hot, dry weather. Use liquid derris as last resort

OTHER ORNAMENTAL PLANTS

Symptoms	Probable cause	Control
Orange or brown swellings on leaves of antirrhinums, carnations, chrysanthemums, sweet Williams	Rust	Pick off diseased leaves and burn
Antirrhinum, aster, carnation, chrysanthemum, lupin and sweet pea leaves and shoots wilt even in moist conditions	Wilt caused by soil fungus	No cure. Remove diseased plants. Switch site for susceptible plants
Straw-coloured tunnels appear in leaf tissue of chrysanthemums	Leaf miner	Pick off and destroy affected leaves
Scorched patches on tulip leaves	Tulip fire	Avoid cold, wet sites. Destroy affected bulbs
Small holes in leaves of young wallflower plants in hot, dry weather	Flea beetle	See page 148
Seedlings collapse and keel over especially under glass	Damping off	Ventilate adequately. Remove affected seedlings. Do not over-water
White, powdery coating on leaves and stems of wide range of plants	Mildew	Water plants regularly. Mulch with compost. Divide border perennials every three years
Leaves and shoots covered with green or black insects on many plants	Aphids (green and blackfly)	See page 143
Mottled leaves, badly-formed buds, stunted growth. Many plants affected	Virus disease	Buy healthy stock. Keep aphids controlled

MONTH BY MONTH
CHECK LISTS

JANUARY

* Complete digging of vegetable plot if soil is workable and finish liming those parts that need it.

* Put cloches in position where you intend to make early outdoor sowings.

* Force rhubarb (see page 95–6).

* Chit seed potatoes (pp 108–9).

* Prepare new borders, working in 84g (3oz) bone meal to the sq m/yd.

* A good time for planting a new hedge.

* Repot fuchsias and take cuttings of late-flowering chrysanthemums.

* Check all fruit and vegetables in store and remove any that have signs of rot.

* Examine stored dahlia tubers. If they have shrivelled, place them in tepid water overnight, then dry thoroughly and dust with flowers of sulphur.

* Sow sweet peas indoors; plant lilies outside any time now until March.

* Indoor bulbs that have finished flowering should be planted outdoors to ripen off.

* Prune ornamental trees, fruit trees and vines before the end of the month.

* Let snow lie on greenhouses and frames, but try to avoid it building up on brittle branches of fruit trees and shrubs.

* Plan the year's cropping for the vegetable garden and order seeds without delay.

* Firm any shrubs that have been loosened by frost or wind rock.

* Cut off canker on apple and pear trees and paint the wounds with Trichoderma paste (see page 137).

FEBRUARY

* Prune summer-flowering shrubs, gooseberries and raspberries.

* Remove suckers from around the base of top fruit and ornamental trees.

* Check stakes and ties and firm any plants loosened by frost.

* Aerate established lawn, make new lawn from turf when ground is workable and frost-free.

* Plant rhubarb after frosting the crowns. Plant chives, thyme, mint and sage or divide established plants to increase stock.

* Protect gooseberry bushes from birds by using Scareweb or draping with plastic netting.

* Continue planting all sorts of fruit.

* Transplant autumn-sown onions.

* Cut Brussels sprouts tops for the kitchen and use the stumps for trench composting (see page 30).

* Sow lettuces, onions, radishes and summer cabbages under cloches or in the cold frame.

* Sow broad beans in soil blocks or peat pots for planting out next month.

* Compost started at the middle of last year will be ready for use now. Turn it in as you dig, use it to line drills before sowing or spread as a mulch on your deep beds.

Storing a wheelbarrow can be the bane of the gardener's life. If you leave it outside, it can rapidly become a rust bucket, while in shed or garage it takes up an inordinate amount of space. So three cheers for this bright idea: the British-made Slimbarro that folds flat when not in use

Two instruments that add more interest to gardening are, left, a simple rain gauge and, right, a maximum-minimum thermometer. The gauge should be positioned in the open where it will be unaffected by buildings, fences, trees and shrubs. The thermometer should be out of direct sunlight. Take daily readings of both instruments and log them in your gardening notebook

'Good home wanted for tadpoles'
says the sign near this garden pool
– a special feature of a small town
garden cultivated organically

One of the most welcome sights in
early spring is the brilliant yellow
blossom on the bare branches of
forsythia, a shrub that loves full
sun and organic soil. Don't be too
heavy with the secateurs. After
flowering, cut back those branches
that have carried blooms

MARCH

★ Sow parsnips, if soil is dry enough.

★ Complete planting of soft fruit bushes and top fruit trees.

★ Plant perennials such as lupins and delphiniums. Complete pruning of all roses.

★ Check over all tools and give the mower a service.

★ Rid the greenhouse of any winter casualties and order replacement plants.

★ Plant out autumn-sown sweet peas as soon as the weather allows.

★ Plant gladioli, lilies and montbretia.

★ Sow leeks, lettuces and radishes in cold frame or under cloches.

★ Under cloches sow beetroot Detroit Little Ball and early carrot Amsterdam Forcing.

★ Towards the end of the month sow parsley and kohl rabi. Plant shallots and garlic, onion sets and asparagus crowns.

★ On the windowsill you can sow verbena, African marigold, gaillardia, phlox, polyanthus, primula and celosia.

★ Start dahlia tubers into growth as early in the month as possible so that cuttings can be taken early next month.

★ If the soil temperature is doubtful for outdoor seed sowing, 8°C (45°F) is the minimum, delay until it warms up.

★ In the greenhouse start preparing the hanging baskets for placing outside when all danger of frost has passed.

★ Under cloches sow early peas, turnips, summer cabbage, Brussels sprouts.

Magnolia thrives best in an organic garden where the soil has been enriched with compost. But it needs shelter from northerly and easterly winds. Avoid planting companion plants too close to the base of the trunk

Daffodils (Narcissus), *are one of the least demanding of spring-flowering bulbs, seen at their best when naturalised or planted in groups like this. Every five years lift and divide the clumps and give the planting holes a feed of compost or well-rotted manure*

*Wire frames, such as this, provide
support for tall herbaceous plants.
Eventually the foliage completely
hides the support*

*From mid-May to mid-September
some shading for the greenhouse is
necessary, along with adequate
ventilation. Try to avoid
greenhouse temperatures in excess
of 32°C (80°F), particularly when
growing tomatoes. You can buy
brush-on liquid shading which
dries white, or fit netting, such as
this, which can be rolled back on
dull days*

APRIL

* Under cloches sow French beans, runner beans, sweetcorn and swedes.

* Make first sowing outside of early peas.

* Plant summer- and autumn-flowering alpines.

* Pot up cuttings of chrysanthemums.

* Set out summer cabbage plants with a collar to protect against cabbage root fly (see page 145).

* Sow winter cabbages and purple sprouting broccoli.

* Spray house plants with tepid water and take cuttings in a jar of water.

* Sow turnips, beetroot, carrots and salads for succession.

* Sow marrows, courgettes and outdoor cucumbers in pots and place in the airing cupboard to germinate.

* Plant out border chrysanthemums.

* Sow celeriac and celery in the cold greenhouse.

* Early in the month sow greenhouse and outdoor tomatoes in trays in gentle warmth. Transfer to the cool greenhouse when seedlings emerge.

* Thin fruit on peaches.

* Towards the end of the month weed the strawberry bed and put down straw or black polythene mulch.

* Stake and tie autumn-sown sweet peas; sow Bijou sweet peas where they are to flower.

* Remove suckers from the raspberry rows.

* Cut the lawn with the mower blades set high, then rake and brush the surface. Sow grass seed on bare patches at 56g (2oz) to the sq m/yd.

* Plant potatoes and when first shoots emerge cover lightly with soil.

MAY

* Sow French and runner beans in situ, sprouting broccoli and winter cabbages in seedbed.

* Stake peas and earth up early potatoes.

* Pinch out growing tips on the broad beans.

* Plant dahlia tubers.

* Take leaf cuttings of African violets.

* In the greenhouse plant tomatoes and sow melons.

* Outside, plant ridge cucumbers, courgettes and marrows.

* Sow salads, peas, turnips for succession. Sow maincrop carrots.

* Put out the hanging baskets and window boxes.

* Lift spring-flowering bulbs and heel them in elsewhere to free the beds for bedding plants.

* Stop chrysanthemum cuttings.

* Shade greenhouse roof and ensure there is adequate ventilation.

* Dust raspberry flowers with derris before they open.

* All house plants now need regular liquid feeding.

* Sow wallflowers, sweet Williams, Canterbury bells in a seedbed.

* Plant outdoor tomatoes after the middle of the month.

* Transplant from the seedbed Brussels sprouts, cabbages and cauliflowers.

* Place netting over the strawberry bed to protect the ripening fruit from birds, but check daily in case birds or hedgehogs get entangled.

* Plant out self-blanching or trench-type celery plants towards the end of the month.

The long yellow tassels of laburnum appear in May or June. Unfortunately, the leaves, twigs and seeds are all poisonous to children and pets

Plant a honeysuckle near to the house where it can clamber over a fence or wall. Its heady fragrance will haunt the garden throughout the late spring

Paeonies are truly aristocrats of the herbaceous border. Plant in early autumn with the crown no more than 2.5cm (1in) below the surface at a site which has been well enriched with compost.

Mulch in spring and again in late summer using compost or well-rotted manure. You will be rewarded with blooms such as this Bowl of Beauty

Chaenomeles (japonica or Japanese quince) is an undemanding shrub, but prefers a humus-rich soil and full sun

JUNE

* Plant out half-hardy bedding plants.

* House plants can be put outside for their summer holiday. Choose a site sheltered from the winds and out of direct sunlight. Don't forget to feed and water them.

* Indoor and outdoor tomatoes need regular feeding and watering and removal of side shoots, except for the outdoor bush types.

* Sow sweetcorn in groups to aid pollination.

* Keep hanging baskets, window boxes and other outdoor containers moist.

* At first sight of aphids on the roses, spray with soapy water.

* Thin developing fruit on the apple and pear trees.

* Prune shrubs that have flowered.

* Sow for succession French beans, radishes, beetroot, peas.

* Feed leafy vegetables, courgettes and ridge cucumbers with liquid seaweed extract, such as SM3.

* Dead-head rhododendrons, azaleas and camellias.

* Lift tulips and outdoor hyacinths and spread the bulbs to dry before storing them.

* Transplant the winter brassicas and leeks.

* Mulch crops after rain.

* Prune gooseberries when the fruit has been gathered.

* Remember to water newly-planted trees, shrubs and flowers.

* Shade the greenhouse, especially during mid-afternoon.

Give your house plants a summer holiday by standing them outside when danger of frost has passed. Choose a site sheltered from strong winds and out of day-long sunlight . . . and don't forget to feed and water them

JULY

*   Sow stocks, pansies, aquilegias, lupins and delphiniums.

*   Sow an early carrot to pull as young ones in the autumn.

*   Spray potato and tomato crops with Bordeaux mixture at first sign of blight (see page 151).

*   Make a final sowing of Little Gem lettuce if the soil is not too hot and dry.

*   Sow spring cabbage and parsley towards the end of the month.

*   Dead-head roses and bedding plants.

*   Harvest shallots as they ripen.

*   Cut out fruited raspberry canes.

*   Take cuttings of border pinks and carnations.

*   Syringe the greenhouse with plain water in hot, dry weather to ward off the red spider mite.

*   Clean up the strawberry bed. Peg down a few runners, but remove all others.

*   Plant autumn-flowering bulbs such as colchicum and crocus.

*   Cut out old wood from the rambler roses.

*   Earth up maincrop potatoes and celery.

*   In the greenhouse sow cyclamen, cineraria and calceolaria.

*   Plant out broccoli, savoys and red cabbage plants.

*   Take cuttings of shrubs and alpines for rooting in a propagator or cold frame.

*   Summer prune bush, cordon and espalier apple and pear trees.

AUGUST

*   Don't forget to feed house plants standing outside for their summer break.

*   Prune regal pelargoniums after flowering, place in a sunny position outdoors and water sparingly.

*   Order bulbs for autumn delivery.

*   Watch out for caterpillars on the cabbages (see page 145).

*   Take cuttings of hydrangea and geraniums.

*   Hedges can now have their hardest trim.

*   Lift and dry onions and garlic.

*   Gather and dry bunches of herbs.

*   Pinch out the growing tips of tomatoes that have set four trusses of fruit.

*   Take cuttings of bay, lavender, rosemary, rue and sage. Simply insert in pots filled with sand and place in a cold frame.

*   Sow green manure crops, winter lettuce and spring onions.

*   Sow hardy annuals for next season.

*   Plant out spring cabbages.

*   Tie in five to eight of the strongest new raspberry canes, depending on variety.

*   Continue blanching the celery.

*   Prune blackcurrants and plum trees.

Clematis, the queen of the climbers, is available in a host of varieties. It likes a rich, organic soil with its roots in the shade and the rest of the plant in the sun

Astilbe is an attractive perennial for the border with feathery plumes of bloom in early summer. It needs a humus-rich soil, adequate moisture and some shade. This is A arendsii Bressingham Beauty

Window boxes and containers of plants brighten this tiny front garden in town

Delphiniums, such as these, need rich, organic soil, adequate water and a sheltered, sunny site. These perennial plants should be divided in the spring every third year

SEPTEMBER

* Ease up on the lawn mowing and give a top dressing of coarse sand.

* Towards the end of the month lift and store carrots and beetroot.

* Grease band fruit trees.

* Plant hardy lilies outside.

* Plant narcissi, hyacinths, crocus, muscari and bulbous iris.

* Lift gladioli and dry off the corms under cover.

* Cover outdoor tomato plants with cloches to assist ripening of final trusses.

* Bring in pot plants that have spent the summer outside.

* Pot prepared bulbs for winter flowering.

* Cut out fruited canes of blackberries, loganberries and hybrid berries, tie in the new growth.

* At the end of the month plant out the wallflowers, forget-me-nots, polyanthus and sweet Williams.

* Take cuttings of hardy evergreen shrubs.

Complete the ripening of outdoor tomatoes by covering with cloches. With cordon plants first remove the supporting stakes and trim off about half the foliage. Then lay the plants lengthways and tuck straw under the trusses. With bush plants trim off surplus shoots and leaves then pack straw around the plants. Leave the cloches open-ended

OCTOBER

* Start digging vacant land if the soil is heavy and allow to overwinter.

* Complete blanching of celery plants.

* Cut down asparagus plants to within six inches of the ground.

* Protect cauliflowers from frost.

* Start pruning fruit trees when they have shed their leaves.

* Remove fallen leaves from ponds.

* Pot geranium cuttings and tulips for indoors.

* Sow sweet peas in pots or tubes and place in cold frame.

* Check the greenhouse for draughts and use a sealant to keep them out. Clear the gutters and clean the glass inside and out.

* The compost heap started in the spring should be ready for use from now on. Until you are ready to start another heap, bag up all vegetable waste.

* Collect all fallen leaves and use for making leafmould (see page 41).

* Plant evergreen shrubs, including conifers, which should be protected from damaging east and northerly winds.

* Plant mint roots in compost in a 15cm (6in) pot and place on the kitchen windowsill for a winter's supply of fresh mint.

* Rake the lawn to loosen moss before giving it the last mowing of the year.

* Take cuttings of gooseberry and currants. Place in sandy soil in a well-sheltered spot.

NOVEMBER

* Divide border plants that have become over-large.

* Lift dahlia tubers, label and store them in moist peat in a frost-free place.

* Dust gladioli corms with sulphur and store in paper bags.

* Bring potted azaleas into the warmth and syringe daily with tepid water.

* Plant roses, tulips, daffodils and soft fruit bushes.

* Bring Christmas flowering bulbs into the warmth and light when the shoots are about 5cm (2in) tall.

* Prune indoor vines and peaches.

* Repaint the exterior of cold frames and lime wash the interior.

* Increase the humidity of house plants in centrally-heated rooms by standing the pots in bowls of moist peat.

* Cut back flowered chrysanthemums.

* Protect tender plants and newly-planted shrubs from frost damage, using sacking or netting or Agryl P17 polypropylene fibre.

* Start turning in the compost as you dig or spread as a mulch on deep beds.

* Tidy up the garden. Burn diseased material, rotting canes and timber, but before setting fire to the heap make sure a hedgehog isn't in residence.

Parthenocissus tricupidata
(Virginia creeper or Boston ivy)
gives a fiery wash to the walls of
this cottage in autumn. A fertile,
quick-draining soil is preferred

DECEMBER

* Complete winter pruning of all trees and shrubs.

* Make sowings of mustard and cress for the Christmas sandwiches.

* Remember to water pots of bulbs still in the cool and dark.

* Nip out the tops of sweet peas when they have made 7.5cm (3in) of growth.

* Give all tools a winter service, cleaning off dirt and debris, then wipe with an oily rag.

* Clean out the greenhouse and wash all pots, trays and boxes.

* Spread compost among the shrubs and roses.

* Treat your bought-in Christmas tree like a cut flower and put it into water as soon as possible. A 1.8m (6ft) tree without roots will take up about 1.1 litres (2 pints) of water a day for the first week after cutting and about .56 litre (1 pint) a day thereafter. Give it this treatment and there will be far fewer fallen pine needles.

* Prepare a seed order, including the seed potatoes, and get it off before the rush begins.

SUPPLIERS

COMPOSTS, MANURES AND ORGANIC FERTILISERS

Betagro, Harding Way, St Ives, Cambridge PE17 4WR.

J. Arthur Bowers, Sinclair Horticulture, Wigford House, Brayford Pool, Lincoln LN5 7BL.

Camland Products Ltd, 36 Regent Street, Cambridge CB2 1DB.

Chase Organics (GB) Ltd, Addlestone, Weybridge, Surrey KT15 1HY.

Chempak, Geddings Road, Hoddesdon, Herts EN11 0LR.

Cornish Calcified Seaweed Co Ltd, Newham, Truro, Cornwall.

Cowpact Ltd, Hollingdon, Leighton Buzzard, Beds LU7 0DN.

Cumulus Organics, Timber Road, Two Mile Lane, Higham, Gloucestershire GL2 8BR.

HDRA (Sales) Ltd, Ryton Gardens, Ryton-on-Dunsmore, Coventry CV8 3LG.

Humber Fertilisers plc, PO Box 27, Stoneferry, Hull HU8 8DQ.

Melcourt Industries Ltd, Three Cups House, Tetbury, Gloucestershire GL8 8JG.

Michael King's Garden Products, Autumn Leaves, Whitley Road, Walton, nr Street, Somerset BA16 9RW.

Leggar Organics, Knapp Farm, Chads Hill, Cannington, Bridgwater, Somerset TA5 2BR.

Maxicrop Ltd, 21 London Road, Great Shelford, Cambridge CB2 5DF.

Organic Concentrates Ltd, Little Chalfont, Amersham, Bucks HP8 4AP.

Organic Farmers and Growers Ltd, Station Approach, Needham Market, Suffolk IP6 8AT.

Scott Wallis Seeds Ltd, 100 Beehive Lane, Chelmsford CM2 9SG.

Stimgro Ltd, Unit 2B, Longfield Road, Tunbridge Wells, Kent TN2 3EY.

Vitaseamin (SC) Ltd, Woodside, Charney Road, Grange-over-Sands, Cumbria.

Warner Knowles, 67 Queensway, Great Cornard, Sudbury, Suffolk.

EQUIPMENT, INSECTICIDES, SUNDRIES

British Earthworm Technology, Harding Way, St Ives, Cambridge PE17 4WR.

Bunting and Sons, The Nurseries, Great Horkesley, Colchester, Essex CO6 4AJ (Biological controls).

Chase Organics (GB) Ltd, Addlestone, Weybridge, Surrey KT15 1HY.

Donaldson Paper and Board Sales Ltd, Suite 9, Essex House, 15 Station Road, Upminster, Essex RM14 2SJ. (Hortopaper, Agryl P17).

HDRA (Sales) Ltd, Ryton Gardens, Ryton-on-Dunsmore, Coventry CV8 3LG.

Hortichem Ltd, 14 Edison Road, Churchfields Industrial Estate, Salisbury, Wilts SP2 7NU.

Hydrocut Ltd, Sudbury, Suffolk CO10 6HB. (Hortopaper, Agryl P17).

Impregnated Tapes Ltd, Lower Penarwyn, St Blazey, Par, Cornwall, PL24 2DS.

Koppert (UK) Ltd, PO Box 43, Tunbridge Wells, Kent TN2 5BY.

Natural Pest Control, Watermead, Yapton Road, Barnham, Bognor Regis, Sussex PO22 0BQ.

Pan Britannica Industries Ltd, Britannica House, Waltham Cross, Herts EN8 7DY.

Wilson Grimes Products, Corwen, Clwyd LL21 0DR. (Soil test kits, pH meter).

SEED FIRMS

Atlas Organic Seeds, 40 Victoria Street, Braintree, Essex.

J. W. Boyce, 67 Station Road, Soham, Ely, Cambs CB7 5ED.

Chase Organics (GB) Ltd, Addlestone, Weybridge, Surrey KT15 1HY.

Chelsea Choice Seeds, Notley Road, Braintree, Essex CM7 7HA.

Elsoms Seeds Ltd, Spalding, Lincolnshire PE11 1QG.

Mr Fothergill's Seeds, Kentford, Newmarket, Suffolk CB8 7QB.

HDRA (Sales) Ltd, Ryton Gardens, Ryton-on-Dunsmore, Coventry CV8 3LG.

Hursts Seeds, Witham, Essex CM8 2DX.

Kings Crown Quality Seeds, Coggeshall, Essex.

S. E. Marshall & Co Ltd, Regal Road, Wisbech, Cambs PE13 2RF.

W. Robinson & Sons, Sunny Bank, Forton, nr Preston, Lancs PR3 0BN.

Suffolk Herbs, Sawyers Farm, Little Cornard, Sudbury, Suffolk.

Suttons Seeds Ltd, Hele Road, Torquay, Devon TQ2 7QJ.

Thompson & Morgan Ltd, London Road, Ipswich, Suffolk IP2 0BA.

Unwins Seeds Ltd, Impington Lane, Histon, Cambs CB4 4LE.

Van Hage Seeds, Great Amwell, nr Ware, Herts SG12 9RP.

FURTHER READING

Companion Planting Gertrud Frank (Thorsons, 1983)
Complete Vegetable Grower W. E. Shewell-Cooper (Faber, 1974)
Composting Dick Kitto (Thorsons, 1984)
Cowpasture: Everday life of an English allotment Roy Lacey (David & Charles, 1980)
Expert Books D. G. Hessayon, PBI (Not organic but packed with facts)
Fruit Garden Displayed Royal Horticultural Society (1986)
Good Fruit Guide Lawrence D. Hills (Henry Doubleday Research Association, 1984)
Green Manures Elm Farm Research Centre (1982)
Know and Grow Vegetables, 1/2 P. J. Salter and J. K. A. Bleasdale (Oxford Paperbacks, 1979/82)
Month-by-Month Guide to Organic Gardening Lawrence D. Hills (Thorsons, 1983)
Organic Flower Garden Sue Stickland (Thorsons, 1986)
Organic Gardening Lawrence D. Hills (Penguin, 1977)

Pests, Diseases and Disorders, Collins Shorter Guide to Stefan Buczacki and Keith Harris (Collins, 1983)
Planning the Organic Herb Garden Sue Stickland (Thorsons, 1985)
Salad Garden Joy Larkcom (Windward, 1984)
Soil Care K. R. W. Hammett (David & Charles, 1986)
Vegetables from Small Gardens Joy Larkcom (Windward, 1976)
Vegetable Garden Displayed Royal Horticultural Society (1961)

Both the Soil Association and Henry Doubleday Research Association publish a range of booklets on aspects of organic gardening. In addition to those mentioned above, the Royal Horticultural Society publishes the *Wisley Handbooks* on a wide range of horticultural subjects, while the National Vegetable Research Station at Wellesbourne, Warwickshire, publishes inexpensive leaflets on vegetable growing. The RHS and NVRS publications give conventional – not organic – advice.

USEFUL ADDRESSES

Biodynamic Agricultural Association, Emerson College, Forest Row, London.

British Organic Farmers, 86/88 Colston Street, Bristol BS1 5BB. Farmers' group to promote contact and disseminate information to those interested in organic farming.

British Organic Standards Group, Elm Farm Research Centre, Hamstead Marshall, Newbury, Berks. Committee of principal organic organisations to create unified standards of organic production.

Commonwork, Bore Place, Chiddingstone, Edenbridge, Kent. A centre for organic farming and self-sufficiency activities.

Elm Farm Research Centre, Hamstead Marshall, Newbury, Berks. A charity, it manages an organic farm, develops organic techniques, and offers an advisory service.

Friends of the Earth, Mitcham, Surrey LR4 9AR.

Good Gardeners' Association, Arkley Manor, Barnet, Herts.

Greenpeace, 29–35 Gladstone Road, Croydon, Surrey. Abuse of pesticides and fertilisers is the focus of a major campaign.

Henry Doubleday Research Association, Ryton-on-Dunsmore, Coventry CV8 3LG. Largest body of organic gardeners in Britain with headquarters at Ryton

Gardens, the National Centre for Organic Gardening.

International Federation of Organic Agriculture Movements, Le Maioun, F84 410 Bedoin, France. Serves as a worldwide network for its member groups mainly for dissemination of information.

Mother Earth, 12 Mason Close, Malvern, Worcs WR14 2NF. Promotes the growing of nutritious food by environmentally sympathetic methods.

National Institute for Agricultural Botany, Huntingdon Road, Cambridge CB3 0LE. Publishes helpful booklets on vegetable varieties.

Organic Farmers and Growers Ltd, Abacus House, Station Yard, Needham Market, Ipswich, Suffolk IP6 8AT. Founded in 1975 as a co-operative for production and marketing of organically grown crops.

Organic Federation, PO Box 8, Malvern, Worcs WR14 2NG. Co-ordinating body for those interested in developing an organic life style.

Organic Growers' Association, 86/88 Colston Street, Bristol BS1 5BB. Represents the interests of organic market gardeners.

Otley College of Agriculture and Horticulture, Otley, near Ipswich,

Suffolk. Runs courses for amateur and commercial growers on all aspects of organic husbandry with associated organic demonstration unit.

Soil Association Ltd, 86/88 Colston Street, Bristol BS1 5BB. Founded in 1946 to promote and protect the delicate relationship between the soil, plants, animals and man and so encourage the organic methods of food production and the reduction in the use of artificial fertilisers, pesticides and fungicides. It is a non-government funded charity.

Well Hall Country College, Well Alford, Lincs LN13 0ET. College of agriculture and horticulture run on biological principles.

Working Weekends on Organic Farms (WWOOF), 19 Bradford Road, Lewes, East Sussex BN7 5RB. To enable people of any age to gain experience of organic farming and gardening and to help the organic movement with additional labour.

WWOOF – Ireland, Carrigleigh, Shenballymore, Mallow, Co Cork, Eire.

Yarner Trust, Beacon Farm, Dartington, Totnes, Devon TQ9 6DX. Concerned with small-scale low-input organic food production.

THE SOIL ASSOCIATION SYMBOL

This is the symbol issued under licence by the Soil Association to farmers and growers who have undergone conversion of a field or holding from conventional chemically-dependent production to organic husbandry according to a plan agreed with the Soil Association Inspectorate.

Produce may generally only be sold with the symbol after a conversion period of at least two years involving the development of biological cycles, sound rotations, the extensive use of animal and vegetable wastes, the use of appropriate cultivation techniques, the avoidance of fertilisers in the form of soluble mineral salts, and the prohibition of agro-chemical pesticides.

The symbol applies to meat, dairy products, eggs, vegetables and fruit, fruit juices, cider, jams, cereals and cereal products.

ACKNOWLEDGEMENTS

The debt I owe to the pioneers of the modern organic movement cannot be measured or repaid. But I am particularly indebted to Lady Eve Balfour, Dr E. F. Schumacher and Lawrence D. Hills for their ideas and their dreams which have been a source of inspiration to me, and many thousands of others, over scores of years.

Acknowledgements are made in the text to source material, while the data in the Fact Files has been compiled from information supplied by Elm Farm Research Centre, the National Vegetable Research Station, the Soil Association and Henry Doubleday Research Association, to all of whom I most grateful. To John Lewis, M Hort, lecturer in horticulture at Otley College of Agriculture and Horticulture; I offer deepest thanks for his assistance in proof reading.

Felixstowe   Roy Lacey
Suffolk

INDEX

T

U

V

W

Y

Z